HELP

THE MARXISM OF JEAN-PAUL SARTRE

By the Same Author

The Tragic Finale, An Essay on the Philosophy of Jean-Paul Sartre.

In hard cover, at the Harvard University Press; in paperback, in the Torchbook series, at Harper and Row.

The Planetary Man, Vol. I, *A Noetic Prelude to a United World.*

Georgetown University Press.

In Preparation:

The Planetary Man, Vol. II.

THE MARXISM OF
JEAN-PAUL SARTRE

by

WILFRID DESAN

Doubleday & Company, Inc.

Garden City, New York

1965

To
Paul, Suzanne, and Christine
this book is dedicated
as to the future which is

Library of Congress Catalog Card Number 65–10631
Copyright © 1965 by Wilfrid Desan
All Rights Reserved
Printed in the United States of America
First Edition

FOREWORD

Jean-Paul Sartre has given us his views on speculative philosophy in *L'Etre et le Néant*.[1] Now in the *Critique de la Raison Dialectique* we are told what he thinks in the realm of sociology.[2] The *Critique* is even more voluminous and in my opinion, more difficult than its predecessor. Yet it contains insights which are as arresting as those of the earlier work, and if such terms as "being and nothingness" and "*Pour-soi* and *En-soi*" are by now commonplace, I believe that this new work will bequeath us a vocabulary that will become equally familiar because it is equally timely. It is for this reason that I have undertaken to lay open the *Critique* in these pages, in a manner similar to that used with *L'Etre et le Néant* in *The Tragic Finale*.[3]

In his recently published autobiography, *Les Mots*,[4] Sartre describes himself as a small boy leaning over the window sill of his sixth-floor apartment and naming the things he saw down below, as if in naming them, he made them his. In the *Critique* the man who has grown from that boy still looks

[1] *L'Etre et le Néant, Essai d'Ontologie Phénoménologique* (Paris, 1943). In English: *Being and Nothingness*, trans. Hazel E. Barnes (New York, 1956).

[2] Jean-Paul Sartre, *Critique de la Raison Dialectique, précédé de Question de Méthode*, Tome I, *Théorie des Ensembles Pratiques* (Paris, 1960). This book will hereafter be referred to as *CRD*. The first section, *Question de Méthode*, has been translated by Hazel E. Barnes under the title *Search for a Method* (New York, 1963).

[3] Wilfrid Desan, *The Tragic Finale* (Harvard University Press, 1954), in paperback, New York, 1960.

[4] *Les Mots* (Paris, 1963).

down upon the world from the windows of his apartment, and in describing the furious activity which he sees, makes it both his and ours. From a bus stop on St.-Germain-des-Prés, man is followed from his powerless position in an unorganized *seriality*, through his feeble gropings toward a primitive form of the *group* and its eventual solidification into an *organization*, to his discovery of himself as once more powerless, this time in the paralyzing inertia of the *institution*. Freedom is still part of the definition of man, however, and if the walls of the prison become too confining, he will be driven to scale them once more.

In the course of his dialectical description, Sartre is confronted again and again with the question of individual and collective responsibility. In the modern world, which has continued to witness persecution and violence on a grand scale, this question is not merely an academic one, and the author's analyses of such questions as the responsibility of individual capitalists and colonialists in the processes of capitalism and colonialism are provocative in this area. The many references and footnotes to the Negro revolution which I have added as examples of Sartre's points attest to their ready applicability. The *Critique* should thus be of considerable interest not only to philosophers but also to sociologists and political scientists as well. And if Sartre is correct in maintaining that man can make his own history more meaningfully as he becomes more aware of what is happening, it is my duty to make more readily available Sartre's own observations, observations which are often controversial but always interesting.

Accordingly, I have attempted to show in Chapter I the evolution of Sartre's social thought toward its mature expression in the *Critique*. A more immediate preparation for the exploration of Sartre's book is given in Chapter II, which contains what I consider to be important in Marx and Hegel for the understanding of Sartre. In no way is this book a critical examination of Marx, even less so of Hegel, but it contains, I believe, sufficient data on both of these thinkers

for the task at hand. Chapter III consists of an examination
of the *Question de Méthode,* an essay originally destined for
publication in a Polish review but now placed at the beginning of the *Critique de la Raison Dialectique* to serve as an
introduction. The *Question de Méthode,* in exploring the divergent *methods* of existentialism and Marxism and possible
ways of combining them, is an attempt to insert the concrete
value of the existential dimension into the abstract framework
of Marxist thought. Whether this section fits precisely where
it stands is debatable. Sartre himself was hesitant, but in the
final editing placed it there, in the fear that were he instead
to place it at the end, "this mountain of pages might seem to
give birth to a mouse."[5] The reader should thus understand
that although the *Question de Méthode* leads us into the
main body of the work, conversely, its own full meaning
comes through only in the light of the whole, and it might
very well be reread and reconsidered when one has the entire
Critique in mind.

The five following chapters of my book bring the reader
into the core of Sartre's *Critique.* I have made strenuous
efforts to present Sartre's view in a detailed and scrupulously
honest way. No doubt, at times my admiration comes
through, as does my criticism, but whether approving or dis-
approving, I have constantly aimed at clarifying his thought
and at revealing the *enchaînement* all through the interminable cascade of Sartre's dialectic. I have not written to absorb him into my own views, as some commentators consider
it their duty to do. Nor is it my intention to replace the original work; the reader, if I may give him good advice, should
go to the original. I have written to clarify Sartre's presentation and to make available what otherwise would remain
dormant. In Chapters III–VIII Sartre is the tree, I merely
the pruner. To that intent, I have added, subtracted and
given other or additional examples where I saw fit. Since I
have used the system of references rather than that of quotations, multiple footnotes refer to the original text.

[5] *CRD,* I, p. 9.

I found this whole enterprise to be a rather laborious task, more complex than I had anticipated at the start. Sartre's book is badly constructed; indeed, it is uselessly obscure and interminable. Our author is definitely at that stage of his fame where he can afford to be non-conformist to the extreme, leaving just enough intelligibility so that the conformist might attempt the struggle to understand him. But whatever may be its limitations, the *Critique* is an impressive performance and undoubtedly makes an eloquent plea for freedom. Sartre, at any rate, had only this one purpose in mind: Marxism is livable, but only after it has understood and accepted the invaluable price of the concrete and of freedom. Whether or not this marriage of Marxism and existentialism is a sound one is explored in the last two chapters. In Chapter IX, I present what are considered to be some problematics unresolved, and in Chapter X, I attempt to offer a more constructive criticism in showing how Sartre's *point de départ* is fatal for any sound collective, be it Marxist or otherwise.

In commenting upon an intricate work, not everything can be said at once, and if certain ideas recur in the successive chapters, it will be seen that they gain in amplitude upon the second meeting. Each new encounter engenders more light. Yet it will be no less apparent—such is the hope and the wish of this writer—that the whole tenor of this book is a progressive one. As in *The Tragic Finale*, I have kept close to the topic and saved the reader useless detours.

Although I have kept abreast with other publications of Sartre, I have paid less attention to his plays than I did in the previous work. This is because I consider them to be less impressive than those of his earlier days, when he gave us such gems as *The Flies* and *No Exit*. Nor have I made use of *Saint Genet*, which recently appeared in English but is already aged on the French market.[6] Although the message

---

[6] *Saint Genet, Comédien et Martyr*, Tome I des Oeuvres Complètes de Jean Genet (Paris, 1953). English trans., *Saint Genet* (New York, 1963).

of these works is vaguely ethical, they cannot be called philosophical in the strict sense. Sartre himself categorized them
under *"Littérature."* What has proved to be valuable, however, was the contribution of Simone de Beauvoir. Her auto-
biographies have no philosophical pretenses, and certainly
intend neither to teach nor to preach, but they do contain
a colorful illustration of Sartre's development from as close
a source as any.[7] She was his constant companion, and echoes
in her own thought what was uppermost in his. Sartre himself came into the game again, and my manuscript was near
completion when we were given *Les Mots*, the first install-
ment of his autobiography. It is short, provocative, and moving in the self-accusation of imposture, which Sartre believes
has afflicted his career. *"Ce vieux bâtiment ruineux, mon
imposture, c'est aussi mon caractère . . ."*[8] Confessions of
insincerity may touch us but they neither erase what has
been said nor completely convince the reader. Writers may
believe in their old age that they never succeeded in saying
what they wanted to say, but posterity may be grateful for
their having made the attempt. If human reality really is that
sort of supple entity which is what it is not, and is not what
it is, no wonder that it keeps projecting itself in writing with
the hope of finally saying what it wants to say. I have upon
occasion used Sartre's sophisticated confessions in footnotes.

These, then, are the documents used in the writing of this
book. A final contribution should be mentioned. I would like
to end this foreword by acknowledging the help of my wife.
Confessions like these have by now become banal, but what
is banal has not lost its truth. Not only am I indebted to her
for correcting my English, but I have understood more than
ever that philosophy is not a soliloquy. Its qualities of clarity
and penetration result from what I have elsewhere called

[7] Simone de Beauvoir, *La Force de l'Age* (Paris, 1960) and *La
Force des Choses* (Paris, 1963). The first has been translated into
English by Peter Green under the title *The Prime of Life* (New York,
1962).

[8] Sartre, *Les Mots*, p. 211.

the "we-language," or the convergent complementarity of the many. Or better still, I have understood that monologue *is* dialogue. For the extraordinary part played by my wife in that sort of intellectual game, I am profoundly grateful.

Wilfrid Desan

Georgetown University

CONTENTS

enfant soumis,
j'obéirais jusqu'à la mort
mais à moi.

SARTRE

In man creature and creator are united:
in man there is not only matter, shred,
excess, clay, mire, folly, chaos; but
there is also the creator, the sculptor,
the hardness of the hammer, the divinity
of the spectator, and the seventh day—

NIETZSCHE

Chapter I

THE ROAD TO A SARTRIAN SOCIALISM

THE EARLY YEARS

Modern life is repetition. Once a pattern is invented, it is expressed mathematically, and once it is expressed mathematically, copies are guaranteed. Since the fundamental structure of our contemporary world has become scientific, its principal creators are the inventors; the others merely repeat a pattern which, once invented, is communicated and then multiplied indefinitely. It is this pattern which modern life implants upon the millions incessantly and, some believe, ruthlessly. Yet we are told that this is a source of happiness: "low-maintenance living" is happy living, the comfort of the machine is the comfort of man. When this scientific and ordered living begins to find its replica in the very behavior of man, however, voices of alarm begin to be heard, and this same man fights for his life against the patterned image. We find more and more titles on the publishers' lists like *The Organization Man, The Lonely Crowd, Growing Up Absurd,* or *The Image Industries.*

All of these protests, and many others, reflect a trend of revolt against the repetition, organization, and conditioning that gets hold of man and crushes his creativity. Existentialism is one of the most powerful attempts to break the strangle hold. Its literary and philosophical publications all desperately fight to protect that mysterious entity called the "freedom" of man, to give him back his uniqueness and his creative powers. That freedom which they seek in common is not merely the freedom that gives man the capacity of saying no, but the freedom that endows him with the power of producing the new as well. This can be said to be, I believe, the main intuition of existentialism, and the central idea that links together Heidegger, Jaspers, Sartre, and Marcel, though through an enormous variety of expressions and amid deep disagreements. In the work of all, the individual man is set against mass production, not because mass production is in itself wrong but because the system places men themselves in danger of becoming things. For the machine steals their creativity and in replacing men, makes men machines. It has been Sartre's obsession to combat this threat, and he has thrown all his intellectual power into the battle. Whether or not he has done so in the right way and with the right means is under debate, and many of my readers may believe that his speculations have led him far astray; but few will deny the urgency of the quest he undertook, and the authenticity and vigor he brought to it. Few will likewise deny the value of following him along the road he chose to take, with all its twistings and turnings through the years.

That road, for all its turnings, nevertheless follows a fundamental "project." I believe that it can be said that Sartre's essential philosophical trend is one of *negation*, a negation of all limitation to freedom, all hampering of man's free movement, all frustration and alienation. Of course, it must be added that if Sartre's fundamental project is one of negation, and if his emphasis is upon a world of darkness, the choice of this particular presentation is for the purpose of bringing light into that world. He apparently believes that one must show the darkness in all its depths in order to understand the need for light, for our first look is into a world of gloominess and oppression. No charity or love lifts the gloom; the only glimmer of hope lies in the relentless pursuit of oppression in whatever form it occurs, human or even divine.

Already as a professor at the *lycée* of le Hâvre, Sartre began to show his dislike for the middle class, to which he himself belonged. He hated the "analytical" intellectuals, all those who have ever on the tips of their tongues the principles of democracy, equality, and brotherhood, as if to profess were to practice. Existentialism, as presented in *La Nausée*, Sartre's first book, was a denial of any and all principles, since to him they are in most cases only a mask that actually serves to hide selfishness. Sartre does not hate people, but he hates people who talk always of charity and piously pray for their fellow men, while at the same time keeping prudently on their own level away from the people for whom they pray.

Simone de Beauvoir, whose autobiography is, aside from Sartre's own works, the best introduction to his soul, tells us how as young university students they kept away from the fashionable bars and restaurants.[1] However much necessity favored the boycott, their preference was supported by their ideology as well. Later on, in their travels, Sartre was always eager to visit and lodge in the poorer sections of cities, as if by physically placing himself in the midst of a lower class, he could morally negate his own.

It is in this opposition to the bourgeoisie and to the soulless abstraction of its ideology that Sartre's flirtation with communism finds its origin. While a teacher, he refused to wear a tie, as if he could shed his class with his tie and thus come closer to the worker. Yet he is not and never will be a worker. Like the *petit bourgeois intellectuel* that he is, he uses more words than the workers, words with which he can analyze their status and rebel in their name. In this rebelling he makes himself; his concern for the worker is the reverse side of his contempt for the strength of the bourgeois, his concern with man the fight against anything that humiliates man, and his rebellion the reaction against all power. It will appear from later pages that to call Sartre a Marxist is an oversimplification, for his efforts to correct the master will be implacable. The freedom that is so deep in Sartre revolts against the voice of suffering itself, whether that suffering

[1] *The Prime of Life*, p. 22.

results from the egoism of the Continental bourgeoisie or from oppression preached in the name of Marx and Lenin.

Sartre virtually grew up writing and attempting to publish his writing, for he was devoted to literature, not as art for art's sake but as a means whereby man justifies himself and at the same time fills a need of others. The term *petit bourgeois intellectuel,* which we have already used, fitted the young *lycée* professor and writer well, and it can also be found in the *Critique de la Raison Dialectique* as a name which he cherished. For if he and others could not be the workers they wished to be, they could at least be a carrier of the revolution in their minds, and thus to an extent escape their class. Furthermore, in extending the new humanism to include all men, they could escape all class whatsoever. At the same time their writing was a kind of action; Sartre at one point during the war had tried his hand at organizing a resistance movement but his "Socialism and Liberty" was greeted with apathy and difficulty on every side and, unsuccessful as an organizer, he returned to his writing, "which represented the one form of resistance work still open to him."[2] For if he had grown up as a writer who apparently had no ethics, he nevertheless placed an ethical topic at the center of each of his plays, as we observe in *No Exit* and in *The Flies.* To him ethics was not some ideal of human action, it was action itself, and brought onto the stage, it could come closer to the life from which he believed it to be inseparable.

The problem of finding a method to express this philosophy of the concrete was one that had always preoccupied Sartre. Simone de Beauvoir has told the story of the day in earlier years when Sartre had a drink with Raymond Aron. Aron, who had just returned from a sojourn in Germany, was able to tell Sartre about some philosopher of whom he had never heard before, by the name of Husserl. He excitedly explained how Husserl had proposed a new method of philosophizing

[2] *Ibid.,* p. 397.

upon the concrete. Philosophy was no longer to consist of an inquiry into origins or of a deductive exploration for invisible substances and causes; philosophy was to be a description of that which appears insofar as it appears, a disclosure of the concrete, a revelation of all that falls under our senses, whether inside or outside ourselves. "You see," said Aron, pointing to his drink, "if you are a phenomenologist, you can talk about this cocktail and make philosophy out of it!"[3] Sartre became pale from emotion, according to Simone de Beauvoir, for this presented him with the very tool for which he had been searching in order to communicate his thoughts. It is no wonder that a philosopher who was later to write plays, stories, and novels in order to bring universals to the ground should have been excited to discover that he could bring that same concrete expression into philosophy itself. A method to observe the concrete in and around oneself and to describe emotions and sentiments, the relation of the self with the outside world, and the world itself insofar as it is noetically shaped by man, all this was what Sartre had been looking for. It was part of a new empiricism that was dependent upon experience and observation, yet kept itself clearly apart from Humean positivism. It was, in short, an empiricism which claimed to find its way between the two extremes of radical materialism and straight spiritualism. Phenomenology was not merely empirical, since its revelations were much more than a discovery of the experimental; in addition, the method claimed to discover relations from man to man, from man to his surrounding milieu, from man to the world, which are beyond the realm of the strictly verifiable. This departure from positivism did not mean that it was on the other hand spiritualistic; its propagators were for the most part atheists who rejected all claims of immortality for the soul. In my previous commentary upon *L'Etre et le Néant* I have given sufficient examples of the phenomenological method.[4] One point remains to be stressed

[3] *Ibid.*, p. 112.
[4] *The Tragic Finale*, pp. 95–126.

here, and this will come out very strongly later: phenomenology attempts a vision of the world and of others *from the viewpoint of the subject*. Sartre had found a method, but it was a method that would solidify his Cartesian seclusion.

This seclusion proved to be more than merely speculative and noetic, for it has had ethical implications as well. Sartre for years had hovered on the edge of the working class, but he no doubt knew that he would never be that which he was not in the past and that he was a prisoner of himself more than he cared to admit, a subject one cannot abandon but must remain forever. I have wondered sometimes whether phenomenology, in addition to being an instrument for achieving brilliant and revealing descriptions, did not serve at the same time as a mask to conceal his own sense of isolation. *L'Etre et le Néant* would then be a strenuous effort to cure himself of this deeply rooted malaise, through the effort to detach man from his past in emphasizing his *freedom from the past* and the constant possibility of change. This intellectual adventure failed, however, to liberate Sartre, as we can observe in his hesitant connections with the Communist party itself. Simone de Beauvoir leaves no doubt of his independence in her report of the prewar era, nor does Sartre himself in his writings. Would he or would he not join the Party? He did not, for he preferred to remain outside it, alone, but sovereign of himself.

The conflict of Marxism and existentialism as Sartre saw it in these prewar days was basically one between group and individual. At one time Sartre was a great admirer of Dos Passos, in whose work he discovered characters who are at the same time both individual and social. A Dos Passos hero is unique, yet a member of the group: "what happens to him could happen to no one else. What does it matter, since Society has marked him more deeply than could any circumstance, since he is Society."[5] Dos Passos' characters need neither psychological mechanism, as was the case with

[5] Sartre, *Literary and Philosophical Essays*, English translation by Annette Michelson (New York, 1962), p. 101.

Proust, nor any complicated physiological background of "explanations," as with Zola. They simply exist, as living animals, inscrutable and yet open. They are tied up in the social without mystery. This does not mean that his creatures are not free, for they are. They are both free and unfree, both interior and exterior, free in their interior or what might be called in their "Kantian noumenal," yet able to be seized and observed in their phenomenal exterior, which is quasi-frozen and coldly determined. Sartre seemed to find in Dos Passos a key to himself, in the insight that one both belonged to the other and yet at the same time did not belong to the other.[6] Sartre knew he himself belonged to the others, to the workers and all those who are in need—this awareness has never left him—yet he belonged also to himself and to his own work. In belonging to himself and to his work, he could now by the same token belong to the others.

In 1938 Sartre published in *Recherches Philosophiques* his by now famous article "La Transcendance de l'Ego."[7] It undertook a speculative examination of Husserl's Transcendental Ego in an attempt to show that human consciousness is impersonal and contains no ego. Consciousness for Sartre is complete translucidity facing the opacity of the object; it is nothing more. By this it is not claimed that the Ego cannot arise from my reflection, for when I reflect upon what I am doing at the present, the Ego does indeed appear. It is Sartre's fear, however, that this introduction of the Ego into the heart of consciousness is fatal, since it would constitute by virtue of its density an obstacle to the perfect and all-out freedom of human reality. Consequently he will allow no Ego other than that which is revealed and constituted in and through reflection.[8]

[6] Simone de Beauvoir describes Sartre's excited discovery of Dos Passos in *The Prime of Life*, p. 113.

[7] *Recherches Philosophiques*, VI, 1936–37. A good English translation is available: F. Williams and R. Kirkpatrick, *The Transcendence of the Ego* (New York, 1957).

[8] For detailed explanation, see *Being and Nothingness*, pp. 102 ff. See eventually *The Tragic Finale*, pp. 27, 144 ff.

This would be a mere speculative discussion without political or sociological impact, were it not for the end of the article, where Sartre unexpectedly warns the reader that his philosophical stand is not an abandonment of the Left. "The theories of the extreme Left have sometimes reproached phenomenology for being an idealism and for drowning reality in the stream of ideas," writes Sartre.[9] He answers that phenomenology has on the contrary placed man back into the world, where he belongs. Idealism is an expression and a relic of the past; phenomenology, with its observation and description, has brought the individual man close to the world of suffering and need which formerly, wrapped up in the cell of his own self, he had ignored. Sartre's insistence upon annihilating the Ego in the depth of consciousness even more emphatically destroys the suspicion of idealism, since from now on there is nothing left but a world revealed and a world transcended.

This is at least his hope. But it was a hope not easily to be fulfilled, for the young Sartre carried in his heart two loves—one for the value of the Subject and the other for the importance of the collective—which were not ready companions. There was Descartes, and there was Marx. How to bring them together would become the mental torture of later years, provoking the synthesis found in the *Critique de la Raison Dialectique* twenty-five years later. The following chapters will give the reader a chance to test Sartre's skill in his combat with Marx. It will be my privilege in the concluding remarks to inquire whether or not Husserl's phenomenology, of which Sartre is still a fervent disciple (notwithstanding his apparent elimination of the Ego) was indeed the best departure for a philosophy of the collective.

Such, then, was the Sartre of before the war, a teacher of philosophy in the *lycée*, a student of Husserl, an independent thinker whose personal views were slowly taking shape in a somewhat anarchic-metaphysical way. Underlying all that he

[9] "The Transcendence of the Ego," p. 104.

did and thought was a strong anti-bourgeois feeling, coupled with a profound sympathy for the worker. "We returned late at night by a road overlooking the Seine, and stopped to look at the Grande Couronne factory buildings on the far side. They were lit up in the darkness, and looked exactly like gigantic but motionless fireworks, a set piece under the black vault of the sky. 'A beautiful sight,' Pagniez said. Sartre rubbed his nose. 'It's a factory,' he said. 'People work all night there.' Pagniez maintained, somewhat impatiently, that this didn't affect its beauty. But according to Sartre, he was letting himself be taken in by a mere mirage. Where was the beauty in sweated labor and exhaustion?"[10]

Nausea AND Being and Nothingness

If Sartre was slow in revealing his purpose, it was nevertheless taking a firmer and firmer hold upon him. Nausea already contained enough discontent with this world to betray a strong desire on the part of the author to change it, but precisely what direction that desire would take did not yet clearly appear.[11] Nausea was an exploration and a promise. Displaying the anti-bourgeois mentality and philosophy of negation that are so characteristic of Sartre, it was a prelude to the more unified and systematic opus which would appear toward the end of the war, under the title L'Etre et le Néant. It has often been said that the latter, appearing as it did in a time of tragedy, merely reflected the sad mood of its epoch. This is oversimplified, for as Sartre himself wrote, it takes no account of time, the immense length of time which is needed to produce such a work. L'Etre et le Néant was in fact started long before the war and was twelve years in the writing, before its completion in 1942.[12] The main thesis upon which Sartre had been working during all these years was a description of the sad futility of all human endeavor;

[10] The Prime of Life, p. 165.
[11] La Nausée (Paris, 1938).
[12] CRD, I, p. 34.

man, he was finding, was merely a "useless passion." If his readers and followers felt that Sartre had led them into an impasse, to a tragic finale, and that they might just as well commiserate with each other in sidewalk cafés or otherwise do just as they pleased, Sartre himself was not in agreement. In his mind *L'Etre et le Néant* was only the beginning, the speculative basis, from which we must set forth with more determination than ever. Once we have recognized that the absolute is forever out of reach but that we are free, fundamentally free, we must ask ourselves what this freedom is to serve. In Sartre's view the capacity for the good lies in the awareness of our freedom and in the possibility of making our own lives, but the possibility of choice means responsibility as well. The problem was not to negate life, to withdraw from the world; it became, rather, "What is man to do with his staggering freedom?"

For Sartre the answer became more apparent and more urgent toward the end of the war. Freedom can never mean immobility, since it is by nature creative; in its incessant actualization, one must choose, and in choosing, one must belong. We have reached Sartre's famous *"engagement,"* or commitment. Just as in the realm of the noetic, consciousness is a revelation of that which is, so also freedom and choice must be the will *of* something. There is no will for nothing, just as there is no consciousness without a world.

We are told by Simone de Beauvoir that around this time Sartre became very friendly with the painter Giacometti. It was both a meeting of minds and also to an extent, a synchronization of methods. Giacometti is described by Simone de Beauvoir as being not only a talented painter but also a man who had brains, "a really first-class mind, the sort that *sticks to hard facts and shakes the meaning out of them.*"[13] Now this is exactly what phenomenology wants to do: it reveals what appears to man and the meaning of that phenomenon as well. Meaning, however, appears against a background, and background for a painter—and here we return to

[13] *The Prime of Life*, p. 386.

Giacometti—implies that a portrait is never painted in isolation but that it is one with its surroundings, just as the mind and the will of man are caught in a situation, Sartre's *engagement*. It was in this mood of commitment that he tried to organize the resistance group which we have already mentioned, a group which in its attempt to embrace and *engage* other middle-class intellectuals was to prove abortive. Sartre learned from this experience that however much he praised direct action and despised contemplation, he was himself made for the latter. More theoretician than actor, his "work" was writing and his action was to take the form of founding a new review to set forth the fruits of his contemplation.

Les Temps Modernes

The review was *Les Temps Modernes,* which first appeared in 1945, with Sartre, Raymond Aron, Merleau-Ponty, and Simone de Beauvoir on its editorial board. Its introductory article, written by Sartre, was a minor masterpiece.[14] Surprisingly enough, it is rarely read, yet it is worthy of greater attention, for it contains the *Critique de la Raison Dialectique* in a nutshell.

In this presentation Sartre outlines the purpose of his review. *Les Temps Modernes* will not take any stand in favor of a political party, but it will take a position toward social and political problems in accordance with the concept of man that it defends. Its content will reflect the editors' conviction that literature must have a social function. It firmly believes in man as an absolute, when considered in *his* time and *his* milieu. In this sense also the individual philosopher can be said to be an absolute, when viewed within his own epoch, surrounded by his friends and followers, working out his ideas and writing his books. In other words, I can say that Descartes is an absolute, while Cartesianism is only a

---

[14] A sound translation of this article has been published in the fine anthology: *Paths to the Present,* edited by Eugen J. Weber (New York, 1962). The translation is by Françoise Ehrmann.

relative value: the man is dead, but the philosophy continues to stroll through the centuries, "where everyone can find what he puts into it."[15]

It is but a short step from the concept of man as an absolute within his own milieu to that of man as revealing himself through his *dialectical* structure, his being shaped by and his shaping of that milieu. The radical innovation which a dialectical approach brings becomes clear when we consider its opposite, the *analytical* method, so dear to the heart of the bourgeois. For the bourgeois, men are like "peas in a can," all alike, juxtaposed, each of them equally available for an examination by the *analytical* mind, that is, able to be defined, classified, and categorized.[16] Thus is man analyzed and placed. The bourgeois philosopher never thinks of the living dialectic, of the movement of reciprocity which links man to man. He does not see man as free creativity, man made by a fundamental "project," which affects his every gesture, every word, and every deed. Man manifests himself always and in every way, whether he chooses a wife or buys a tie; man is everywhere, "he is the whole earth."[17] *Les Temps Modernes,* in helping men to become aware of what they are and can do, will liberate them.

It may appear at first glance that the bourgeois with his analytical approach, whereby human beings are juxtaposed and separated, protects the individual more than the *dialectical* and *synthetic* approach, which attempts to tie people together. The truth of the matter is that Sartre wants to see both methods combined, for within the global scheme of the dialectical and the synthetic, one must also take into account the analytical. The place of both these elements is not yet clearly defined and the author will in the years to come show where they belong.[18]

[15] *Paths to the Present,* p. 435.
[16] *Ibid.,* p. 436.
[17] *Ibid.,* p. 439.
[18] Sartre has kept his promise. The *Critique de la Raison Dialectique* contains among other things an elaborate clarification concerning the distinction between the *dialectical* and the *analytical.*

This was the end of the beginning; *Les Temps Modernes* was launched and promptly set out for the open sea. It was from the start an enormous periodical, appearing ten times a year and totaling close to a thousand pages annually. It was avant-gardist, leftist in the world of politics, though without formal ties with the Communist party, existentialist in the realm of philosophy, socially minded, though without a definite program in the domain of literature. The list of editors changed over the years. After a while the name of Merleau-Ponty was dropped from the inside cover, as was that of Aron and even that of Simone de Beauvoir. The one name which never disappeared, however, was that of its most prolific, possibly its most talented writer, Jean-Paul Sartre himself. If he was the pillar of the review, it was in turn his tribune, for it gave him the chance to publish whatever he wanted of his own work and an outlet for his flowing discourses, aptly called *articles-fleuves*, which spilled his ideas over the market place. Keeping in mind the purpose of our study, I shall merely give here those ideas appearing in *Les Temps Modernes* that can be considered milestones along the way to the *magnum opus*. For *Les Temps Modernes* is an invaluable source book to uncover the genesis of the later work, and anyone who reads both the *Critique de la Raison Dialectique* and *Les Temps Modernes* will have no difficulty in noticing that some of Sartre's views were reshaped through their contact with the incisive criticism coming from such men as Merleau-Ponty, Albert Camus, and Claude Lefort. Sartre, like all of us, owes much to his opponent, for writing about dialectic goes hand in hand with practicing it, and in publishing his review, Sartre performed an old feat: he well knew that sails move on opposing winds.

His most famous, perhaps also his best article appeared under the title "Matérialisme et Révolution."[19] It made a deep impression everywhere and has remained to this day an

---

[19] A selection of articles from *Les Temps Modernes* came out in the collection *Situations*. Some were translated into English under the title: *Literary and Philosophical Essays*.

undigested piece for his Marxist opponents. It consists mainly of an accusation against the materialistic dogma of modern Marxism. Young men are told to choose between materialism and idealism, Sartre claims, yet the sophism of such a choice should be obvious. For the modern Marxist, the *subject* is always *object*, that is, he is a product of matter and of the evolution of matter. The Marxist has barely stated that dogma when he turns around and acting as if he were subject and not object, formulates his own dogmas concerning God, History, Finality, etc. How, asks Sartre, could a Reason that is a captive of blind forces still be a Reason which is capable of dictating truth and discovering a world structure?[20] Where is materialism as a general philosophy when, after having buried the subject, one all of a sudden exhumes him again, to make him the Prophet and Metaphysician of History? The final irony is that Soviet Marxism has killed the dialectic in burying the Subject, for if the Subject is a fossil and subjectivity nothing but matter, there can no longer be any living dialectic.[21]

The remedy in Sartre's view is the rejection of matter as the sole infrastructure of the world and of men. The very meaning of *revolution* implies a *going beyond* the present situation, a process that is more than material. The new philosopher—as for example Sartre himself—is the one who embodies "the thinking of the oppressed insofar as they rebel against oppression."[22] He is both thought and action. His thought is more than idealism, for in its unmasking of reality it is at the same time a modification of the real. This approach can already be discovered in Marx (in his *Theses on Feuerbach*) where it is called "practical materialism." But Sartre protests that it should not be called materialism when the oppressed can be shown a way to transcend the present situation toward a world scheme yet to be fulfilled. Transcendence is in itself Freedom, and the revolutionary shows

[20] *Literary and Philosophical Essays*, p. 203.
[21] *Ibid.*, p. 216.
[22] *Ibid.*, p. 227.

by his revolt that he is not a thing, but the master of things, not an object, but a subject. The Revolution plainly demands a new humanism, and this Sartre hopes to offer in the *Critique de la Raison Dialectique*.

SARTRE *vs*. MERLEAU-PONTY

If the previous article ("Matérialisme et Révolution") was unpleasant to the eyes of the Parisian Communist, another series also published in *Les Temps Modernes*, under the title "Les Communistes et la Paix," was more agreeable to read. This series contained a factual defense of the Party and an attempt to convince the workers to join it, since it contained their hopes *portées au rouge*, carried to a white-hot intensity.[23] Sartre maintained that the revolutionary disposition of the worker is fruitless unless organized, for the worker in juxtaposition with other workers is ossified and helpless. Later on, in the *Critique*, Sartre will use the more elaborate term "seriality" to characterize the helplessness inherent in separation and to set out upon a brilliant analysis of the formation of the group. But in these articles we already see the ideas of the *Critique* germinating; conversely, in the light of the later *Critique*, we can better understand the positions he took in these earlier days, positions which at the time were so startling and incomprehensible to his contemporaries.

The French worker, Sartre continues, needs politics, and they must be those of the Party, since a democratic vote, as practiced in the so-called democracies, merely perpetuates his separation. Political democracy will keep the worker isolated and impotent in a world where all the power and money belong to the bourgeoisie. The worker, therefore, needs Authority around which to rally—and Sartre surprisingly launches into an enthusiastic praise of the dictatorial power in the Party—and he needs orders. Playing upon the similarity of the words and of their meaning, Sartre calls the

[23] *Les Temps Modernes*, octobre 1952, p. 697. The entire series is in the following issues: juillet and octobre 1952, avril 1954.

Communist party an "order," a monastic order, with a mission that is absolute and cannot tolerate any criticism.[24] Obedience on the part of the worker now is a guarantee of his freedom in the future. Although Sartre still does not approve of the Marxist position of uncompromising materialism, he nevertheless considers the Party to be the only available organ for conveying the aspirations of the worker.

In the series of articles "Les Communistes et la Paix," the French existentialist has undoubtedly come closer to a Marxist position. There is something pragmatical in his attitude, somewhat resembling that of Charles Maurras, who, although an unbeliever, considers the Catholic Church to be the most valuable instrument for the accomplishment of his nationalistic purposes. So also Jean-Paul Sartre, although an unorthodox Marxist in the eyes of Soviet Marxism, emerges as a fervent believer in the power and efficiency of the Party.

Sartre's articles did not go unopposed. One of his severest critics was an old friend and collaborator; in Merleau-Ponty, Sartre all of a sudden met an opponent of his own size. Merleau-Ponty's criticism came in the form of a book, *Les Aventures de la Dialectique*,[25] which attacked above all certain totalitarian trends in Sartre's position, such as his granting of unlimited power to the Party and of obedience alone to the worker. Sartre wants the proletarian to play a role of complete submission to the Party, to be *passif comme une femme*, maintains Merleau-Ponty, but in preaching that sort of passivity, he seems to have forgotten what happens when the Party has unquestioned mastery. This is all the more strange when we have such a ready example at hand —modern Marxism as realized in Russia should have taught him quickly what happens when the Party wields an exclusive control.[26]

Merleau-Ponty finds the old dualism of *Pour-soi* and *En-*

[24] *Les Temps Modernes*, octobre 1952, p. 759.

[25] Maurice Merleau-Ponty, *Les Aventures de la Dialectique* (Paris, 1955).

[26] *Ibid.*, pp. 146, 148, 149, 175.

soi to be another of Sartre's weaknesses, since the distinction between mind and matter is too neat and too radical, as it is in Cartesianism.[27] This is, ironically enough, unlike the conclusions of Marx himself, who accepted the mediation of things and saw the "presence" of man everywhere—in the tools he uses, on the walls which surround him, in the social group to which he belongs. Sartre, in accepting only *man* and *things*, overlooks the *intermonde*, that in-between-world of history, symbolism, truths to be achieved, etc.[28] In ignoring these realities, Sartre loads upon the individual man too great a weight of responsibility and accomplishment, as if individual consciousness alone counts and the social order is something alien and totally extraneous. One might even go so far as to say that the "social dimension is a scandal for the Cogito."[29] Its existence, while not denied, is nevertheless accepted merely as an activity on the confines of the subject: the world of the Other appears "either as a trap, or a menace, or as a task, either behind us as a remorse, or ahead of us as project," but always as something which has in one way or another made *me* incomplete or otherwise oppresses *me*.[30]

For Sartre, then, there is no *world* of literature. He accepts "a Julien Sorel of Stendhal *and* one of Taine *and* one of Leon Blum *and* one of Paul Bourget" but refuses to co-adunate these entities into a world.[31] The world of literature, emptied by Sartre of all inner consistency, becomes nothing but a construction of the *Pour-soi*. Merleau-Ponty

[27] *Ibid.*, p. 185.

[28] *Ibid.*, p. 269. This is an instance where Sartre, feeling the opposing winds, took another tack in the *CRD*. Whether he veered sufficiently remains to be seen.

[29] *Ibid.*, p. 208. Here again Sartre has made great attempts in the *CRD* to emphasize the dialectic and to improve his philosophy of the intersubjective. I am still of the opinion that on that point Merleau-Ponty was right, and although starting from a totally different viewpoint, I shall draw conclusions similar to his. My attempt will be to show that Sartre is not so much an Hegelian as he is a Cartesian.

[30] *Ibid.*, p. 209.

[31] *Ibid.*, p. 190.

concludes that Sartre has no real dialectic, since the break between the *Pour-soi* and the *En-soi* is too radical to allow for an authentic circularity, nor has he a real philosophy of intersubjectivity, since the social dimension is merely built up from the viewpoint of the Self. Between the *Pour-soi* and the *En-soi* there is indeed nothingness.

Merleau-Ponty goes on to question Sartre's assertion that truth in the social order is what the poorest of the poor see, in other words, that truth is the accusation we read in their eyes.[32] This, he believes, clearly shows how Sartre *speculates,* yet does not *observe,* or rather observes what his speculations have led him to look for. Caught in a position, he is unable to see the whole clearly. Instead of taking the look of the poor as a norm, one might better look at the whole world and its present situation, observe events impartially and see how they have evolved. This means keeping an eye not only upon the poor but upon the bourgeois as well and noticing how he may have moved away from the positions of his grandfather. Sartre's implication becomes even more unrealistic when the Revolution has achieved its course. Shall we in that hypothesis still apply the same norm? Is the look of the poorest of the poor in Russia still a criterion of truth? It must be, since there is no other. And if so, it is doubtful whether that look will be one of unqualified blessing and approval.[33]

The peculiar situation of *Les Temps Modernes* is that like everything else in Sartre's world, it had to be an example of creative freedom. Starting from a present that is permitted no past, its contributors were to belong neither to church nor to political group. They and the review itself had to start from nothing beyond the belief in man's freedom itself. Merleau-Ponty asks whether this attitude does not hide a fundamental error, that of calling for a continual start from zero and of dreaming of an incessant creation, when in fact this is impossible. There is no *creatio ex nihilo;* there is only creation with the material at our disposal, material that is

[32] *Ibid.*, p. 207.
[33] *Ibid.*

already shaped before it reaches our hands. Our judgment has always a pre-predicative basis, of which it is often not aware and which in his own situation Sartre seems to ignore. In actual fact his review itself started moving in a definite direction, toward the Communist camp, whether it wanted to or not. It reached a position which it had not exactly intended to reach when it started, and at no point along the way was an article brought into the world *ex nihilo*.[34]

Merleau-Ponty also brought up Sartre's greatest vulnerability, a criticism the eternal would-be Communist had to hear more than once: Is it fair to appoint oneself judge and theoretician of the Party and yet refuse to become a member?[35] Sartre believes that this can be done, but why, then, is he less tolerant for the French worker, whom he obliges to carry a card membership and thereby deprives of the freedom he so generously offers to himself. Is communism, perhaps, the sort of organization that one admires, envies, looks at, but doesn't ever join? This attitude might be defensible when one confronts some other world vision, but can it be upheld by a Marxist, who so radically rejects all idealism to preach action and total engagement?

While Sartre himself did not directly answer the penetrating critique of his old friend, Simone de Beauvoir went to the rescue in a carefully documented article, "Merleau-Ponty et le Pseudo-Sartrisme,"[36] the gist of which is that since Merleau-Ponty had not understood Sartre, his statements were a mere tilting at windmills. Sartre's philosophy, she claims, was never a philosophy of the Subject only, but one of the Subject conditioned by the world, for without a world there is no Self.[37] To prove her point, the author combs the works of her friend and extracts a great number of texts which emphasize the unavoidable interrelation of world and

[34] *Ibid.,* p. 258.
[35] *Ibid.,* p. 216.
[36] *Les Temps Modernes,* juin 1955, later published together with other essays under the title *Privilèges* (Paris, 1955).
[37] *Privilèges,* p. 206.

self. Against the accusation that Sartre has no grasp of dialectic and reduces every action to spontaneous creation, Simone de Beauvoir insists that action is never born from nothingness but that it results from a concrete situation and that this situation is one of *need:* I act not for the joy of acting but because I am hungry or because in one way or another my situation is untenable. The Revolution is not *un article de luxe,* it is a need. It is not so much the echo of freedom—the poor do not even know what freedom is—as it is the result of unbearable frustration.[38] "The bite of nothingness upon being is not in this case called freedom but need."[39]

The same observation can be made concerning History. History is neither mere action, nor vertiginous freedom, nor frivolous creativity, but it is the persistent attempt to do the best we can with the knowledge of the moment. If we are told that "truth lies in the look of the poor," it simply means that the falsity of society lies in its oppression, which, however much it is masked by idealism and argumentation, is revealed by the poorest of the poor.[40] Finally, in answer to the reproach that Sartre's flirtation with communism does not *really* involve him, since he prudently remains outside the fold, Simone de Beauvoir claims that although Sartre is not a member of the Party, he is nonetheless exemplary in his understanding of the poor and their needs, while Merleau-Ponty, living in a world of ideas and nursing in his heart a nostalgia for the religious, refuses to acknowledge a world which is human, all too human.[41]

Such, then, is the duel of two old friends. No literary duel

[38] *Ibid.*, p. 236.
[39] *Ibid.*, p. 235.
[40] *Ibid.*, p. 254.
[41] Comparing Merleau-Ponty's prose and Mlle. de Beauvoir's answer, I found the latter harder, almost to the point of being insulting. Later she became aware of the difference of tone and wrote: "*Quant à lui, il ne m'en voulut pas, ou du moins pas longtemps: il pouvait comprendre les colères intellectuelles. D'ailleurs, tout en ayant l'un pour l'autre une très grande amitié, nos disputes étaient souvent vives; je m'emportais, et il souriait.*" *La Force des Choses*, p. 342.

was ever taken too seriously in France, including this one.[42] Yet the sharp thrusts and ripostes revealed a fundamental opposition which philosophically speaking was never bridged. To this writer it appears that Merleau-Ponty has raised some crucial questions, and although he himself was the first to agree that Sartre was *célèbre*, tacitly implying that he did not share the same widespread fame, it is not so obvious whose impact in the long run will be the more pervasive.[43] One should add that Merleau-Ponty's opposition has affected Sartre's philosophical position in the *Critique de la Raison Dialectique*. Further study will reveal that in his later work he attempts to give the dialectic more room and to curtail the impact of the human Subject. Whether he does so sufficiently is something else again. In any case *Les Temps Modernes* was for Sartre an excellent sounding board. It was an organ where he could express his own views, where his opponents in most cases found ample occasion to answer— Sartre was generous in allotting them space—and where some of his followers like Simone de Beauvoir, Francis Jeanson, or Marcel Péju were in charge of administering the *coup de grâce*.

The Dispute, Sartre–Camus

Although this event is of lesser importance for our purpose, I mention it here as one more example of Sartre's growing Marxist sympathies and the unavoidable result, the loss of another good friend. When Albert Camus published *L'Homme Révolté* in 1954,[44] it was reviewed by Francis Jeanson in *Les Temps Modernes* under the title "Camus ou

---

[42] For an account of their later reconciliation see *Merleau-Ponty Vivant*. This was a special issue of *Les Temps Modernes*, bearing no date, but published between the issues of July and November 1961 and numbered 184–185.

[43] On this topic, see James Collins in *Cross Currents*, XIII, No. 2, p. 197.

[44] English trans., *The Rebel* (New York, 1954).

l'Ame Révoltée."[45] The title in itself was insulting and
clearly implied that Camus' position was no longer in line
with that of *Les Temps Modernes*. Actually Camus' *l'homme
révolté* does believe in revolt, but not in an extreme form.
Similarly he believes in unions, but without political affilia-
tion, in socialism, but not through totalitarian methods, in
action, but only in fulfillment of a transcendental Idea.
Sartre, with his distrust of anything abstract, could not accept these qualifications of his own concreteness. Ironically,
it will be his persistent problem later on to discover a way
of writing history without drawing up an abstract blueprint,
to take a stand without positing ultimate norms, to construct
a system that is supple and elastic enough, without falling
into Platonization.

Camus wrote a letter of reply to *Les Temps Modernes*
which he addressed directly to Sartre, calling him "*Monsieur
le Directeur*."[46] This was an unfortunate beginning. The letter that followed was extremely well written; it was sensible,
prudent, polite, but just a little too elegant. It was this slight
touch of artificiality which Sartre ridiculed from the start.
In his answer, an enormous river of prose that is a prime
example of his *articles-fleuves*, he made huge fun of the sol-
emn tone of Camus: Why should he, close friend for ten
years, now be called "*Monsieur le Directeur?*" Sartre point-
edly countered with "*Mon Cher Camus*." But whatever may
be their prose—they were in their own ways both first-rate
writers—their opinions were divergent. Sartre's attitude was
more combative and radical, Camus' more sensitive, with a
deeper *sens de la mesure*.[47] Here again, as with Merleau-

[45] *Les Temps Modernes*, mai 1952.

[46] *Les Temps Modernes*, juillet 1952.

[47] Sartre's break with Camus was for all practical purposes a definitive one, and the two old friends were never really reconciled. Although Simone de Beauvoir had been somewhat close to Albert Camus,
she took the side of her friend in this split and subsequently judged
Camus rather harshly. See *La Force des Choses*, pp. 60, 126, 144,
and 279. I, for one, find her judgment of the author of *The Plague*
and *The Stranger* too severe. Whatever Simone de Beauvoir may say,
it is undeniable that Camus' influence is great and that his books
have a strong fascination upon students, as any professor can attest.

Ponty, Camus was not uninfluential upon Sartre. Since he was less of a philosopher than Merleau-Ponty and lacked his technical precision, his influence was more vague, but I think we may say that the example of his restraint kept Sartre from taking any more extreme positions than he did.

A dramatic blow came with the massacre of the Hungarian freedom fighters in the revolt of Budapest in 1956. A few weeks before, I had met Sartre in Paris and at that time he still expressed great hopes in Khrushchev, whom he considered to be a man who would give a new turn to Russian politics and to Marxism in general. *"Il a du respect pour l'homme en tant que tel!"* Sartre told me. His high hopes were sadly crushed along with the young idealists with the entry of Russian tanks into Budapest.

A six-hundred-page copy of *Les Temps Modernes* was devoted to "La Révolte de la Hongrie."[48] Although the opinions of the contributors were various, the general trend was emphatically anti-Russian, with the repressive action of the Soviet sternly condemned by all. Sartre himself wrote a long introductory article under the title "Le Fantôme de Staline," in which he considered the Russian intervention to be a remote effect of Stalinism. He no less fiercely condemned the attitude of the French Communist party for its slavish submission "to the dictates of Moscow." "The time of revealed truths, of the words of the Gospel is gone: a Communist party is possible in the West only when it has the right of free examen."[49] A similar attestation was published by Sartre in the Parisian weekly *L'Express* on January 6, 1957. The conclusion of both articles did not imply a total break with Marxism—Sartre will remain a Marxist, though always on his own terms—but it definitely contained a severe condemnation of the Russian intervention and marked at the same time a cooling off in the relations between the Party and its intellectual critic. In the *Critique* he makes it quite clear that *his* kind of Marxism is not to be equated with communism.

[48] *Les Temps Modernes,* janvier 1957.
[49] *Ibid.,* p. 693.

Sartre has never changed his position on Budapest, as we shall see later, and for this honesty, at times even blunt sincerity, he deserves our respect. The very fact that the philosopher can find himself caught between *praxis* and theory, however, points to a basic problem. Sartre, as a philosopher, cannot avoid philosophizing and as a man of ideas, cannot avoid theories. The difficulty arises with the idea of *engagement,* which links *praxis* and theory together. Accordingly, the philosopher cannot live and think apart from events and from the masses which carry these events. By essence *engagé,* he comes down into the cave and like Plato's visionary, mixes with the prisoners. His is the temptation, even the task, of continual commitment, with its attendant risk of making mistakes. Sartre's political thought can be said to rest upon empiricism, but, in being continually dependent upon the pragmatical, it lacks by principle any fundamental norm beyond a vague resentment toward all that is bourgeois, a current that runs all through *Les Temps Modernes.* "Bourgeois" is used here in its broadest sense as the incarnation of all that is inert and traditional.

We may conclude that what the French existentialist opposes is often eloquently described, but just what global truth he wants to see fulfilled is often left in the darkness of the cave. No wonder, then, that many of his admirers were hopefully looking forward to the publication of the magnum opus which they knew Sartre had been working upon all these years and which was finally published in 1960 as the *Critique de la Raison Dialectique.* When its 755 pages of small print came from the press, it became clear once more that the philosopher was not himself going into the street, for its depth of penetration and brilliance of insight proved that when all is said and done, he has no greater commitment than that to his desk.

Chapter II

MARXIST SEMANTICS

Although the Communist party had already existed for many years in France, the introduction to Hegel, and with this, a genuine Marxist intellectualism did not take place until around 1936, when Alexandre Kojève, a leading Hegelian, began to give his courses on *The Phenomenology of Mind* at the Ecole des Hautes-Etudes.[1] His early audiences included an intellectual élite—Sartre, Merleau-Ponty, Hyppolite, Fessard, and others—and through them the immense significance which Hegel holds for the modern world erupted upon the French intellectual scene. The impact of Hegelianism was immediately apparent in the recognition of its importance to Marxism and the increasing and more knowledgeable use among intellectuals of terms like "dialectic" and "alienation." More subtly, the study of Hegel was inspirational in the launching of three separate, singularly powerful movements. These were, in brief: the Phenomenological, led by Merleau-Ponty, whose work showed the profound influence of Husserl as well as of Hegel; the Existentialist with Sartre; and the Personalistic with Emmanuel Mounier, whose leftist periodical *Esprit* was characterized by its outspoken political and social defense of the concept of person.[2] All three of these movements, with the excep-

[1] These lectures were later published under the title: *Introduction à la Lecture de Hegel. Leçons sur la Phénomenologie de l'Esprit* (Paris, 1947).

[2] This triple division was given by Henri Lefebvre in an article entitled "Le Marxisme et la Pensée Française," *Les Temps Modernes,* juillet–août, 1957. The article is short but provocative. Sartre and

tion of Gabriel Marcel's particular form of existentialism, sympathized with Marxism in a more or less pronounced degree. It is therefore vital for us to have firmly in mind the speculative position and terminology of Marx, as he was influenced by Hegel, in order to understand this important part of the modern intellectual world, and in particular, that segment we have chosen to examine in detail, the first volume of Sartre's *Critique de la Raison Dialectique.*

THE CONCEPT OF NEED

Sartre's project in *L'Etre et le Néant* might be said to have been an incessant attempt to fill the void which is man. His speculative approach in that work showed strikingly that the depth of the nought in man desperately wanted *to be* and that the desire for being brought a permanent attraction toward all that which is *En-soi.* It is toward this plenum that man is incessantly carried. Sadly enough, the identification of the nought of human consciousness with the solidity of the outside world was doomed to failure.[3]

In the *Critique* the essential line of this approach has not changed. It has received, however, an even *more concrete and urgent mode,* for the *Pour-soi* is now shown to be a being of need, a being which in order to live *must* have an object capable of assuaging its hunger. On this level Sartre makes no claim of originality. More than a hundred years before, Marx had already asserted that since man is a being of nature, a being which is part of nature and lives from nature, he is also a being of need. "Hunger is a natural need; it requires therefore a nature outside itself, an object outside itself in order to be satisfied and stilled."[4] Hunger is of course only *one* need. Man also seeks clothing, sex, habitation, and

---

Lefebvre do not see eye to eye in the domain of Marxist interpretation, but Sartre nevertheless gives his opponent a hearing.

[3] See *Being and Nothingness,* pp. 615 and 627.

[4] Marx, *Economic and Philosophical Manuscripts of 1844,* in Erich Fromm's *Marx's Concept of Man,* p. 182.

it would be naïve and unrealistic to study the history of man-kind either at its inception or at any stage along the way without considering these needs and the continual attempts to fulfill them. Such attempts are inseparable from produc-tion, and we can assert without hesitation that material pro-duction lies at the beginning of and *is* History.[5] Even saints and men of ascetical detachment were not exempted from this imperative. The founder of the Trappists, wanting noth-ing more than a walking stick, had to go into the forest in order to cut one from a tree. In this simple feat St. Bruno was performing an act of material production.[6] Few men are satisfied with so little, of course, for generally as soon as needs are satisfied, new needs arise. The only way to satisfy this incessant, unremitting claim of nature is through labor, for need, in becoming passion, stirs man to action.

Since it is in the light of the notion of *need* that the *Other* gets his particular significance, the concept will become piv-otal for Sartre. We should be prepared, however, to find in the *Critique* that he more frequently uses the word *scarcity* to point to a situation that engenders need. Sartre will repeat over and over that it is in a world of scarcity (*dans un monde de la rareté*) that need originates. In this world where there is not enough of everything, the presence of the Other threat-ens the satisfaction of my own needs. It is in such a world that the Other appears to me even more harshly than he did in *L'Etre et le Néant*, where his Look provoked my reaction and his presence was a source of shame, or of pride, or of humiliation,[7] for now he has become a danger for my sur-vival as well. In short, he is more than a mere Self whose recognition I desperately require in order to consolidate the dimension of my own Self, as he was in Hegel and in *L'Etre*

[5] Marx, *German Ideology*, in Fromm's *Marx's Concept of Man*, p. 200.

[6] *Ibid.*, p. 206.

[7] *Being and Nothingness*, pp. 369, 379, 404 ff.; *The Tragic Finale*, pp. 67 and 71.

et le Néant. He has now become the Opponent who threatens me in my very survival.

ALIENATION

Alienation is not an easy term to define, but if we first go back to Hegel and Feuerbach, we shall be able to fix its meaning in Marx himself. In pursuing *alienation* as the enemy of genuine accomplishment and freedom, Marx drew heavily upon Hegel's use of the concept in *The Phenomenology of Mind.* Hegel gives the word most of its original etymological sense, whereby to be alienated means to be estranged, or in one way or another not to be at home. A consciousness which projects its substance outside itself, or in other words, exteriorizes itself is alienated. In a vain attempt to reach this myth which it has projected outside itself, whether in the form of a god or any other, human consciousness becomes unhappy.[8] Alienations are multiple, as one can easily imagine, but all are in common characterized by some form of exteriorization and by an incessant craving that is never satisfied. Hegel's *Phenomenology* is the long journey of consciousness looking for itself. Where Proust builds up a meticulous description of a mind recuperating time past *à la recherche du temps perdu,* Hegel, absorbing the past, moves onward *à la recherche de son âme,* which eventually after a long dialectic he claims to discover in the identification of the Self with the Absolute.

In the post-Hegelian tradition, the term *alienation* points to the unnatural situation of the individual who has built for himself a visionary world of abstractions and dwells in that empyrean of dreams instead of facing reality as it is. Feuerbach presents us with a well-known example in his *Essence of Christianity,* where man is shown to embody each one of his main faculties—mind, will, and heart—in a Superior Being. In positing his aspirations as fulfilled in the Deity, man deems himself to be by contrast weak and powerless.

[8] Hegel, *The Phenomenology of Mind,* trans. J. B. Baillie (London, 1931), pp. 253 ff.

This conception of a Being which exists at a great distance in all the splendor of his isolation results in alienation for man. In an attempt to overcome this alienation, man loves "God" and through belief in the incarnation of his Son finds a means of reunion with the distant Deity. All this is, in Feuerbach's opinion, not only deceitful but actually harmful. Man must confront the earth and make his happiness *there*, rather than live in the vain desire of a nonexistent God. "*Homo homini Deus!* Man is God for himself!"

In taking over the notion of alienation from Hegel's speculations and Feuerbach's application of those speculations, Marx attempted to give it a more forceful and aggressive character. He was more pessimistic than his predecessors, for to him alienation has been an enormous source of grief, far surpassing that of the unhappy consciousness. Marx, wary of all abstraction, disregards the dialectic of *The Phenomenology of Mind,* where Hegel slowly but with great depth unrolls for us the gradual enrichment of the soul as it climbs toward its identification with the Whole. This is too remote for Marx, for whom alienation immediately takes a concrete form; to define means to diversify, and alienation is either intellectual, economic, or political. Something which can be pinned down can be more easily removed, and this removal of alienations, one by one, becomes the concrete form of man's earthly combat against all suffering.

One may wonder of course just what that complete human being is whose alienations are successively cancelled, and one may ask as well just what his ideal fulfillment ought to be. On this no clear answer seems available. Marx—and Sartre after him—is more successful in telling us what man must not be: the free man who emerges from all his entangling alienations is still an unknown.

INTELLECTUAL ALIENATION

In October 1836 Marx went to study in Berlin and was immediately caught by the philosophy then in fashion—he became a Hegelian. His Hegelianism was of the left wing variety, whose adherents, unlike those of the right, claimed to have given up all acceptance of the Hegelian speculative doctrine and kept only its dialectical method. In addition, the left wing Hegelian was more liberal politically than his opponent, who tended to be conservative. This explains Marx's first defeat: he became editor of the *Rheinische Zeitung*, but after a few years, the censors no longer permitted the newspaper to appear.

This experience taught Marx that philosophy by itself was insufficient and that in order to reach the masses and break through the opposition which inevitably confronts speculative dreams, action is necessary. It became clearer every day to Marx—it was to become an obsession later in his life—that one must transform the world, not merely interpret it philosophically. He wrote in 1845 his *Theses on Feuerbach* (unpublished during his lifetime), in which he attempted to prove that the best way to realize a philosophy was to suppress it as an entity of mere contemplation and speculation. A similar position is developed in another book, *The Holy Family*, where philosophy is accused of soaring above *praxis*. It will be Sartre's constant preoccupation in his *Critique de la Raison Dialectique* as well as in certain minor publications to convince the reader that revolution is action almost to the exclusion of planning.[9] On a similar topic Henri Lefebvre writes, "Truth is the concrete."[10] This is the bridge connecting Marxism and existentialism, upon which Sartre himself will linger. For Marx as for Sartre philosophical abstractions in themselves have no efficacy. "There is no immobile absolute, no spiritual beyond. The propositions of the *philosophia perennis* are either nothing but tautologies or receive definite meaning only through an historical and empirical context."[11] In passing, one cannot refrain from noting that these radical assertions do not seem to have cut down upon

[9] See, for example, the collection of articles published in English under the title *Sartre on Cuba* (New York, 1961).

[10] *Le Matérialisme Dialectique* (Paris, 1949), pp. 54–55.

[11] *Ibid.*

the number of Marxist theoreticians who are prolific writers or in any way inhibited them from replacing "obsolete and traditional speculations" by a no less verbose dialectic.

Religious Alienation

In this attack against all abstraction and alienation, the religious man comes in for heavy criticism. There is no doubt in the mind either of Marx or of his followers that religion estranges man from this earth and prevents him from becoming completely human. It is doubly dangerous in that it not only affects man in his individual condition but also contaminates his social standing, for the problem of religion is tied up with the political structure of the state. According to Marx, a state which is religious, whether officially or by way of the private convictions of some of its citizens, is an unhealthy state, for the ascendance of religion is a sign of political decline. Here Marx is more radical than other non-Christian philosophers, such as Bruno Bauer, who still tolerated religion in private practice.[12] For Marx, as soon as a private citizen is something more than a mere citizen, he is a divided man. Living on this earth, which it may be well to remember is very earthly, he wants to play his part, and yet he wants at the same time to bet upon the supernatural. The separation of Church and State does not in Marx's opinion provide a solution to this "contradictory" situation. As long as the private citizen remains a religious man, one may as well keep the two identical.

Marx's principal objection to religion is summed up in the well-known formula, "Religion is an opium for the people." He believed that religion, in giving people a justification for the evils of this world through promises of hope in some future happiness, lulls them into an attitude of resignation. The inspiration for this is Feuerbach, who first pointed out

[12] Bruno Bauer (1809–82) was a German theologian, a Hegelian, and a radical opponent of Christianity who published a great number of works on theology. He also became an ardent admirer of Bismarck.

the myth-making mania of the sufferer in *The Essence of Christianity*. Marx goes beyond his predecessor, however, in wanting, above and beyond an explanation of the religious attitude, its elimination as well. This will only take place, of course, after social and economic reforms have been made.

Marx's position is debatable at this point. He does not consider the possibility that religion in itself might be a natural phenomenon, which neither attachment to the world nor dialectic are able to cure. It is possible that the metaphysical structure of man may be one of dependence upon a Supreme Being which is the origin and end of life, and that the act of invocation is not addressed merely to a Myth. From a purely pragmatic point of view, one may wonder whether an atheistic position, in which man becomes an all-powerful and self-sufficient center, goes farther toward the elimination of economic alienation. Might not atheism lead to a hardening of relations between men, while the recognition of God could bring with it a recognition of all men as brothers?[13] All these are questions which a social reformer might consider worthy of consideration. But neither Marx himself nor his existentialist disciple lose much time on the topic of religion. "*Je ne m'occupe pas de Dieu, je m'occupe de l'homme!*" Sartre once told me, and it appears that he has followed this rule to the letter in his *Critique de la Raison Dialectique*.

POLITICAL ALIENATION

In the clarification of Marx's political ideas, we find ourselves once more face to face with Hegel, for he is responsible for Marx's position on the concept of the State, this time not as master, but as opponent. This is not surprising when we recall that in politics Hegel was an arch conservative. For him the State is an advanced form of civilization, a form

[13] *Cf.* Jean-Yves Calvez, *La Pensée de Karl Marx* (Paris, 1956), pp. 98, 632 ff.

which the Spirit takes on in the latest phases of its evolution
through History and in which the freedom of the individual
reaches its fulfillment. Freedom thus goes together with an
ideal State, but this freedom must be understood strictly in
the sense of obedience and devotion, based upon personal
conviction, to a rationally organized State.[14]

According to Hegel, this ideal State was actually being
fulfilled, or in his terms, was "real" in the constitutional and
hereditary monarchy of Prussia, a regime which was basically authoritarian and left to its Parliament merely a con-
sultative vote. Hegel believed that the "rational" works itself
out gradually but inevitably in the "real" course of History,
and that this had indeed happened in his own State, which
was rational as well as real. This being so, any attempt of
revolution or any thought of clandestine activity would be
"irrational." Impatience is unwarranted in any case, for History in the long run will successfully implement the concept
of an authentic State.[15]

At this point Marx voiced his opposition. He could not
consider patience to be the mark of a reformer, or approve
of the concept of the State as an objectification of the Spirit,
or as one more phase in the grandiose panorama of the Ideal
fulfilling itself through the ages. All this he could only consider to be part of a speculative and ideological structure
which diverts attention from the real and the important,
which is, in Marx's understanding, the masses. Instead of
walking on its head, the Hegelian system ought to be turned
about and placed on its feet: the "real" political world is
constituted by the masses and by class structure, not by any
ideal political superstructure. It is precisely this inversion of
values which in Marx's eyes constitutes political alienation.

In a comment upon Paragraph 261 of Hegel's *Philosophy*

[14] *Philosophy of Right*, Paragraph 149. See also his *Philosophy of
History*, Preface.
[15] *Philosophy of Right*, Preface. For comment on the famous apho-
rism: "The rational is real and the real is rational," see Franz Grégoire,
Etudes Hégéliennes (Louvain, 1958), p. 314.

of Right, Marx reasserts his view. According to the paragraph under discussion, the State is a necessary entity which is exterior to private and civil rights and superior to both. Marx objects that this exterior entity is endowed with a real dimension and real power, whereby the average individual is divested of all control and becomes politically alienated.[16] In this case, the state is not fulfilled in the people and the masses are not sovereign; on the contrary, something unreal and idealistic, which is embodied in the sovereign and is exterior and superior to all the others, holds the reins. Hegel's Prussia certainly cannot be called a democracy.

Marx proposes an alternative: real democracy is the identification of the State with civil society. In this view the State is no longer incarnated in the prince and is no longer a "superior" and "exterior" concept. Real universality refuses to be confined within the "particularity" of a prince, but is spread out among the people. But—and this is an interesting progress—the reason for political alienation lies in the class system, which engenders the opposition of classes, with the superior class being that which in princely fashion holds the reins of government. This typically Marxist position, followed so enthusiastically by Sartre, leads to Marx's position on social and economic problems, for the only way to overcome the political problem is first to take care of the social and economic situation.

Economic Alienation

We have arrived at the last alienation on the road toward "perfect" self-achievement. If economic alienation can be overcome, man will have reached his complete restoration.

As far as practical applications of economic alienation were concerned, Marx found ample examples in the country where he had established himself, though he could have found equally sad examples elsewhere. This was the England of

---

[16] *Critique de la Philosophie de l'Etat de Hegel,* MEGA, I, I, pp. 425 ff.

child labor. Between 1820 and 1850 hundreds of children between the ages of four and five were brought to factories to work.[17] In 1835 the English economist Ure discovered among the workers in the factories which he visited over ten thousand children who were less than eleven years old. It was an epoch when proletarian misery and capitalistic abuse were at their peak and Marx could observe it all at first hand.

[He turned once more to Hegel for his theoretical interpretation of the economic alienation that was behind all this misery. This return to Hegel is important not only for a clear grasp of Marxism but of Sartre as well, since Sartre's method in the *Critique* is much more Hegelian than Husserlian.

It is Hegel's claim that the Self asserts itself through negation, that is, a Self which is merely in the *an sich* state (or what we may call an immature and unreflected state) becomes *für sich* (clearly and fully itself) through its negation of the Other.[18] This happens through the encounter of Self *A* with Self *B*: upon meeting *B*, *A* proceeds to cancel or to negate *B*. But in the selfsame act of (mental) cancellation, it discovers itself to be mediated. The same process appears in reverse movement, coming from *B* to *A* and returning to *B*. Each in and through the mediation of the Other returns into itself and realizes in truth and in objective certainty its own existence through the Other. I am only a Self if I make myself recognized by the Other, and if I recognize the Other in the same way. This dialectic, a form of rebounding reciprocity, will be much used by Sartre, and we shall come back to it later in a further clarification from Sartre's own examples.

Marx himself was less attracted by this particular game. The content of the later pages of the *Phenomenology* seduced him more, where Hegel develops his ideas on Master and Slave.[19] According to this theory, when two egos face

---

[17] G. Weil, *L'Eveil des Nationalités et le Mouvement Liberal, 1815–1848* (Paris, 1930), p. 327.

[18] Hegel, *The Phenomenology of Mind*, Ch. IV, p. 229.

[19] *Ibid.*, p. 235.

one another, one asserts itself with greater power and makes the other "unessential." The other then is vanquished and becomes the slave, while the first becomes the master. The slave is caught up in "thinghood," that is, he shares in the dependency of the matter, while the master is liberated and able to live fully. The existence of the master is nonetheless dependent upon the slave both for recognition (he *is* only through recognition) and for the things which the slave makes. The slave cannot, of course, enjoy what the master enjoys. He labors upon the matter in fear and trembling, but a reaction comes, for the hard labor and deep fear trigger what I may call, translating Hegel into modern terms, a "psychic shock" toward gradual recovery and freedom. The wheel of history turns and someday the slave will become the master.

In the *Manuscripts,* Marx very cleverly exploited the Hegelian dialectic of Master and Slave, above all the observation that the slave puts his labor into the thing which the master will later enjoy. The proletarian in a capitalistic regime will be compared to Hegel's slave in four ways: (1) The object or "objectivized labor" which the worker manufactures is taken away from him. While he himself remains dependent, he builds up a capital which is extraneous to himself. The worker produces palaces and lives in hovels.[20] (2) His labor itself is alienated, for it is not freely chosen, but forced, and he is not happy in his work. (3) If man is alienated from both his product and the act of producing it, he is likewise divorced from nature. In order to understand this statement, one must keep in mind that in the Marxist sense, man is coextensive to nature, that is, he lives from the inorganic like animals, only more so, since he is himself more universal. Through his labor, he comes in contact with nature and to an extent identifies himself with nature, but in the world of capitalism, the worker does not in a natural and human way approach the inorganic. His approach to nature is one of compulsion so that it has an artificial character which

[20] Marx, *Economic and Philosophical Manuscripts,* in Fromm's *Marx's Concept of Man,* p. 97.

causes him to revolt and draw into himself.[21] (4) Finally it appears that the worker is alienated in his relation to man, for his resentment breaks up the harmony between men. It should be kept in mind that every alienation which affects the worker has its repercussions upon the capitalist. Even without the opposition engendered by resentment, the capitalist lives an artificial life. Like all men, he should have a close contact with nature, and in refusing to work, he ignores the vocation of his birth.

Even in this brief summary of Marx's views, it clearly appears that he is interested in what may be called the "material dialectic" rather than in Hegel's gradual reconciliation of the Self with itself. What counts for Marx is not a speculative dialectic of reason, but an analysis of the actual relationship of opposite forces within the social order. It is to be expected, then, that Marx will also cast aside Hegel's belief in a redemption of the slave through his own valor and assert that salvation can come only through a reconstruction of the social and economic order, in the course of which the bourgeoisie will be eliminated. The dialectic must be kept moving between man and object, and man and man, and it must do so *scientifically*.

This "scientific" presentation of the dialectic was the object of Marx's study in later years and reached the public toward the end of his life in *Das Kapital*. In that work a famous distinction was first made. The product of labor was shown to have a double value, a *value in use,* when the object satisfies certain needs, and an *exchange value,* when it can be employed as an article of exchange; so, for example, a car has a definite use, yet it can also be used for exchange. Different commodities all have one thing in common—the labor involved in making them. To calculate this element of "common" labor is intricate. It can perhaps be determined when only two commodities are at stake, but it becomes vague and undefined when one is confronted with the universal ex-

[21] *Ibid.*, pp. 100 ff.

change of commodities. Values then must become embodied in something and that something is money. Money becomes value.

Marx will now apply this distinction to the labor of the worker and distinguish between its *exchange value* and its *value in use*. The *value of exchange* is the amount the worker is paid strictly for living and subsistence, while the *value in use* is the amount the labor itself is actually worth. The difference between the two is the *plus-value* of the commodity. The laborer is paid for his living and subsistence, not for the plus-value, which is pocketed by the industrialist as profit. The continual addition of profits results in an accumulation of money which is called *capital* and inversely in a growth in poverty for the laborer. This is the structure of capitalistic society, breeding a fundamental alienation which is at the start of all other alienations. The wealthy capitalist helps to perpetuate an inhuman society, where the opposition of classes is rendered more and more violent.

Opinions differ as to whether or not the younger Marx was more humanistic than the older, with his scientific presentation and his socialized, materialistic economy. Some believe that he was merely expressing in his old age that which was already in him as a young man, while others think that he moved in a totally different domain. Whatever may be the truth, let us merely state at present that to call *Das Kapital* a positive science may be imprudent. Theories on value and plus-value cannot be called scientific in the strict sense of the word. They are not the result of a strict inductive method, nor are they verifiable point by point. In my opinion they are a philosophy, merely a more extensive application of the philosophical views of the younger Marx and *Das Kapital* is nothing but an analysis of the fundamental alienation. It is an economic theory, grounded upon a philosophical view.[22]

[22] *Cf.* Jean Hyppolite, "De la Structure du Capital, et de quelques présuppositions philosophiques dans l'oeuvre de Marx," *Bulletin de la Société Française de Philosophie*, 1948, Vol. 42, pp. 171 ff. As we shall see later, Sartre shows little enthusiasm for Marx's scientific method. This is indeed one of the points where he conflicts with Marx.

One may wonder of course how at the very beginning, chronologically, society developed as it did. If one accepts a form of economic determination within the evolution of society, how shall it be explained at its inception? From whence comes the first "capital"? For Marx, the answer is violence and will to power. History shows us that the law of brutal force had everywhere and always the upper hand and that the primitive accumulation of capital had no other origin.[23] This is a topic which fascinates Sartre, for the question immediately arises whether in addition to the automatic and mechanistic evolution of the material dialectic human factors also play a role, such as human violence, in Marx's formulation—or human choice, in Sartre's terms. For Sartre there is no hesitation. Capitalists have *chosen* to be what they are and have fought for the execution of their free decision. In other words, there is a participation of man in the Marxist machinery and this participation should be recognized.

DIALECTIC

The term *dialectic* inevitably enters into any discussion of Hegel or Marx, and, as the title indicates, of the *Critique de la Raison Dialectique,* so that it might be well to attempt a certain clarification before launching into a detailed examination of Sartre's views.

In Plato's time the term was being used to indicate a movement of the mind, whether that movement be the search, through dialogue and discussion, for the clarification of a concept, or the ascent from a grasp of the concrete form to the contemplation of the universal essence. An example of the latter is given in the *Symposium,* where the soul rises from the concrete form of beauty to the enjoyment of Beauty in itself. In Socrates' view the disciple must start with the love of beautiful forms in the concrete, at first one form only, and then another, and another, until he perceives that beauty in

[23] Marx, *Capital,* English translation by Samuel Moore and Edward Aveling (New York, 1936), pp. 784–85.

every form is one and the same. From then on he will no longer view beauty under this or that form, but growing beyond the relative, he will reach for the contemplation of absolute Beauty.[24]

Aristotle uses the term *dialectic* in opposition to *apodictic*. The apodictic method is a demonstration in the strict sense of the word, while the dialectical can claim only probable results. This is the meaning which was followed by the Scholastics. Kant used the term to indicate all reasoning beyond the stable activity of the understanding and as such, conducive to illusion. To this world of illusory entities belong the metaphysical discoveries both of the soul, with its spiritual qualities, and of the existence of God. This does not imply that Kant rejects their existence altogether but merely that he asserts that they can not with certainty be discovered through reasoning and demonstration.

Hegel picked up the term *dialectic* to indicate his method, and it is this meaning which is more or less understood today. To understand this meaning, we must first of all keep in mind that it is Hegel's constant aim to reconcile *subject* and *object*. The world can no longer be considered to be divorced from the mind. Hegel furthermore ties together all aspects of the real (whether mind or matter) from the most abstract, such as *being* and *becoming, quality* and *quantity,* etc., to the more concrete such as the succession of different philosophies or civilizations over the ages. To tie different elements together is to show that they have a relative structure and that term *A* implies sooner or later the existence of *B*. The relational structure by which the one *requires* the other is fundamentally what is understood by *dialectic*.

Dialectic becomes a more complex procedure when the two related entities, called "thesis" and "anti-thesis," through their coming together engender a third entity. The two previous entities then are "*aufgehoben*" or given up and absorbed in the third. This third entity, called "synthesis," turns

[24] *Symposium,* 210 ff.

into a new thesis and provides the beginning of a new dialectic. Incidentally, the familiar terms *thesis, anti-thesis* and *synthesis* were not used by Hegel who instead used *affirmation, negation,* and *negation of negation.* A classical example often presented is the case of an authoritarian regime (*thesis*) provoking the rise of an *anti-thesis* (revolution or revolutionary regime), which in turn becomes over the years a moderate form of democracy (*synthesis*). Not every dialectic is equally clear-cut, however, and there may be a running reciprocity between two extremes, as, for example, master and slave, which does not result in a neatly defined synthesis. What counts is the referential structure of both elements and their mutual interaction. Sartre will use similar dialectic abundantly, as we shall see later, whether between human beings (two *subjects*) or a *subject* and an (inorganic) *object*. It will become a more important approach than the mere phenomenological method of *L'Etre et le Néant,* since within the reciprocal rebounding between subject and object, it will allow Sartre to underline the importance of the *Subject.* But before exploring in detail the Sartrian dialectic, let us observe the Marxist position.

We are often told that Marx is against Hegel's "ideas." Indeed, it is well known that he rejects without hesitation Hegel's a priori point of departure, the so-called absolute Idea. We should add that he goes even further and is a "realist," that is, that he accepts the objective reality of the world as it appears to be. Labor is the test of such a reality, for the work of man upon matter is the proof of its existence. Work is considered, once more in imitation of Hegel, to be negation: my work on the land is a negation of the land. Unlike Hegel, however, Marx would claim that when man plunges into his work and becomes object, he somehow remains such and finds himself at the end of the dialectic to be a part of nature, however privileged a part it may be. For Hegel, on the contrary, although the value of labor is not denied, the dialectic of man leads ultimately toward an identification with the Absolute and an abandonment of his object-character. We have already seen that this is the conclusion of *The Phenomenology of Mind.*

Notwithstanding this continual insistence upon the exclusion of "ideas," Marx does not really favor a total rejection of philosophical discussion, so long as it aims toward the improvement of some abuse. Thus, arguments in favor of atheism help to cure mankind of its religious alienation, and others in favor of common possession and against private property have the ultimate purpose of righting the economic disequilibrium. Since philosophical views like these alter a debased state of affairs, they are not *mere* speculations. Knowledge worthy of the name is oriented toward action and is preserved in and through action. Work and action are uppermost, and while "ideas" may be an accompaniment, they are not the mainspring of accomplishment.

Marx insisted that the propelling force of History lies not in ideas or theories but in matter: it is economics that commands the historical process, consequently called *Historical Materialism.* As historical process, it will go its dialectical way until freedom for all and everyone is obtained. This will of course mean the end of all alienations, as well as the end of all dialectic. This end, and the new beginning, are not yet in sight. In the meantime, action is necessary, even violent and "illegal" action, for that, too, is part of the *negation* within the dialectical process.

At this point a question arises that is of some importance for the understanding of Sartre's position: Does dialectic need man, or is it possible to have a dialectic of nature all by itself? Engels believed that the same laws of dialectic which govern history and the development of human thought *were* applicable to changes in nature, and he attempted to defend his position in his *Anti-Dühring.* His attitude seemed to be confirmed by the recent inventions of his day: the discovery of the cell in 1839, the Clausius-Carnot law of the transformation or conversion of energy, the Darwinian revolution (1859). Observing these examples of movements and evolution in nature and of action and reaction both in the organic and inorganic, Engels felt that he was justified in proclaiming the existence of a dialectic in nature.

Sartre disagrees radically. His view is in accordance with that of Kojève, who believes that any dialectic of nature independent of man or of History (which is still man) is not acceptable. "There can be no truth, strictly speaking, unless there is discussion or dialogue, that is, antithesis or negation of the thesis."[25] This negation is the negation of nature through the intervention of man. Later on, commenting further upon Hegel, he writes in the same vein, "Without man, being would be deaf; it would be there (*Dasein*) but it would not be true (*Das Wahre*)."[26] Texts like these have an existential ring, for they make room for the intervention of man as organizer of a world where he is made not to be ruled but to rule. It will be no surprise to the reader to discover that Sartre, who likewise sees man as a meaning-giving center, will be reluctant to accept any dialectic without human interference. For him, too, nature without man would be a deaf mute.

[25] Kojève, *Introduction à la Lecture de Hegel*, p. 455.
[26] *Ibid.*, pp. 462 and 483, footnote.

Chapter III

A QUESTION OF METHOD

GENERAL COMPARISON OF MARXISM AND EXISTENTIALISM

From the start Sartre makes a distinction between *analytical rationalism* and *dialectical rationalism*. *Analytical* rationalism is a philosophy which considers man and matter to be juxtaposed, with man, however, clearly supreme over things. He judges the world as if he were a god, uninvolved and unprejudiced. This position implies a profound trust in man and a confidence in his reason, but it involves, one will readily concede, a certain pretentiousness as well. *Dialectical* rationalism, on the other hand, recognizes not only human interference in the organization of the world but also its contrary, a shaping of the mind through the rebounding of this "organized" world upon it. There is still a mind behind actions and judgments, but that mind is one which cannot escape the impact of the incarnation in which it dwells. In short, the world affects the mind of the judging man, however humiliating this admission may be. This *mutual* involvement of man and his universe—a radical departure from all previous thought—was, according to Sartre, introduced in the philosophy of Hegel and turned into a sociology by Marx.

This distinction between the *analytical* and *dialectical* reason is of the utmost importance and will be picked up again and again throughout Sartre's text, gaining in meaning as it reappears, and later we shall see that the *analytical* reason, as a true expression of the Cartesian era, is no longer an adequate expression of our own.[1] Though in making men critical it served in the hands of the bourgeoisie as a social instrument against the old feudalism ("The abstract revolt precedes by some years the French Revolution . . ."),[2] it gave a false service in the period that followed, since it attempted to preserve the gains which had been made, to maintain the *status quo,* through a "liberalism" that preached non-intervention, non-intervention on the part of a proletariat that was becoming increasingly powerless through its "atomization."[3] At this point it was necessary for the analytical reason to become but a moment in a dialectic that was the discovery of a new age.

For this is, according to Sartre, the only meaning and task of philosophy. Philosophy is "born from the movement of society and is itself a movement."[4] It is "a certain way for the 'rising' class to become conscious of itself," it is the totalization of all knowledge up to its day, it is a *praxis* (action) that forms the future.[5] In terms of this definition, by which a philosopher must be the expression of his own era and the forerunner of the next, there are of course very few philosophers who are truly giants, and very few periods of philosophical creation over which they tower. Sartre sees only three since the seventeenth century, the period of Descartes and Locke, that of Kant and Hegel, and that of our own day —of Karl Marx. Each of these philosophies fulfills Sartre's demand that it be an expression of the rising class of its own

---

[1] I will later attempt to show that however much Sartre repudiates Cartesianism, he himself nevertheless never quite escapes from its postulates.

[2] *CRD,* I, p. 16; Barnes trans., p. 6. As noted earlier, the section under discussion in the present chapter has been translated into English by Professor Hazel Barnes, as *Search for a Method.* Footnotes will refer to both the French and English texts. I should inform the reader, however, that this chapter was written before the English translation was available, hence that literal quotations are mine and not the translations of Professor Barnes.

[3] *CRD,* I, p. 16; Barnes trans., p. 5.

[4] *Ibid.;* Barnes trans., p. 5.

[5] *Ibid.;* Barnes trans., p. 4.

time. Thus Marxism is *the* contemporary philosophy, since it expresses the movement of our own epoch, and it will last as long as the "movement" of the masses lasts; to combat its fundamental position is only a vain attempt to reintroduce an outdated philosophy. Even existentialism is not an independent philosophy but merely a parasitic appendage to that of Marx. When one goes back to the origins of existentialism, to the work of Kierkegaard, one finds not a philosopher but rather a man in revolt, a man who is passionately rejecting Hegel's intellectualism. For Kierkegaard the existing man cannot be caught in a system of ideas. Men are not changed by ideas; their suffering, need, passion are realities which cannot be surpassed or changed by knowledge, they can only be lived and fought against. Thus he was fighting for his very life (existence) when he refused to be made a concept by Hegel.[6] Hegel himself would of course have accepted Kierkegaard as a "moment" of his own dialectic and equated his desperate struggles to the "unhappy consciousness" which must be surpassed. Kierkegaard becomes part of—we could even admit an objection against—Hegel, but as such, he is himself absorbed in the Hegelian dialectic.

The protest of Marx against Hegel (to whom he was nevertheless much indebted) was of a similar nature in that it, too, objected that realities were not to be changed merely by a system of thought. Marx felt that Hegel had erroneously tied together the two concepts of objectification and alienation, as if they were reducible one to another.[7] Objectification, as the projection of oneself through one's work into nature, need not inevitably lead to alienation, the turning back of this work against man, which brings with it that feeling of frustration and "homelessness" that is so characteristic of modern man. The very statement that alienation is characteristic of *modern* man implies that while it does indeed exist and that many workers truly are not enjoying the results of their labor, it nevertheless need not be, for alienation is tied not to

---

[6] *Ibid.*, p. 22; Barnes trans., p. 16.
[7] *Ibid.*, p. 20; Barnes trans., p. 13.

objectification per se but to an *historical* condition that can be changed. In the Marxist view the remedy lies not in mere knowledge, as if the unrolling of the different phases of man's knowledge and the final identification of the Self and the Absolute could cure the evils of modern man. Salvation lies, rather, in labor, material labor and revolutionary *praxis*. Action is called for, action rather than cognition, for the human situation cannot be turned back from its course toward disaster by knowledge alone.

Thus we see that in the Sartrian interpretation Marx's position parallels that of Kierkegaard in its attempt to rescue the existential from the Hegelian Idea, yet repudiates Kierkegaard and rejoins Hegel in eliminating the overemphasis of Kierkegaard upon the subjective and in defending the objective. For Marx it is the concrete individual in his world who matters, the man who works, needs food, and must live. Marxism thus makes room for both Kierkegaard's "specificity of human existence" and Hegel's "concrete man in his objective reality."[8]

Notwithstanding all its emphasis upon the concrete, acting individual, however, Marxism needs correction in its turn, and it is at this moment that we must look to present-day existentialism, keeping in mind that the modern existentialist, like Kierkegaard, is only a man in revolt, this time against the *misuse* of Marxism. Sartre wants to make it perfectly clear that the authentic Marx must not be confused with the modern Marxist; it is one of his major worries to keep Marx on his side against the modern Marxist theoreticians, who have ossified the tenets of their master into a priori judgments and ceased to follow the historical process.

Marx himself was "convinced that facts are never isolated appearances, that if they are produced together, it is always within the higher unity of a whole, that they are tied to one another by internal relations, and that the presence of the one profoundly modifies the other."[9] This being true, he set

[8] *Ibid.*, p. 21; Barnes trans., p. 14.
[9] *Ibid.*, p. 26; Barnes trans., p. 25.

out to discover the underlying totality by the facts. For him history was a moving, dialectical totalization, a totalization unceasingly totalizing itself, a "philosophy becoming the world."[10] Particular facts must consequently be related to the totalization in process. Marx himself was always careful never to force a concept upon a particular situation. On the contrary, in his study of an historical event, as for example of the Eighteenth Brumaire, he sought to understand the concept of the *petite bourgeoisie* not only as it was prior to 1848 but also as it had evolved. He explored slowly and in detail the concrete situation in order to check whether or not the "abstract" concept need not be modified in the light of new evidence. For Truth is not static, it is constantly a becoming.[11] History must then be seen as a totalization, that is, as *a growing totality which we must attempt to reconstitute*. There is in Sartre's opinion no achieved totality but only one in the process of being made, and the attempt to encompass this totality-in-the-making, with the awareness that any exhaustive encompassing is impossible, is what he meant by *totalization*. The failure to appreciate this insight can lead to gross simplifications and even outright errors, for if history is arrested, if theory (*Savoir*) is divorced from *praxis*, then judgments will be made a priori and reality forced into a preconceived mold.

This the modern Marxists have not understood, or if they have understood, have not appreciated. It is, indeed, the sclerosis of modern Marxism, which has so indurated its victims that such an interpretation as that of Budapest could result. Sartre still condemns the Russians for their cruel intervention. In his opinion the condemnation of the Hungarian freedom fighters is the rigid result of an "oversimplified" judgment, a blind spot. The Russians have not seen that "imperialism" has many faces and that they have tragically misread this one; the rebellion in Hungary is not to be equated to an imperialistic move instigated by the Western camp, but

10 *Ibid.*, p. 30; Barnes trans., p. 30.
11 *Ibid.*; Barnes trans., p. 30.

rather, one having its own character and its own origin. Hungary had and has to a great extent an agrarian population, one which, though not eager for a return to the old feudalism, nevertheless is equally opposed to the imposition of communistic kolkhozes. Fiercely individualistic, the Hungarians are a people who would naturally rebel against any hasty form of collectivization, whether or not their rebellion was provoked by the West. The Russians have forgotten that any change in a civilized group needs an "explanation." Be it propaganda or not, the Hungarian felt entitled to know what the future had in store for him. Knowing only one form of socialism, the Russians were unable to envision any other possibilities.[12]

Sartre's criticism of Marxism in its modern applications does not prevent him from sharing Marx's fundamental principle that "the mode of production of the material life in general dominates the development of social, political and intellectual life."[13] Man is above all a "worker who produces the conditions of his life"; he is what he does.[14] Sartre also believes with Marx that progress follows the usual triad, namely, the contradiction between thesis and antithesis, which, once overcome and totalized in some new form of synthesis, may then again become the start of another conflict. Marxism is still for him the answer so long as we have not overcome the problem of *scarcity*, the unequal distribution of those material things which can satisfy our needs.

[12] *Ibid.*, p. 29; Barnes trans., p. 29. On the origin of the Hungarian tragedy according to Sartre, see also his article in *L'Express*, November 9, 1956. Sartre's condemnation of the Russian intervention in Budapest did not kill his friendship for the Soviet Union, though his sympathy went through a severe crisis at that time. Since then Sartre has visited Russia several times. He admires the Russian intellectual for his incessant effort "to overcome the contradictions" of the Stalinist era and to find a place in the modern world. The Pasternaks, the Evtushenkos learn to think for themselves. All this gives them "a depth, which is unusual in this epoch of extero-conditioning." Simone de Beauvoir, *La Force des Choses*, p. 667.

[13] *CRD*, I, p. 31; Barnes trans., pp. 33–34.

[14] *Ibid.*, p. 24; Barnes trans., p. 20.

For scarcity is the cornerstone of the entire Sartrian building; when it has disappeared as a factor to take into consideration, it will be time to lay another cornerstone, and to build another building, housing some new philosophy of freedom which we cannot even imagine at the present.[15] In the meantime, however, the world is divided into those who "understand" and those who don't. In an interview with Fidel Castro, published as a foreword to *Sartre on Cuba*, Sartre reflects the deep feeling of rapprochement among those who do appreciate the importance of scarcity, as between Fidel and himself. Words were few, silences meaningful, answers predictable.

"Man's need is his fundamental right over all others," said Castro.

"And if they ask you for the moon?" asked Sartre.

". . . it would be because someone needed it," was Castro's reply.

Sartre had found a friend, one who understood that the one humanism that is possible is founded "neither on work nor on culture . . . but on need." In a sense, his entire work in the *Critique* is a philosophy of those, who, in the words of Castro, "have the courage to understand their suffering and to demand that it be ended, in short, who are men."[16]

To the Marxist the meaning of history can only be the unification of the exploited masses and the gradual growth toward a classless society. The Proletariat must become conscious of itself and thus become the subject of History, become "men," not objects pushed around by History. It must not let its *praxis* (action) be stolen or alienated. This happens when men are not united; history escapes them when others make it as well, for the differing actions cause each group to lose the real meaning and control of its actions. This is exemplified by Engels in his book *The Peasant War in Germany* where the various provincial movements, though achieving

[15] *Ibid.*, p. 32; Barnes trans., p. 34.
[16] Sartre, *Sartre on Cuba*, pp. 134 ff.

local objectives and victories, actually lost in the final result, through their separation from one another.

We are still at the point where the Proletariat is separated into various groups with various interests so that History is still being made without knowing itself. Sartre believes, however, that we have a greater degree of self-awareness than ever before; we are able to situate various groups and events (colonialism, civil war, etc.) more accurately within the total picture and to discover the diverse meanings of History. He looks to the day when we will be still more aware, when men, no longer separated, will make History in common and it will have "only one meaning," one which will correspond to the intentions of those who make it.[17]

This is the humanism which Sartre wants to introduce to replace the old bourgeois humanism, which "was shattered when we sensed around our town the immense crowd of 'sub-men conscious of their subhumanity.'"[18] When the moment comes that all will share alike in the abundance of things, and consequently in humanity itself, freedom will again triumph in all its sovereignty, completely independent from all economic dictatorships. At that moment *"le marxisme aura vécu,"* writes Sartre.[19] In reading this exposé, one is tempted to ask whether Sartre has said farewell to his cherished freedom. He has not, as we shall see, but in the concrete it is no longer the absolute and unlimited force that it was in the abstract presentation found in *L'Etre et le Néant*.

THE "MEDIATING ROLE" OF THE INDIVIDUAL

If Sartre is Marxist in his adherence to the Marxist formula of History, he is nevertheless existentialist in his reading of that formula. To him, the errors of modern Marxism become more and more apparent. They stem from a blind devo-

[17] *CRD*, I, pp. 61–63; Barnes trans., pp. 88–90.
[18] *Ibid.*, p. 23; Barnes trans., p. 19.
[19] *Ibid.*, p. 32; Barnes trans., p. 34.

tion to an "a priori" stand, as we have already seen in the
case of the Hungarian rebellion. Traditional Marxism has provided a framework into which its followers think they must
force History, instead of letting the events speak for themselves. In short, the modern Marxists have ceased to live with
History, but try to force History to live with them.

The work of Georg Lukacs provides, in Sartre's opinion, a
typical example of this rigidity.[20] His claim that German
existentialism became "activist" under the influence of the
Nazis or that French existentialism is a wartime reaction of
the *petit bourgeois* against the occupation forces is naïve
and grossly oversimplified. As for the first, Heidegger was
never "activist," at least not in his philosophical writings—
furthermore, "activism" is itself nothing but "an empty concept which permits opponents to liquidate a certain number
of unrelated ideologies" that they haven't taken the trouble
to read and comprehend. Concerning the second, Sartre can
himself attest that he started the research on *L'Etre et le
Néant* in 1930, which makes the assertion that it was an
"echo of the war" absurd.[21] The blunt truth is that the Marxist theoreticians are incapable of understanding the complexity of the existential situation, whether philosophical or
otherwise. They do not bother to read the Other, but merely
impose a preconceived theory—theirs! In so doing, the modern Marxist loses sight of the fact that there is no real totality
(*un tout fait*) but merely a totalization (a never-ending
succession of events kept together by human intervention),
hence that as commentator he cannot and should not draw

[20] *Ibid.*, p. 34; Barnes trans., p. 38. Lukacs is an Hungarian-born
Communist, famous for his numerous publications on Marxism. He
lives at present in Moscow. For his relations with Sartre, see De
Beauvoir, *La Force des Choses*, p. 190.

[21] And it makes equally absurd the statements that *L'Etre et le
Néant* is *merely* an Hegelian product, as some German commentators
at present imply. To be Hegelian in method does not mean to be Hegelian in one's fundamental intuition. Sartre learned to study Hegel
in the classes of Kojève just before World War II. By that time Sartre
knew what he was going to say although he was not yet determined
concerning the method.

conclusions concerning that which is as yet unfinished. Indeed, his greatest limitation perhaps is that he cannot resist the temptation of constructing universals: from a concrete event he builds a universal, under which subsequent concrete events are to be classified.

Thus the literary work of Paul Valéry is regarded simply as "an expression of bourgeois idealism." The Marxists, in their eagerness to assimilate and to universalize, do not bother to *differentiate*. There is no attempt to understand "the originality of a bourgeois thought," only a hastiness to classify it under "idealism."[22] What they are doing, actually, is to reduce the concrete—this man, this book—to an abstraction—example of capitalist imperialism or of idealism—in the supposition that the abstraction—idealism—is the concrete reality.[23] They are only taking out of their work what they themselves put into it, and in the meantime, Valéry has completely disappeared.[24] In actuality, Valéry must be considered in his particular and concrete milieu to "explain" what produced him, for while "Valéry is an intellectual *petit bourgeois*, not every *petit bourgeois* is a Valéry."[25]

This sentence is pivotal. It points to the correction which Sartre wishes to introduce into modern Marxist interpretations, namely, to bring Valéry (and other men, other events) back into history. One must search out his unique qualities by attempting to discover the "mediations" which link him to others and to his historical surroundings. His relation to idealism is only a part of the whole story; Marxism, contenting itself with the part, misses the whole and thus does not enable us "to grasp the process which produces the person and his product inside a class and inside a given society at a given moment of history."[26] This kind of thought leads to such bizarre statements as that of Engels according to which

[22] *CRD*, I, p. 40; Barnes trans., p. 49.
[23] *Ibid*., p. 41; Barnes trans., p. 51.
[24] *Ibid*., p. 43; Barnes trans., p. 54.
[25] *Ibid*., p. 44; Barnes trans., p. 56.
[26] *Ibid*.; Barnes trans., p. 56.

the appearance of such a man as Napoleon at a certain moment in history was pure chance; if there had been no Napoleon, there would have been some other Napoleon to fill his place. Existentialism wants to bring into relief the individual concrete, the particular, against its general background of productive forces.

Similarly, it is not enough to say simply that Flaubert's *Madame Bovary* is a potent weapon against a class and a regime, the expression of an epoch, determined solely by the economic forces of that day. Other shaping influences were at work, influences which the modern Marxist ignores, as for example, those of childhood and growth. Psychoanalysis must be used for a better understanding of the genesis of a person, and subsequently, of the value of his work. It is only in this way that the mediation between the particular individual and the universal class can be discovered, since it establishes the way the child "lives his family relations inside a given society."[27] It is only in this way that one discovers the difference between, say, a Flaubert and a Baudelaire, where such details as the paternal "fixation" of Flaubert and the oedipal complex of Baudelaire enter into the picture. These details reflect both the objective structure of society —Flaubert's father was of the new bourgeoisie and invested his money in land and his mother was of the faded nobility, while Baudelaire's family was urban and invested in stocks and bonds, characteristic of the new nobility—and the childhood of the two men—Flaubert's in the company of a father who felt socially below the industrial families in his care and carried his resentment into violent personal relationships, Baudelaire's under the influence of a mother who could afford to be independent and vain, and was. Psychoanalysis used in the framework of a dialectical totalization takes all of this into account.[28] The Marxist, on the other hand, will consider the individual only as the recipient of an income or salary, forgetting that before "reifying" himself in his work,

[27] *Ibid.*, p. 47; Barnes trans., p. 61.
[28] *Ibid.*, p. 48; Barnes trans., pp. 63–64.

he was discovering "reification" and the "alienation" of labor in the work and life of his parents. Sartre has no wish to deny the relation between culture and economics, but he simply wishes to deepen the meaning of that relationship through showing that both are "mediated" through the individual, whose work is the concrete accomplishment of many contributing elements.

Existentialism can supply still another corrective to the interpretations of modern Marxists with its recognition of the role played by the personal involvement of the evaluating mind. The Marxist believes that, keeping things at a distance, he can look at them with complete detachment, but in actuality, there is no ontological autonomy, either of the object or of the subject. A sociologist cannot be *non-engagé* in his description of a sociological event, as if he himself were not a part of history or the member of a group involved in historical movements. Both he and his topic constitute a pair, and they must be interpreted one by the other.[29] To believe otherwise is again to shut one's eyes to the facts as they are. For the sociologist is in himself an object of history, and his sociological attitude a moment in its flow. Lewin's Gestaltism, which views completed totalities from the outside, rather than totalities in the becoming, in which the viewer himself is involved, has grown from his personal experiences of exclusion. Thus Lewin, persecuted by the Nazis and exiled from Germany, considers Germany from afar, and his sociology reflects both the fixed totality which must be rearranged (ignoring both past history and present conditions) and the non-involvement of the arranger (an exile). Similarly, empiricism in its extreme form, which overlooks connections with the past, is a common failing of American sociologists, whose outlook is only reflecting the short history of their own country. It is possible that had they been steeped in the past, they would have included it in their sociology.[30]

This mutual coloration of the writer and his object does

[29] *Ibid.*, p. 53; Barnes trans., p. 72.
[30] *Ibid.*, p. 52; Barnes trans., p. 71.

not preclude, however, a certain measure of objectivity. Sartre praises in this respect the work of Abram Kardiner, the American sociologist, who was earlier under fire for his concept of the "basic personality"—Sartre could of course not agree with Kardiner's assertion that a static essence could impose itself upon the members of a group, for that would be placing the definition *before* the man.[31] Although Kardiner's ideas may be opposed to dialectical materialism, his research is still useful, for through its empiricism it extracts sound information, in this case on the inhabitants of the Marquesas Islands, which can later be of value to those who do believe in the dialectical method. Ironically, he can show contemporary Marxists how to enlarge the meaning of "material conditions" beyond that of mere technique in the simple sense of the word (which is all they consider) to include certain *human* situations that are present. Thus the scarcity of women is a material factor which influences not only productivity but also the "style of life"[32]—the problem is lived in a certain way on these islands. So the scarcity of women results in polyandry, which in turn engenders a certain hardness that is found in the character of the women, a tendency toward homosexuality as a form of revenge in the men, etc. It is unnecessary to go into the details of Kardiner's studies here; we wish merely to point to the importance they give to the reciprocal and circular influence between concrete men with their own unique ways of surpassing the material conditions of their life, and to the interrelationship between human relations and the facts of production. For no social event stands by itself. All are tied together and mutually react, one upon the other.

Sartre is insistent upon the importance of these interactions, for to him, as to Marx, "group" can mean only a number of people who are together in some way, their mutual relations and the relations of these relations; it has no ontological entity in itself. He does not deny that the group has a

[31] *Ibid.;* Barnes trans., p. 70.
[32] *Ibid.,* p. 53; Barnes trans., p. 74.

status—its rules and administration—but this status is not and cannot be closed. Each totality is *detotalized,* that is, open to further growth.[33] The terminology is Sartre's, for the Marxists have never turned their attention sufficiently to these matters to supply a vocabulary. For example, they have never fully explored the concept of the "collective," Sartre's term for these groupings around some object.[34] So they can come to consider the market a *thing* and the workers in its power an abstraction, whereas Sartre will show that the power of the market actually rests upon the separation of individuals who are very real indeed, that the market is an absence rather than a presence, a flight rather than a consensus.[35] Furthermore, these collectives have themselves to be placed within a social "climate." Marxism has barely touched upon the infinite complexity of our social situation, with explorations into what it means to belong to clubs, to a church, to a factory or a school, to a street, even to a certain position or way of looking at things. Man lives his class not only as a worker working but as a worker living in the milieu of his products. Sartre reproaches the Marxists for having overlooked the multiple connections which make up the individual life and having kept only the abstract skeleton of universality. "The result is that it (Marxism) has completely forgotten the meaning of what a human being is; and to make up for this lack, it has nothing but the absurd psychology of a Pavlov."[36]

[33] *Ibid.,* p. 56; Barnes trans., p. 78. Sartre himself places a footnote here to the effect that he will develop these ideas later, so the reader should not be concerned if their import is not clear.

[34] We will deepen this meaning later, in Chapter V, page 116 ff. where Sartre probes into the matter of collectives. Indeed, he goes on from there to give the detailed philosophy of the group which he feels Marxists have neglected. In the course of his discussion many of the statements we are making here will be enlarged upon. I have transferred the extremely interesting development of his ideas on the market (*CRD,* I, p. 56) to Chapter V, where the reader will be better prepared to understand them.

[35] *CRD,* I, p. 56; Barnes trans., p. 78.

[36] *Ibid.,* p. 58; Barnes trans., p. 83.

Man must be brought back into Marxism, through the integration, within its framework, of a concrete anthropology. Though critics have called Sartre's methods "irrational," he protests that they aim, on the contrary, at an elimination of the obscure and the indeterminate, of the part played by chance. Dialectical materialism, in its pursuit of historical totalization (Knowledge), must make use of the empirical data provided by sociology and psychoanalysis.[37] The method for doing so, for integrating man as an existential being into the philosophy of Marxism, Sartre calls "the progressive-regressive method."

The *Project* as the *Maker* of History

It is almost a commonplace to say that according to Marx, man is entirely determined by anterior conditions, economic in nature, in other words, that he is merely a passive element which is subject to conditioning. Yet Sartre claims that Marx really meant that this "passive" entity can also influence history more positively, either by resisting it or by collaborating with it.[38] There is a circular movement, with man partially in control of the motion, not merely a wheel turning in one predetermined direction, in the spinning of which he is hopelessly caught. Man is admittedly conditioned by his social environment, but he nevertheless makes himself in the way he *surpasses* this given and thus he turns back to condition his environment as well.

We have already made clear that Sartre shares the Marxist dream of a classless society; it should also be evident by now

[37] If a living Marxism needs sociology and psychoanalysis, these two disciplines in their turn need Marxism. For unless their data are integrated into the movement of History, their givens will, if they don't become lifeless, at least "sleep side by side" (*CRD*, I, p. 59; Barnes trans., p. 84).

[38] *CRD*, I, pp. 60–61; Barnes trans., pp. 85–87. Sartre quotes various references which could be used to support either view, as, for example, the second preface of *Das Kapital*, where the passivity of man is dominant. Actually the texts are not clear, but Sartre claims that their very ambiguity points to the rich complexity of Marxist thought.

that he does not agree with those Marxists who would see it come about through some sort of mechanistic determination. For Sartre, too, man is "alienated," but the alienated man is still not a thing, and alienation is not brought about by the same kind of physical laws that regulate the natural order.[39] Alienation can change the intended results of an action, but not the human reality of the action itself. The German peasants in Engels' *The Peasant War in Germany* did not achieve the goals they thought they had achieved, but this does not mean that they were mere things caught in the force of History; they were still real men making real, if alienated, History.[40] A little later in his text Sartre accuses the contemporary Marxists of having forgotten that man, however alienated or reified he may be, is nevertheless still man and claims that Marx meant by "reification" that they were "condemned to live *humanly* the condition of material things"[41] (italics mine). It is at this point that a typical existentialistic dimension of man, which was so prominent in *L'Etre et le Néant*, is exploited. Man is seen to be above all capable of "going beyond" his given situation through his "project," which is his attitude toward the multiple possibles open to him. "To say what a man is implies to say what he can," and conversely, "to say what a man can is to say what he is."[42]

It is an irony that the Marxists, who live so naturally in the future of "Five Year Plans," have ignored this basic dimension of man and of society and considered only the past as a determination, working in a mechanistic way upon the present, whereas in truth, man's projected flight into the future is equally important in shaping his present. Although society determines for each man his objective situation and "the truth of a man is the nature of his work" (and his salary), he lives this truth nevertheless in going beyond it toward another objective, in surpassing his given and going on

[39] *CRD*, I, p. 63; Barnes trans., p. 91.
[40] *Ibid.*, p. 61; Barnes trans., p. 88.
[41] *CRD*, I, p. 70, footnote; Barnes trans., p. 104.
[42] *Ibid.*, p. 64; Barnes trans., p. 93.

to produce a new condition.[43] We continually go beyond ourselves, that is, we go beyond the contradictions of a past childhood into a present adulthood through an objectification of deed and act (the production of an object or an event in the social world) with the hope of liberating ourselves from the tensions of the status to which we belong. The new status, however, is itself conducive to new contradictions. So we are once more propelled into the search for a new attitude, in which a fresh effort toward *dépassement* is attempted. At the core of the inner contradition of man lies a material or economic situation—here Marx is right—but this situation is not a frozen reality weighing upon a present event. It is, rather, a challenge *looking for its solution* in the future.

When prices are high and wages low, the workers demand an increase in their salaries. Their rebellion is based not upon some inevitable "effect" or law but upon a lived reality: the worker is hungry and tired and resents his condition, and his resentment is already a going beyond toward the possibility of change.[44] When the result is a change in conditions, we can see in that result both the lived reality that has been surpassed, that of the hungry, tired, resentful worker, and the projected change, the rebellion in the form of a strike, secret resisting of work quotas, etc. If the worker had been a mere thing, he would have been incapable of feeling hunger and fatigue, of resenting this, and of rebelling in such a way that a new set of conditions is reached. This is what Sartre means when he sees history as a totalization forever being totalized and when he rejects both a mechanistic materialism and a dialectic that imposes itself on the universe, a metaphysical force behind the historical process that replaces man (Hegelian idealism).[45] For Sartre man is the totalizer, and without man, there would be no totalization, and consequently, no history.

[43] *Ibid.*; Barnes trans., p. 93.
[44] *Ibid.*, p. 67; Barnes trans., p. 97.
[45] *Ibid.*, p. 68; Barnes trans., p. 99.

Sartre gives a striking example which may help to clarify his position.[46] A colored ground-crewman stationed at an air base near London was condemned to remain forever on the ground, since his race barred him from ever becoming a pilot. This was his objective situation; the only possibilities open to him were to remain a part of the ground crew, or to rebel, that is, to objectify his rebellion through the production of some object or event.] This could have ranged from a simple feeling of resentment to the writing of a book to the spectacular means he actually chose. This *particular* man, refusing the prohibition, stole a plane, piloted it across the Channel, and crashed to his death in France. His individual project involved the internalization of the possibles open to white people, the piloting of a plane, and this he did, even though for him, lacking their training, it meant death. In this individual choice the general revolt of the colored against the colonizers is reflected, as well as the present status of the conflict—passive resistance is over, but organized resistance has not yet come (or the possibility of colored pilots was still "in committee"), and individual acts of protest are still necessary. We might compare this example to recent events in our own country, where the colored race has also passed the stage of passivity and internalizes for its own members the same range of possibilities—decent wages, good housing, educational and occupational opportunities —that is open to the rest of the population. In its beginning stages the revolt called for individual acts of protest that were dazzling in their heroism—men carrying placards of protest along lonely Southern roads, families moving into homes in white neighborhoods where they were not welcomed, students enrolling in universities under police protection—until the day when organization had reached a point where thousands could march together with their placards to the very steps of the White House. The historical process which is unfolding does so through real men with

46 *Ibid.*, pp. 65–66; Barnes trans., pp. 95–96.

real projects; it is not some closed, inevitable system, whether mechanistic or dialectical.

The material conditions of a man's existence (the social, historical reality) of course determines the number of possibilities that are open to him. What a man does reveals both what he was, for in going beyond, he reveals what was the need which he negated and surpassed, and what he can do, for in going beyond a need, he realizes positively one of his possibles. These may be very limited—in a bourgeois society where the cost of a medical education is high, the worker may not be able to dream of his son's becoming a doctor. He can, however, join a union, vote to go on strike, etc., in an attempt to change the situation more remotely, for the sake of his son's son. It is the project, "as a mediation between two moments of objectivity, which makes history."[47] When we speak of human *praxis*, we mean the subjective surpassing of one objectivity, a given condition, to the realization of another objectivity, which at one time was merely one of the possibilities internalized as the project, or one of the ends which called forth the action. (We will recall here the definition of man in *L'Etre et le Néant* as a flight out of the present into the future.)[48] In the objective process, then, there is necessarily a subjective moment between the two objectivities, between the starting point and the end result in an object or an event.[49] This surpassing which is the project (it has no content) Sartre calls "a long work"; although a life continually changes, there is an underlying permanence, an underlying orientation. "A life unrolls in spirals; it passes over and over by the same points but on different levels of integration and complexity."[50]

Thus in the life of Flaubert one could find a continuous movement from his childhood onward, all of which gets its coloration from the relationship to his father. The rejection

[47] *Ibid.*, p. 68; Barnes trans., p. 99.
[48] *Being and Nothingness*, p. 149; *The Tragic Finale*, p. 43.
[49] *CRD*, I, p. 68; Barnes trans., p. 97.
[50] *Ibid.*, p. 71; Barnes trans., p. 106.

of a medical career because the brother had already succeeded in medicine so brilliantly, the choice of law as an alternative, the attacks of hysteria to avoid the hated career, the final objectification in literature, all are moments in an unrolling spiral. Sartre does not deny that the drama that was Gustave Flaubert was played out against an economic background, upon a stage with particular props, but he wishes to restore to the actor his power to act. Furthermore, if there is this dialectic between a man and his given starting point and between a man and his fellows, if the movement of a life is synthetic, it is our task to reconstruct it if we wish to discover its truth. Our old methods of thought, which push us toward the linear and the analytical, do not equip us for this task, and as an alternative, Sartre, "following Hegel and Marx, demands nothing less than a new rationality," a dialectical rationalism.[51]

THE PROGRESSIVE-REGRESSIVE METHOD

The progressive-regressive method bases itself upon this one fundamental supposition, which we have already explained, that man is defined by his work, or as Sartre puts it, *"dans son projet."* "Project" implies that man is always beyond himself towards . . . This striving toward objectification takes different forms according to the individual, but its ultimate explanation lies in choice, not in a mechanistic, scientifically conditioned choice, but one that is hidden away in the complex mystery of the Self or *Pour-soi.*[52] The project betrays the secret of the Self: it is the purpose, the finality in the

---

[51] *Ibid.*, p. 74; Barnes trans., p. 111.

[52] Although Sartre does not explicitly go back to his formulation of *L'Etre et le Néant,* it will occur to the reader that the method described is based upon his earlier dualism of the *Pour-soi* and the *En-soi* and that it constitutes an attempt to get hold of the *Pour-soi,* or human consciousness. In order to review the earlier position, the reader might read pages 102, 149, and 588 in *Being and Nothingness.* For comment, see *The Tragic Finale,* pp. 35, 43, and 201. Concerning the use of the old terminology in *CRD,* see the discussion in Chapter X.

future which commands the essential choice and direction of a man's life. The problem which this method sets for itself is to find this tension, this project, this movement which extends from one objectivity to another, to reinvent the movement by discovering its beginnings, *regressively*, and going along with it *progressively* through its possibles, or field of instruments to its ends, both intended and unintended (alienated).

If man is always beyond himself towards, then none of his actions are understandable without going beyond the present and looking at them in the light of the future or in the light of their ends, as that future or those ends appeared to him.[53] Sartre calls this understanding "comprehension." A simple example will be helpful.[54] I am talking with my friend in a room when he suddenly jumps up and starts toward the window. I understand the meaning of his action; the room is too hot, and he is going to open the window. My "comprehension" is possible only because first, I, too, as a man, feel the heat and can live with my friend what he is going to do in order to surpass this given and because second, I am able to unify the act by a *regressive* movement back to the original situation of being too hot and simultaneously by a *progressive* movement to its remedy of letting in air. I know also the field of instruments through which he must pass—the table he must avoid, the window he must open, etc. Thus this relatively simple enterprise has a rich complexity of meanings, each unified with the other—the room itself defines my friend's action (it defines his path, provides the window or lack of a window, etc.) but conversely, my friend's action unifies the room—his opening of the window shows its use, etc. The action is that which defines the original given—if my friend had not jumped up, it would have been because the heat was not unbearable. Or it is possible that we were so absorbed in our discussion that we did not notice the heat. A third man entering the room finds it un-

---

[53] *CRD*, I, p. 96; Barnes trans., p. 152.
[54] *Ibid.*, pp. 96–97; Barnes trans., pp. 153–55.

bearably hot, and seeing the closed window, he can through a regressive movement to the given that has not been surpassed reconstruct for himself our absorption.[55]

It is because we ourselves have projects and objectify ourselves in things (the opened or closed window) that we are able to comprehend project and objectification in others. The movement of my comprehension ascending toward the objectification of a "project" of a human being is *progressive*, while the attitude by which I simultaneously grasp his original condition is *regressive*. This is not a matter of mere contemplation; we are understanding the Other as a dimension of our own life. Modern positivism, which has permeated Marxism, refuses to study man as this flight into the future, as one guided by and pursuing ends. Sartre protests, for although it is indeed wrong to attribute the properties of man to the inorganic—anthropomorphism must be eliminated from the natural sciences—it is equally wrong to banish those properties of man which rightfully belong to man and to consider him merely as an object.[56]

It is also in the light of this position that one can understand Sartre's insistence upon considering man as the *signifying* animal, for obviously man is the entity through which meaning is introduced into the world.[57] *L'Etre et le Néant* has made it abundantly clear that man is responsible for the world: it is man who attaches a purpose to objects and equally it is man who reads the purpose which has been inscribed in the object. To come back for a moment to the overheated room, we can see now that if the window is not opened, the newcomer entering the room will feel the need of the deed-to-be-done-and-not-yet-done, that is, he will read a purpose into the window, as that which could be opened to ventilate the room. He not only understands the window as an instrument, but as we have already seen, he can also deduce from the non-use of that instrument the fact that the

[55] *Ibid.*, p. 97; Barnes trans., p. 155.
[56] *Ibid.*, p. 98; Barnes trans., p. 157.
[57] *Ibid.*, p. 96; Barnes trans., p. 152.

people who were in the room were so involved in their conversation that they did not feel any discomfort. The closed window was a sign in many ways, a sign of what could be done, pointing toward the future, and a sign of the indifference of the two occupants of the room, pointing toward the past. One thing is certain: man goes beyond the object and endows its naked materiality with a meaning, causing the naked and brute object to become a *sign*.

This is one of the old tricks familiar to the movie producer, for in the world of the image, more than anywhere else, the visual goes beyond its material existence and is endowed by man with meaning. In the bullet holes, I discover the fight, and in the broken glasses, the drunken party.[58]

This still does not fall into the abuse called anthropomorphism, for I do not attribute the characteristics of man to the lifeless, but merely recognize the world as human and acknowledge that the depth of the world is nothing more than the depth of man.[59] To *comprehend* therefore is in most cases nothing but a return (*regressive* method) into the genesis of an act or an opus: in the depth of his act man has built up his future and then executed the act that was to bring about that future. The drive toward his future is his project, and as I follow its movement in the *progressive* act, I can read as in a sign the author himself and the complex world in which he has lived.

When we apply this method to Robespierre and the Revolution, or to Flaubert and his objectification in *Madame Bovary*, we should keep in mind that the *regressive* steps will be much more complex to trace than those that merely lead back from the window in the overheated room to the occupants of the room, but in principle it will be the same method. It is not always possible to penetrate both an epoch and a man living within that epoch without deep and exhaustive study and without the use of all the tools at our disposal. The task is less tiring, of course, for the present-day Marxist, who

[58] *Ibid.*, p. 98; Barnes trans., p. 156.
[59] *Ibid.*, p. 92; Barnes trans., p. 145.

always knows in advance what he wants to find . . . and finds it.[60] One could, for example, merely apply the universal Marxist slogan at the beginning in order to understand the French revolutionary Robespierre. It would be far simpler than making a careful study of his past, his growth and his milieu, and reconstructing the "reciprocity" of the relations between himself and his period, as Sartre would have us do. Robespierre's mind worked dialectically (as do all minds): there was an action and reaction between himself and his surroundings, both of which we must seek to understand, one through the other, by means of a continual "cross reference." It is imperative, in order to achieve any real grasp of an epoch, to study its "instruments," that is, its modes of thought, since this is the field through which Robespierre must pass, the window which he must open. Thus, we can see that he was under the influence of the Idea of Nature, as were all in his time, and that for him and his contemporaries the Revolution was a growing totality, not an achieved fact. We must establish the significations of these ideas, both for those of his day and for Robespierre himself. In short, one must put oneself back into this period in order to understand Robespierre, "a man fitted, in some luckier settled age, to have become one of those incorruptible Pattern-Figures, and have had marble-tablets and funeral-sermons,"[61] and then discover those details which differentiated him from others of his day and led him, jaw mangled, to the guillotine. Carlyle's Pattern-Figure is of course as false to reality as was Engels' "some other Napoleon" for it is the peculiar reactions of a particular mind to the challenge which confront it that makes the man what he is, and it is impossible to imagine any other Robespierre than the one we know. It is *this* Robespierre facing *this* challenge in *this* period into whom we wish to descend through the *regressive* method.

Sartre's use of the method to descend from the novel *Mad-*

[60] *Ibid.*, p. 86; Barnes trans., p. 133.
[61] Thomas Carlyle, *The French Revolution* (Modern Library ed.), p. 698.

ame Bovary into its author *and* into its epoch is perhaps more ingenious. It should be stated once more that the bare assertion that *"Madame Bovary* is a product of its epoch" is a gross oversimplification. The *regressive* method will reveal much more than that. It will reach as far as possible into the genesis of the masterpiece, and by this very fact into the life of the author himself and into the spirit of this epoch. Analysis—and this is precisely in what the *regressive* method consists—will show us that Flaubert was somewhat feminine, that he was a solitary, even lonely person, that he was narcissistic, etc.[62] This alone does not reveal the work to us in all its complexity. We have still to place it in its epoch, an epoch of capitalism on the one hand—Flaubert was a landed proprietor himself—and of great poverty on the other. We add that in *that* epoch and to *that* author, who was at bottom a mystic and a metaphysician, no other instrument was available than the instrument of his times: he had *to tell a story*. Flaubert then will go through this instrument and tell a story, but what a story it will be: *"l'ouvrage monstrueux et splendide . . . Madame Bovary."*[63]

CONCLUDING REMARKS

The concluding pages of the *Question de Méthode* are printed in italics to underline their importance.[64] They contain the core of the theory which has already guided our author in the preceding pages and will also direct his method in the further sections of his book. They are difficult. I have attempted to clarify his thought and I beg the reader to bear with me in the effort of understanding. Some of the dark spots that still remain after the preliminary presentation will be illuminated as Sartre gives still more practical applications later on.

In Sartre's opinion, certain anthropologies take man as the

---

[62] *CRD*, I, p. 91; Barnes trans., p. 143.
[63] *Ibid.*, p. 94; Barnes trans., p. 148.
[64] *Ibid.*, pp. 103–11; Barnes trans., pp. 167–81.

object of their study but tacitly omit that in their inquiry he who interrogates is *man* as well. In the very omission lies the admission that the human beings who constitute the topic of their examination are being considered merely as *objects*. This is regrettable. It should ever be kept in mind that the interrogator is in fact the same as the one who is interrogated, that *man* is studying *man*.[65] Anthropologists who ignore this fact behave like geometricians, who can work with space and time in the concrete without being concerned with the notions or concepts of space and time. They exert themselves in formulating laws on the workings of human society, but in so doing, they do not reveal what man himself is. *"Les sciences de l'homme ne s'interrogent pas sur l'homme."*[66] The true anthropologist, on the contrary, is obliged to explore *what man is*. This, as we know already from the speculative study on man in *L'Etre et le Néant*, he feels is a difficult undertaking, however urgent it may be. For as we have seen, Sartre believes that any conceptual definition of man is impossible, since human reality *becomes* and *is not*. "Human reality makes itself and invents itself continually. So it appears that existence precedes essence." Essence (what we are) is a result of what we make ourselves to be.[67]

Sartre's former resolution of the problem lies at the basis of the present view. Human reality, although resisting any abstract formulation, can be understood through its *project* within the framework of society. Man is a dynamic entity—and it is this which modern-day Marxism has forgotten—man is *pro-ject*, and the fluid becoming of human reality escapes all methods of knowledge which approach man as if he were a static entity. When we say that man is *project*, we imply that in his continual act of *existing* he (1) cannot be conceptualized, that is, understood by way of clear con-

---

[65] *Ibid.*, p. 104; Barnes trans., p. 167.

[66] *Ibid.*; Barnes trans., p. 168. Notice the reflective structure of this quotation. In quoting Sartre, I have not always italicized his italics, since the choice of the quotation was sufficient emphasis in itself.

[67] *Being and Nothingness*, pp. 25 and 61.

cepts, but (2) he can be _comprehended_. To make this act of _comprehension_ more explicit does not mean to make it _ipso facto_ part of Knowledge, Knowledge being understood as that achievement of man's intellect in which universal statements and general laws are formulated. This Sartre calls _Le Savoir. Comprehension_ is not _Knowledge_. It may very well prepare the ground for Knowledge, but for the present we should insist that _comprehension_ is nothing but _that movement of the human consciousness by which it reproduces the project of the Other_.[68] It is a kind of pre-Knowledge, but it can never be universalized as _intellection_ because the project is constantly in flux. Comprehension is thus _act, the act by which one lives the existence of the other_.[69] This approach in motion is only possible because both the interrogator and the interrogated are themselves human beings, constituted of _project, negation, transcendency,_ and _need_.

Comprehension, then, can be said to be existence itself or better still, a way of existing. It is the incessant growth of existence, which can never stand still. It cannot be frozen into concepts, for it sweeps away all concepts in its onward movement. Comprehension, in the Sartrian interpretation, is itself action and simultaneously an understanding of the other's existence—his existence falls under my comprehending pro-ject. Obviously, this pro-jecting dimension of man prevents him from being a thing, since he is always beyond being a thing.

Sartre fears that his approach may be called irrational. He radically protests that this qualification is not at all suitable for _his_ approach (though it may be for that of Kierkegaard). The term anti-intellectualistic would be more exact,[70] for he does admit that not everything can be seized by the intellect. So, for example, when man uses language, he makes himself clear through words and becomes what may be

---

[68] _CRD_, I, p. 105; Barnes trans., p. 171.
[69] _Ibid.;_ Barnes trans., p. 171.
[70] _Ibid._, pp. 105, 106; Barnes trans., pp. 171, 172.

called "object of [the other] man."[71] But at the source of this "becoming object" lies the incessant growth of existence itself, a growth which escapes the intellect and can only be *comprehended*. It can also be pointed at in the process itself of language, which in its act of expression returns upon itself: I understand X because to an extent I am X myself and constitute a project on the basis of the spoken word.

The anthropologist who really wants to be complete must add to intellectual *Knowledge* a comprehensive *non-Knowledge*, by which he feels the motion of that existing, projecting, transcending entity called man. This comprehensive *non-Knowledge* grows into an intellectual grasp when it reaches the stages of conceptualization, but even then the very words themselves point regressively at the comprehension. The mutual interaction of both *comprehension* and *intellection* must therefore be incessant if knowledge wants to be real and not merely misleading through sheer ignorance of the deeper structure of existing man. Nor should one forget that *comprehension* can only be obtained when one studies man in his concrete situation, that is, when one sees a project as fulfilled in a particular time and place and discovers this by reaching retrogressively into the elemental subjacent structure of that man in that concrete milieu.[72]

Such a correction would have been welcomed—to give these speculations a more concrete shape—in the assessment of the Hungarian revolution in 1956, the example of misjudgment that came up in previous pages. Sartre does not reintroduce it here, but I believe that I can very well do so for him in order to clarify his arduous dialectic. What the Russians lacked in their brutal repression was precisely a *comprehension* of the Hungarian collectivity. They approached Hungary with an "intellectualistic" scheme, that is, with a Marxist dogma that was frozen and unchangeable. They possessed only Knowledge, with no supple grasp or comprehension of the diversification of the projects involved.

[71] *Ibid.*, p. 106; Barnes trans., p. 172.
[72] *Ibid.*, p. 107; Barnes trans., p. 174.

It is also their fundamental, continuing mistake in Africa, where the same unnuanced "intellectual" approach of a Marxist dogma is imposed upon a totally diverse culture and civilization.

Sartre now feels at peace with his present position: he is both a Marxist and an existentialist.[73] The two views do not conflict: they merely complement one another. There is only one anthropology, and it is the Marxist, which takes man "*a partir de la matérialité de sa condition.*"[74] It needs, however, a corrective and this corrective can only be, as we have seen, existentialism, for existentialism will forcibly remind Marxism that both the interrogator and the interrogated are the same: they are both man, and in man lie "free" existence and unique project. Later on Sartre will approach all the familiar Marxist idioms such as reification, alienation, and labor from the same deepened point of view and show that the complete grasp of any one of them presumes an existentialistic *pro-ject*. The individual man objectifies himself in his labor, but his performance is a result of his fundamental *project*, by which he "transcends himself toward" such accomplishments. In all this it should and will appear that existentialism is not anti-Marxist. It is, however, definitely anti-deterministic. The Sartrian brand of Marxism is, in the hopes of our author, true Marxism, a Marxism which accepts a dualism of being and knowledge, and which in propounding that dualism does not level man to being a mere part and fragment of Nature, but respects him as a human being. It is from that human being that knowledge comes as a "moment" of its activity. From whence man himself comes, Sartre does not make clear, and I am afraid, never will.

Whatever this limitation may be, it can not be denied that within the total frame of his thought, Sartre has respect for man. "*Ce qui m'interesse, c'est l'homme,*" he once said, and everyone will agree that his immense intellectual

[73] *Ibid.;* Barnes trans., p. 174.
[74] *Ibid.;* Barnes trans., p. 175.

energy has indeed been directed into the defense of what he calls *"l'indépassable singularité de l'aventure humaine."*[75] In 1949, the walls of Warsaw were plastered with signs reading: "Tuberculosis slows down production."[76] This was indeed tragically true. Statistics do not lie, and they relentlessly demonstrated the authenticity of the equation. Sartre wondered, however, about the tubercular worker himself, who to the Marxist was no more than a "variable," a cipher dissolved in the production processes. Existentialism is a protest against just such an expulsion of *man,* until Marxism itself, realizing its oversight and "comprehending," fulfills its obligation. By that time, existentialism will have achieved its aim and having no longer any claim for survival, will disappear in the dialectic.

[75] *Ibid.,* p. 108; Barnes trans., p. 176.
[76] *Ibid.,* p. 109; Barnes trans., p. 178.

Chapter IV

SOME PRELIMINARY OBSERVATIONS

CRITICAL DIALECTIC *vs.* DOGMATIC DIALECTIC

It will quickly appear to the reader of the *Critique de la Raison Dialectique* that Sartre in his abundant use of dialectic is more Hegelian than Husserlian, as he was in *L'Etre et le Néant*. The descriptive method is not completely abandoned, but we find it subordinated to a constant call upon the Hegelian approach of a "rebounding" reciprocity. Most French intellectuals are in one way or another Hegelian. Having absorbed two influential forebears, Descartes and Bergson, during their *lycée* years and at the university, they are eager to apply research both for motion and for clarity to other philosophies. In Hegel they discover the perfect terrain, for his philosophy provides both a moving dialectic for the Bergsonian-minded and an obscurity which every Cartesian finds an ample challenge to his powers of clarification. In this respect Sartre is no exception, and this not only makes for difficult reading in his work, but also means that to an extent his theory stands or falls with the Hegelian dialectic.

The grounds for this dialectical approach could eventually be demonstrated by induction, but in Sartre's view this would be an endless task, and for all practical purposes it need only be stated a priori.[1] One is moved to ask, however, how dialectical materialism, which claims to be the basis of everything, can become the basis of itself. Hegel himself made

[1] *CRD*, I, p. 117.

no claim that his dialectic was demonstrable, but left it to stand upon its own power of evidence. For him the knowledge of nature and of the world ultimately came through a knowledge of the Self.[2] According to Sartre, Marx believed that on the contrary Being could not be reduced to Knowledge, although the two are dialectically related.[3] This interpretation would imply that we can never come to an ultimate self-identification with the Whole, as we do in the Hegelian dialectic. The defense by Marx of a dualism of "matter" and "mind" conflicts with their identification in the scientific mechanism which surprisingly enough is professed by *modern* Marxism. These "positivistic" Marxists, in accepting determinism and mechanistic succession, claim that prophecy is possible, since History is nothing but a mechanistic repetition and the future lives in the present as an unavoidable effect of the present *cause*. Sartre protests against this view, and in tracing the *human* element integrated within scientific trends, shows their consequent unpredictability. One might even go so far as to say that this is the *raison d'être* of his book.

Here already he points to an inconsistency in Marxism, which claims that every ideology is merely an expression of an economic situation but that its own position is independent of and can explain History. Man, who is only a piece of matter, an object like all other parts of nature, can suddenly turn on his heels and become Lenin making statements on the nature of History that are dogma to all those other "parts of nature" which happen to belong to the Communist party.

Sartre, as would be expected, bluntly rejects this sophism. Not only is man more than an object, more than a victim of a dialectical matter that is governed by the laws of nature, but even if he were *object* only, how could he suddenly become subject and make laws concerning the nature of the Real and the course of History? If I am a victim of the uni-

[2] *Ibid.*, p. 121. *Cf.*, also the end of Chapter I in this book.
[3] *CRD*, I, p. 121.

verse and ideas are only a passive occurrence in me, how can I know that they are indeed a truthful reflection of the real?[4] Sartre continues relentlessly with his questions. Why should the Marxist have the right to impose upon Nature as a whole a dialectic which has barely been discovered in the social order? "How can a human being, lost in the world, crossed by an absolute movement which reaches him from everywhere, how can he *also* be that consciousness which is certain of itself and of the Truth?"[5]

Lenin introduced a slight modification through his claim that human consciousness is nothing but a reflection—*un reflet*—of being, a reflection which at its best is only approximately correct. In making this claim, however, he invalidated the content in its very enunciation. For how can a "reflection" which is "approximately exact" or which is sheer passivity make any infallible pronouncement concerning the propelling forces of History?

Sartre himself comes to the rescue, he believes, by finding sufficient data spread all through Marx's work to build up a more realistic epistemology, by which Marx can be defended against Marx. In so doing, he draws heavily, of course, upon his own theory of knowledge, with which *L'Etre et le Néant* has made us familiar.[6] At the heart of this theory lies the fundamental dualism of *Pour-soi* and *En-soi*, the *Pour-soi*, or Being-for-itself, being human consciousness, which is nothing but the revelation of that which is, while the *En-soi*,

---

[4] *Ibid.*, pp. 123 ff. These pages are extremely interesting. At times they fall prey, however, to Sartre's volubility and are repetitious. The topic also comes up in a very good footnote on page 30 of the *CRD*. Those who have read Sartre's famous essay entitled "Matérialisme et Révolution" will find striking resemblances to these passages, with one important difference. The older Sartre, author of the *CRD*, wants Marx on his side and takes great pains to demonstrate that the dualism which he defends in the world of knowledge was already present in Marx, although it was not always explicitly recognized as such by the latter.

[5] *CRD*, I, p. 126.

[6] *Ibid.*, p. 131, see also footnote, p. 31. For more detailed information, see *Being and Nothingness*, pp. 172 ff.

or Being-in-itself, is the world as hunted and revealed by man. Both *Pour-soi* and *En-soi* are irremediably tied together, yet the one is not the other. It should be added—and this is of vital importance here—that the *Pour-soi* "knows" through negation, that is, it knows an object in the very act of "negating" what it is not: the object which confronts me is not a tree, it is not a car, it is not a barber's pole; it is a lamppost. In this mutually rebounding, "annihilating" dialectic between the Self and its object, the lamppost appears for what it is. It should furthermore be kept in mind that there is no *Pour-soi* without an *En-soi*, since all consciousness is consciousness *of* something. Without an object there would simply be no consciousness.

No one would claim of course that this formulation comes directly from Marx. It is definitely Sartrian, yet it does present us with an interpretation of the world in which "being is the negation of knowing and knowing gets all its strength from the negating of being,"[7] an expression which can in its roots be discovered in some Marxist and Hegelian texts. The very important conclusion is that for Sartre and for Marx (at least in Sartre's view of Marx) mind or consciousness is divorced from Nature, and Nature has no power of command upon the mind of man. Although it is unavoidably related to matter, mind for Sartre is definitely not matter. It should be made clear, however, that Sartre's purpose lies far from any attempt to make the *Pour-soi* a soul and to give it any subsequent claims to immortality. He wishes, rather, to show that since it is outside being, it is free and responsible, not merely thrown about in some causal chain of being. Moreover, in the act of knowledge, the *Pour-soi* reveals a world, which, without man, would not be in the light and not being in the light, would not be.

It is by now obvious that Sartre could not agree with any claim that there is a dialectic in inorganic nature *all by itself*. In his view this thesis cannot be demonstrated.[8] If there

[7] *CRD*, I, p. 131.
[8] *Ibid.*, p. 129.

is dialectic in nature, it can only be insofar as human *praxis* confers upon matter its particular "importance," or stated differently, insofar as material conditions affect the *human world and in turn themselves receive the impact of human* interference. Only within the social orbit of man can matter have dialectical implications. Outside man and without man, dialectic is mere hypothesis.

The *dialectic which Sartre accepts is the reciprocity between man and the world, man and man, the individual man and the group*. This dialectic moves through history in a succession of contradiction and totalization. It is precisely the awareness of this dialectic which makes the world, its structure and its history intelligible. It will appear as a necessity only when lived as such by man. (Man is used here not as mankind in the abstract but as the concrete existent.) This dialectic will be materialistic only in the sense that the individual discovers it in his "exteriority," which is actually his labor and the results of his labor. It will appear then that dialectic is not a blind law but a *lived reality* resulting from the multitude of men acting within themselves and with one another dialectically. It will appear as necessary and intelligible to the individual observer when *lived* as such *by him*. *Dialectic is only understood and accepted when lived by the interrogator*. "The individual [then] discovers the dialectic as a rational transparency insofar as he practices it himself, and as an absolute necessity insofar as it escapes him . . . and the others do it."[9] There is here, of course, a reciprocity at work according to which the dialectic is exterior to all because *in its totality* it is interior to no one, but nonetheless really exists.

This, then, is precisely what Sartre proposes to do in the pages to come: *he wants to live with the reader all forms of life* and to show their dialectical structures, then submit this to a "critique." His purpose is to show that there is place for a *Critical Dialectic* to replace the *Dogmatic Dialectic*

[9] *Ibid.*, p. 133.

of certain Marxist theoreticians; the resulting study will be, as its title indicates, a *Critique de la Raison Dialectique*. In doing this, Sartre does not claim to introduce an interpretation of History that is counter to the Marxist view, that is, to dialectical materialism, but he wants merely to become aware of the dialectic, and through this awareness, to show its rationality (when well understood) and necessity. Any effort to show the rationality of dialectical materialism, or to make it intelligible will of course consist in protecting the place of the human Subject.

CRITIQUE OF THE CRITICAL EXPERIENCE

Sartre now gives a critical prelude, in the course of which he hopes to bring the dialectical process to the surface and prove its reality. For if dialectic is an inner dimension of being and of knowing, it must manifest itself as intelligible and in one way or another as translucid, that is, at least partially open to conceptualization. This will be possible, the dialectic will manifest itself as such, if a totalization takes place and is accessible to a thought which itself continually "totalizes." *Totalization* is a key term which will appear again and again in Sartre's discussion, and it is important at this point to distinguish it clearly from another Sartrian concept, that of *totality*.[10] A totality is not to be identified

---

[10] Sartre is not the first to use the term "totalization," and I am certain that he claims no monopoly in that field. See on that topic Georges Gurvitch in the Appendix to *Dialectique et Sociologie* (Paris, 1962), p. 173, and Proudhon, *La Création de l'ordre* (Paris, 1927), p. 233. In his article "Sartre and Metaphysical Stalinism" (*Dissent*, Spring 1961), Lionel Abel makes the valuable suggestion of "translating" the term *"totalizer"* into *"maker-of-the-whole."* As a further help in clarifying the meaning, I would like also to indicate the pertinent remarks of G. Lichtheim in his article "Sartre, Marxism and History" (*History and Theory*, 1963, No. 2) to the effect that totalization cannot be contained within the contemplative consciousness alone but must spill over into action or *praxis*. This is indeed Sartre's intent. Lichtheim's article is most useful in placing the Sartrian position in its historical context.

with "the sum of its parts"; it is constituted, rather, through
an internal relation of its parts, a relation which results from
some previous intervention but which is now stabilized and
inert as, for example, a picture, a symphony, a machine, a
tool. Each of these constitutes a "totality." These totalities
are important, and I would like to call them, although Sartre
himself does not use the term, "catalyzers" of human relations. Further along in the text they will be called the
pratico-inert. The making or using of a totality is called
praxis. In addition to the *totality*, there is also *totalization*
or the unifying aspect of an act which is, as Sartre puts it,
en cours, that is, of an act which is not terminated but nevertheless can be considered synthetically *when one views every part as connected with every other part*. An empty house
—to cite the example given by the author—would be *pratico-
inert*, but once inhabited, it becomes a home and the center
of that unifying activity which is called "totalization." We
can now understand how dialectic is nothing but this totalizing activity,[11] which can be known when the knower is himself part of the inner dialectic. For only one who participates
can know and is consequently able to take a critical attitude. It follows that in such an hypothesis no abstract universal is possible. This would be a contradiction in terms.
Sartre at this point, not without an air of triumph, once more
buries the abstract universal—"*La totalisation ne peut être
qu'une aventure singulière*."[12] All reflection, in the very act
of participation in a dialectic, takes as its object a particular
slice of the dialectical reality.

Sartre confesses without hesitation that a "critique" in
the line of his own effort is only possible through the use of
the tools bequeathed us by Hegel and Marx. The Stalinists,
however, have corrupted the natural flow of historical dialectic through their improper methods and falsified epistemology. Thus there is an urgent need for a *critique*. Such a
critique as this which is being presented by Sartre could

[11] *CRD*, I, p. 139.
[12] *Ibid.*, p. 140.

also be made by others, as is indeed happening, but whoever takes up the task, it is one which needs to be done now. When Sartre writes, *"Il s'agit de n'importe qui aujourd'hui,"*[13] this must be understood literally. Any one—indeed everyone—in the post-Stalinian era could and should avoid rigid thinking and totalize the dialectic on his own behalf. Sartre claims no monopoly. Others have attempted what he has done; the efforts are *"tentatives . . . nombreuses —toutes intéressantes et toutes contestables (y compris naturellement celle-ci . . .)."*[14]

It is in this critical rethinking of history that the individual will realize how Marxism must be truly understood. For unlike traditional Marxism, which starts with production, moves from there to the structures of group and of society, studies the contradictions which these impose and finally reaches the individual, the *critical* experience will start with the individual. It will proceed from the individual in his abstract *praxis*—Sartre uses the term "abstract" in the Hegelian sense of *incomplete*—analyze his relations with the Other, trace the growth of groups and other collective forms, and end with the absolute concrete entity: the historical man.[15]

One might object that this inner experience carried by the individual—and for all purposes this individual may be myself—omits an experience of the past, since the past escapes my immediate awareness. To this Sartre answers, "I myself am conditioned dialectically by a past which is totalized and also totalizes the human adventure: as a man of a culture (this expression fits every man, whatever his culture may be, even the illiterate), I totalize myself from a whole past and to the extent of my culture, I totalize this experience."[16] The entire past is present in me and in my experience, and this past knowledge—all the knowledge that has been gathered up to now—should be available, theoreti-

[13] *Ibid.*, p. 141.
[14] *Ibid.*, p. 142.
[15] *Ibid.*, p. 143.
[16] *Ibid.*, p. 144.

cally at least, to our regressive dialectic. We should not confess that we know nothing, as did Socrates, for actually we are on the way to knowing *all*, since in our dialectical experience, we can use all which the past has gathered.

In speaking of the past, Sartre brings in once more the familiar idea of *reciprocity*; it is almost a *leitmotiv* in his publication, and we will see it appear again and again, with an ever-deepening meaning. At this meeting it is used to describe that complex structure of mutual relations which links me to the other, in whatever moment of the present or the past. So, for example, I am linked to Socrates, and although I have not actually lived *that* moment in Athens, I am linked to it through the intermediacy of culture. This *reciprocity* reveals both me and the other and replaces any universal definition of man: I am that which Socrates has made, and it is I who make Socrates, for only through me can he survive.

THE PLACE OF POSITIVISM

At this point in the text, Sartre once again considers the applicability of dialectic to nature, still with a certain displeasure, but this time from a new vantage point. There is still in his view no dialectic of nature without man, but nature obviously exists and is open to the probings of *positivistic reason*, since it is only reason working upon nature that is capable of measuring quantities with precision. Yet this approach can only be a "moment" within the larger embrace of the *dialectical* method. Analytical and positivistic thought with their quantitative approach have their place, but that place must be clearly demarked: one must see that it is merely the inert which is measuring the inert. In the analytical method, *la pensée doit se faire chose*,[17] and in this "thingification," thought absorbs the quantification of the outside reality. Man's mind becomes quantitative in a world

[17] *Ibid.*, p. 148.

of quantity, inorganic in a world of the inorganic. This attitude is provisional, but is continually reinvented and then dropped once more by the *dialectical* reason. For it is dialectic which dominates History. It can reveal many things which are hidden to the positivist, since only dialectic, in moving beyond its contradictions, can uncover the new, while in positivistic analysis, the *new* is constantly reduced to the *old*.

The emerging of the entirely new must be part of a complete dialectic, but the genesis of the new, that which is not reducible to the past, is nevertheless intelligible. One can understand it, however, only if one sees it as part of a process and as segment toward an end. *"Comprendre . . . c'est voir le tout,"* writes Sartre.[18] Within the totalizing view, the new part falls into its place and can be understood. One understands the new, furthermore, in the act of producing it, not insofar as it comes to one from the outside.[19] It will be our task to develop this argument further, but we should add here, as a hint to the line which will be pursued, that intelligibility will be considered to be not merely applicable to an individual adventure; it is the *total* human adventure which is understandable, or as we call it here, "intelligible," although there is no grand Totalizer who holds it all in his mind.

In excluding the possibility of a grand Totalizer, Sartre of course manifests his atheism.[20] He does not go into a demonstration here, as his reasons have been sufficiently developed in *L'Etre et le Néant*. Although in the earlier work Sartre attempted to give several arguments for his atheistic position, the main "proof" grew out of the impossibility of bringing together the *Pour-soi* and the *En-soi* in one unified entity which would be all and everything. Such Being is non-existent. Sartre's atheism results from this dual structure of the *Pour-soi* and *En-soi*, which leaves no room for a third

18 *Ibid.*, p. 149.
19 *Ibid.*, p. 150.
20 *Ibid.*, p. 152.

entity. Even if there were a God, he still could not see the totality, for, asserts Sartre, "No consciousness, not even God's can 'see the underside'—that is, apprehend the totality as such. For if God is consciousness, he is integrated in the totality. And if by his nature, he is a being *beyond* consciousness (that is, an In-itself which would be its own foundation) still the totality can appear to him only as *object* (in that case he lacks the totality's internal disintegration as the subjective effort to reapprehend the self) or as *subject* (then since God is not this subject, he can only experience it without knowing it). Thus no point of view on the totality is conceivable; the totality has no 'outside,' and the very question of the meaning of the 'underside' is stripped of meaning. We cannot go further."[21] Since there is no Totalizer, it is our task to show that totalization, that is, this comprehensive grasp of the dialectic, is necessarily a concern of the many. The different ways in which this is accomplished will be shown later.

Sartre next summarizes the work to be done in the following pages. It would not be advisable to summarize his summary, since the outlines he gives would only be puzzling without a knowledge of the details he later fills in. I shall instead merely point to the double structure of the book which follows. The first part starts from a dialectical examination as comprehended and understood through *individual praxis*. We soon discover, however, that this dialectic reveals to us the *inert*, which consists of the series (individual men juxtaposed) and other forms of passivity called the "anti-dialectic." The dialectic is free, controlled, planned; the anti-dialectic comes into play when the actions of man escape him and he becomes unfree, inert, passive. In the former he is master of his fate, in the latter, victim. Against this menace of stagnation and in an attempt to regain control of the dialectic, man has united with others to form a

[21] Sartre, *Being and Nothingness*, p. 302. For an attempt to defend the existence of a *totalizing* God, see my book, *The Planetary Man*, I, Chapter VIII.

group, the second type of dialectical action. The analysis of *group* makes up the second part of the book, where Sartre uncovers the circular movement linking both group and individual and series and group, for *groups* will be distinguished from *series* and from what Sartre calls a *collective*. All this constitutes only the horizontal phase of what may be called the content of history or the intelligible structures of society. A second volume is projected, in which Sartre plans to analyze these constructions chronologically and to show the truth and intelligibility of History itself.[22]

Our exploration is actually nothing but the *experience of the identity of an individual life and human history*.[23] This identity is still the object of future demonstration, but it can be said already that its truth will be experienced in our analysis. If there is a dialectic, it will appear as the totalizing force which envelops us, in all our freedom, as a necessity. Both freedom and its "rocky foundation,"[24] or necessity, will be the object of our experience. Necessity results from the continual interiorization of an external reality—we act and through our action contaminate a world—and the exteriorization of an internal dimension—in action we produce an external object. We are very clearly caught in nature or in the power of the inorganic, as will appear later more forcefully. Sartre makes a brief but unequivocal admission of the material connections and dependence of man upon matter.[25] He is still concerned above all with human freedom, and he has no intention of burying it underneath scientific determinism, but nevertheless, his thought has somewhat evolved, and freedom is no longer as detached from the matter as it was in previous publications. Indeed, the conclusion to which these very interesting pages lead is that matter is the motor of History, but it is *"matière ouvrée,"* that is, matter touched by man. Man is an object of History

[22] *CRD*, I, p. 156.
[23] *Ibid.*
[24] *Ibid.*, p. 157.
[25] *Ibid.*, p. 158.

when he looks backward, since man's "past" belongs not to himself but to the past; he is a robot, an essence, forever "frozen" and reified.[26] Man in the present is still free to go beyond himself, and far from being a robot, he constantly makes himself.

Our critical experience will show us at all levels this indissoluble unity of "organic and inorganic," on the level of the individual himself, of the series (of individuals), of the group and as a consequence, of history itself. In this statement we have the main structure of the coming pages. Sartre will at the start discuss what he calls the "constituting" dialectic (on the individual level), then the anti-dialectic (as we have seen, the menace of the inert) and finally, the equilibrium re-established through the "constituted" dialectic in the group. This will then be synthetically and progressively brought together in one global totalization, the ground and starting point of History.

[26] *Ibid.* See also *Being and Nothingness,* pp. 114 and 328. For eventual comment see *The Tragic Finale,* pp. 38 and 78.

Chapter V

FROM INDIVIDUAL *PRAXIS* TO THE PRATICO-INERT

THE FORESTER, IN CUTTING DOWN A TREE, MAKES THE
FOREST, OR THE INDIVIDUAL ACTS, AND THROUGH HIS ACT,
TOTALIZES

"The most important discovery of dialectical experience
. . . is that man is 'mediated' by things to the extent that
things are mediated by man."[1] This is one of the core statements of Sartre's book, and it implies what he calls a *dialectical circularity*. The Hegelian overtones are, of course,
obvious, but Sartre will incorporate them into his own ordering and give them new meaning, as we will see in the following pages.

We may state without hesitation that the individual lies
at the beginning of all historical dialectic, whatever may be
the later impact of collective entities upon him. The first
dialectical manifestation originates with *need*, which reveals
a lack in the organism itself.[2] As lack, it may appear to be
negative, yet it has a positive result: it compels the organism
to act in order to preserve its existence. The living organism
goes beyond itself to explore the environment as a possible
field where it can gratify its needs. Nature is the medium to
fulfill the lack—man wrests his livelihood from it—but it is a
danger zone as well, since it hides the possibility of death
for the organic entity. To protect himself and to subsist,

[1] *CRD*, I, p. 165.
[2] *Ibid.*, p. 166; see also in this book, Chapter II, pp. 26–28.

l'homme du besoin[3]—the "man of need"—uses both tools and his own body, to the extent that it is material and "inert," for man, in his approach to nature, becomes inert in a world of the inert.

It immediately becomes apparent that *organic function, need*, and *praxis* (and by *praxis* we understand the action taken) are correlated. When nature *negates* man through its menace, man offsets this threat by negating nature. It should be well understood, however, that that negation which comes from nature and reaches man is ultimately provoked by man himself and not by nature, whatever the claims of Engels may be. Sartre here defends a position which he has already proposed in the beginning of *L'Etre et le Néant*, where human intervention was so strongly emphasized. In that work, it is the *Pour-soi*, the consciousness of man, which introduces non-being into things. The *En-soi*, or nature, is massive and full being, and as such, it cannot know itself.[4] Sartre continues to place heavy emphasis upon the *Pour-soi* (without using that term), which in this work, in the form of "man" or "labor" or "human *praxis*," continues to confer meaning upon the *En-soi*, or matter.

We have mentioned that *need* is at the origin of all human activity, since it compels man to do something in order to overcome some lack. This need—as the reader will remember from the study of Chapter II—is identical with the fundamental *pro-ject* of the individual man toward the surrounding world.[5] This essential attitude of the individual *unifies and totalizes the surrounding plurality* as future possibility and constitutes by this very fact a passive and inert totality,

[3] Sartre's colorful term does not lend itself easily to translation.

[4] *CRD*, I, p. 168; see also *The Tragic Finale*, pp. 16 ff., and on p. 19: "This annihilation, the specific activity of the For-itself, is possible only if the For-itself is 'out' of Being-in-itself. If human reality were a massive and full being like Being-in-itself, if it were engulfed in the density of being, then all capacity for negation (or annihilation) would be excluded. *Only* 'what is not' is able to understand 'what is.'" See also *Being and Nothingness*, p. 11.

[5] *CRD*, I, p. 173.

a totality which in turn forges an obstacle to man and in this sense negates him, but this negation, we repeat, comes to man as a result of his own initiative. His labor not only has an impact upon the surrounding field of action, but also is in its very essence a mediation of the worker with himself. In addition, within the external totality, *it opposes a part to the whole*. It is man who through his labor introduces in nature the awareness of the whole and supplies a consciousness of the tearing apart of the whole, *le tout et la déchirure du tout*.[6] Sartre introduces here the example of a forester who chops down a tree in a virgin forest. His labor recognizes nature as a whole and within that whole cuts its part (through negation); in so doing, it understands the whole or "totalizes" through the implicit negation of its own negation. Thus, if and when the forester cuts a tree, it is a negation—the tree is removed—yet he implicitly recognizes the whole, which is the forest intact. Similarly, when I erase the vestiges of a certain event, through this act I recognize a differentiation within the co-ordinated whole. What Sartre wants us to see is that between man and his instrumental field an incessant *"chassé-croisé,"* or reciprocal exchange, is at work. Man is always dominated by the *end,* which is ever present, and this *end* is dictated by the need, or project. *"On guette à la chasse"*[7]—one incessantly stalks his prey.

This is the dialectic of the working man. It implies a variety of movements—the "shaping of the present through the future, the interchange of the inert with the inorganic, negation, contradictions overcome, negation of negation, in short, totalization in action."[8] All this, it may be well to remember, does not explain the origin of the organic entity which we call man, but merely shows it to us in action, as a living, existing, and free entity. Sartre himself is reserved concerning any explanation of the origins of the organic. In his view, we are certain only of the existence of human life;

[6] *Ibid.*
[7] *Ibid.*, p. 174.
[8] *Ibid.*

we have no strict proof of its evolution from the inorganic. The theory of evolution he considers to be merely an interesting hypothesis, one which is far from being demonstrated apodictically, and which as it stands requires more "faith" than he is prepared to bestow upon it.[9]

If the intelligibility offered by the *dialectical* reason does not solve the problem of origin, the *analytical* reason does no better. Actually the *analytical* reason is only "a moment" within the dialectical movement, and although the average man is not aware of it—he may very well be convinced that life consists merely of the mechanical and the analytical— he will, if he pays sufficient attention, easily see that in any act of labor is buried the dialectic.[10]

THE *petit bourgeois* LOOKS FROM HIS WINDOW, OR MAN AS LINK AND MEDIATOR

This section of Sartre's study has unusual interest, not so much for its conclusion as for its penetrating phenomenological description, combined with the use of a dialectical reciprocity à la Hegel. The method is both Hegelian and Husserlian, and Sartre shows himself a master in manipulating the combination. The description may be long and diluted, but to one who has said farewell to the deductive method, no other road seems possible.

Human relations are, in Sartre's view, not so much a result of History as a phenomenon which runs concomitant with History. One must examine them carefully before tying them up with the problem of production as the Marxists eagerly (and prematurely) do. For modern Marxism, as we very well know, human reality is nothing more than an inert and pas-

[9] Sartre's reluctance to accept the theory of evolution must be linked to his position in *L'Etre et le Néant,* where, as is well known, the *Pour-soi* and the *En-soi* are kept strictly distinct. The origin of the *Pour-soi* is not so simple and Sartre confesses not to have an answer at hand. The surprising conclusion is that Sartre somehow in this domain is more conservative than the Jesuit Teilhard de Chardin.

[10] *CRD,* I, p. 176.

sive entity, pushed around by the forces of production. Such
an hypothesis not only cancels History—how could there be
History, if man is a mere robot—but also contains a defense of
bourgeois philosophy as well, since above all the bourgeois
wants man to be passive and hence susceptible to conditioning.[11] For Sartre, on the contrary, human relations are a result of human activity. They are human insofar as they result
from the *praxis* of men. In the example of language, Sartre
agrees that *le mot est matière*.[12] History has made the word,
but it has done so only because there was man first. Language presupposes man and his interindividual structure.

Sartre now launches into the strange description of a *petit
bourgeois intellectuel* looking from a hotel window and observing two men working in neighboring fields but separated
by a fence and unaware of each other. Obviously the observer does not belong to their class. Their worries are not my
worries, reasons the *petit bourgeois* staring from his window,
their hopes and plans are not mine, but the very insight I
have into these differences englobes and constitutes them as
part of my understanding.[13] In the grasp of my own self, I
understand their work, how their individual aims shape their
labor, and how all this locates them in a class. Any one of
these multiple negations—*they are not what I am*—reveals
to me what they are. I see their gestures, their tools, etc., not
only in their *present* meaning but also as significant of a *future*, for it is against this future that their present is understood. But all this emphasizes my own limitations as well,
—in status, I am only a *petit bourgeois intellectuel*—and in
skill, I am not able to do what they do.

But this is not all. I am always the subject, the living subject, and as such I am also a link.[14] In being the third man,

[11] *Ibid.*, p. 180.
[12] *Ibid.*
[13] *Ibid.*, p. 183.
[14] This is another idea dear to the heart of Sartre. Man, introspec-
tively *subject*, becomes *object* through his being-known-by-the-other.
See *Being and Nothingness*, p. 339.

I am the one *who brings their mutual ignorance of one an-other into being*. Through me this mutual ignorance obtains a real and objective dimension, not merely a subjective quali-fication, for phenomenology—it should not be forgotten—dis-covers realities which a mere empiricism does not see. I am also the one through whom each of them gets an "objective" standing, just as I become "object" in their presence. There is in all this no Grand Maker of essences at work; there is nothing more than a human individual, the presence of an-other individual, and the dialectic born out of the *praxis* be-tween both. In case of mutual ignorance—as was the case here—there is, of course, the need for a third man, but the latter may very well be dropped when the two know one an-other. Even when they are aware of one another's presence, however, the third man still plays a role when his presence creates the *us-object* feeling of the two. The *us-object* emerges when the relation—any relation—between two peo-ple is observed by a third man. Both of *us* become object in the world of a third person. In this new relation I and the other suddenly become unified.[15] The third man may some-times be the enemy, or he may be god or somebody whom *we* ought to placate with a gift. The gift then implies reciprocity and signifies upon its acceptance a cessation of hostilities. In our society all these relations, whether between two or among three persons, are fluent and unstable, they come up and dis-appear and then come up again.

Coming back once more to our two workers, still occupied on opposite sides of the fence, one must emphasize that their relation of reciprocity is always concrete. It is neither abstract *comme la charité des chrétiens*,[16] nor the result of some Kantian-like decision to treat one another as an end. Kant's approach in the *Metaphysics of Morals*, which treats man as a universal, is of no value to Sartre, nor is the third formula-tion of the *categorical imperative*—that man is his own law, with a static, rational element within himself commanding his

15 *Being and Nothingness*, p. 415. (In *The Tragic Finale*, p. 92.)
16 *CRD*, I, p. 189.

actions. There is no human nature, or universal character of man; there is only *this* farmer recognizable by his tools and his clothes or *this* construction worker, known through his *praxis* and his pro-ject. Everything on them and around them makes me recognize and accept them for what they are. At the start of all human relations lies this fundamental recognition, or what I might call *acceptance of the other for what he is*, an acceptance which is based upon his *praxis* or individual performance. Strangely enough, there is even a mutual recognition between the worker and the employer who will exploit him. For although the worker will be exploited, at the start of this exploitation lies his freedom, his free acceptance of the contract, and of all that it implies.

We observe in all this Sartre's continual attempt to discover a *human* world, a world which is indeed matter and yet has at the same time a dimension which is more-than-matter. Man lives in a material world which he needs to change for his very subsistence, and it is in this act of transforming matter or a portion of it that he "makes" himself and builds up the flexible relation of reciprocity with the other man. Similarly, we have that reciprocity called *exchange*, when two men agree to become means for one another *in* the object they have manufactured, with the hope that this mutual subordination will serve their individual aims. There is *struggle*, however, when one man, recognizing the instrumental value of the other man, attempts to use it against his will, and when the other man refuses to be used instrumentally. Once more, we have a *human* decision, but that human decision is imbedded in materiality, with matter not only supplying the means of implementing it but also lying at the origin of the struggle itself.[17] Incidentally, the matter which lies at the origin of struggle may actually be the absence of matter, that which we call *scarcity*. Scarcity is of major importance to Sartre, as we shall see again and again.

In conclusion, Sartre feels the need to emphasize once

[17] *Ibid.*, p. 192.

more the importance of the third man, in our example, the *petit bourgeois intellectuel* gazing from his window. His presence is, indeed, that "which keeps alive the objective meaning written in things, and (also) that which constitutes the group as totality."[18] One remarks Sartre's continual insistence "to cover" man through the presence and the ever-active awareness of the other man. This *object*-ification of man happens always through matter, for every individual, although not matter himself, is sunk in materiality. From all this it clearly appears that there is nothing more active than Sartre's *Pour-soi,* yet it is itself nothing but the revelation and manipulation of what it is not. It is forever involved, in Sartre's terms continually *engagé,* but it has no consistency of its own and must hang upon what it is *not* in order to *be*.

For the purpose of showing what the third man does in this strange function of "objectifying" an event, Sartre gives the example of a taxi driver who, while driving along the Seine, observes a group of people who are leaning over the low stone wall along its banks and watching something in the water. Their movements and gestures are caught by the taxi driver and reveal to him a specific action of men, a common intention. In keeping this intention alive, the third man is mediator between a form of universality (the common deed and purpose of these men) and the different individuals themselves. *Unity is imposed upon them from the outside.* This is a pivotal point; Sartre continually attempts to abandon the universal and to substitute for it a link, which, not in itself an abstract common entity, constitutes nevertheless a means of combining the one and the many.[19]

This attitude of the third man carries with it the possibility of a hierarchy, since it builds up a synthesis between himself and the others, which at times is not reciprocal, as for example when one person commands and the others must submit to his orders. This may eventually be a turning movement, since each one may in turn become the *third* man. This

[18] *Ibid.,* p. 197.
[19] *Ibid.*

question, obviously not a simple one, will be more thoroughly explored later. At this point in the text, one thing is certain: human relations exist "and they are actually nothing but the relation of man's *praxis* with itself."[20] Human relations result from the turning back of man's activity upon itself.

It would be well to recapitulate where we now stand. We have discovered that at the start there is an individual *praxis*. Upon leaving this "abstract" moment, we have seen the relations of men arise as an unavoidable dimension, each man with his own pro-ject and totalizing mental activity embracing the other. We have noticed also how these connections were cemented in and revealed through the inorganic materiality.[21] Human beings are organisms, but these organisms live in a world of matter, use matter and constitute a plurality spread open over the inorganic. Their activities, each one of them, are caught up in diverse matter. This multiplicity and variety of material (and inorganic) conditions shape the relations of men and give them their individual and peculiar character.

We have not yet reached History and indeed, we still have a long way to go. For first we must acquire the tools to understand groups, such as classes, nations, and society itself. Still, we have started well on the way in seeing the human individual at work, his *praxis* and incessant vitality, his totalization and the slow growth of relations from man to man through the diverse materiality which conditions each of them. We must pause once more to see how this matter that is "touched" by man hits back at him.

L'enfer c'est l'autre, OR THE IMPORTANCE OF MATTER

The paradoxical purpose of this section is to show that notwithstanding all our protests to the contrary, a part of human history has an inhuman dimension. This inhuman dimension lies in the cruel and desperate dependency of man

[20] *Ibid.,* p. 198.
[21] *Ibid.*

upon his negation, that is, upon his labor, insofar as it comes back to him in the form of *inertia*. This will of course require more comment in the following pages, but it should be noted at the start that this tie between the individuals in our history and their surrounding materiality is characterized by *"une lutte acharnée contre la rareté."*[22] Scarcity is considered by Sartre to be the very foundation of human history, that which in our world has made it to be what it is. One could, of course, imagine a world where this sad feature would be lacking, but it is *not* the present world, where after thousands of years three quarters of its population is still undernourished. For there is no "man" in general, there is only our man of today, and it is this man who interests us.

The topic itself is not new, but what is new, in Sartre's opinion, is the dialectical point of view; it will be seen that in the phenomenon of scarcity in human history, materiality is merely rendering to man what man had beforehand inflicted upon matter. Scarcity reaches matter through man and man through matter. There are primitives who live in "scarcity" and extreme poverty, yet lack a history, so it is clear that scarcity alone does not impart reality to history; man's confrontation of matter, or of the absence of matter, is also important. We note again a circularity at work, a circularity which must be closely studied if history is to be at all intelligible.

If the only field of action open to man must contain scarcity as an inevitable part (as it does in our world), then we may say that "scarcity defines a particular relation of the individual to his environment."[23] It is from scarcity, which is in its very default a "materiality," that the threat of destruction reaches the individual man. We must concede that there is an *inhuman* dimension, a dimension which has a quantitative character: *of a certain thing there is not enough, therefore I must negate you.* In other words, scarcity is *the negation of man through the presence of other men.* These other

[22] *Ibid.*, p. 201.
[23] *Ibid.*, p. 204.

men threaten what I have because there is not enough for all.

This formulation can also be expressed in another way: "scarcity realizes the passive totality of the individuals of a collectivity as an impossibility of coexistence."[24] As a consequence, there is a trend toward a reduction in the number of inhabitants of that collectivity, manifested in various ways. One does not have to kill directly, but one can let children die, or through the practice of birth control not let them be born at all, thus eliminating the future consumer. This is the way it is done in bourgeois democracies as well as in Communist China, until production can catch up with population. It should be added that every member of the group, although surviving, is a possible candidate for elimination and that everyone is as a result questioned *in his very being* by all the others. Sartre observes that "man's own activity thus rebounds against man himself."[25] Man becomes, through matter, other than himself; he becomes the *inhuman* man. Every man is for the other man something demoniacal in that although the Other is the same as I am—I discover in him what I discover in myself—he is nonetheless other, since for me "he carries in himself the menace of death."[26]

Every man, then, is both factor and victim of scarcity. It is because of scarcity under one form or another that man kills. Sartre feels that he is in opposition to Hegel when he states that the death of the other man is not an end in itself but merely a means to survival.[27] For it now appears that the notion of evil is conceived through the Other because of the threat which the Other poses. Man perpetually faces

[24] *Ibid.*, p. 205.
[25] *Ibid.*, p. 206.
[26] *Ibid.*, p. 208.
[27] Sartre's position may be defensible as far as content goes, but to formulate this in the form of an opposition to Hegel is another matter. I am not at all certain that Sartre has understood Hegel correctly on this point. Hegel's man wants recognition above all and stakes his very life on that condition. The death of the other is not an end in itself. In fact, Hegel's dialectic rejects the death of the opponent, since that eventuality would cancel the possibility of recognition. See Hegel, *The Phenomenology of Mind,* p. 133.

anti-man,[28] even where scarcity is less apparent, as, for example, in the case of the primitive nomads who wander over the prairie with enough space and sustenance for all. This does not argue against Sartre's case, for even where all needs are fulfilled, the anxiety still remains that some day they may no longer be, and from this anxiety grow distrust and hate. Life is a play of reciprocity, a treacherous reciprocity, from the heart of which ethics is born.

Sartre seems to give way to a Manichean trend, whereby Evil gets its incarnation. He does so brilliantly, however, and substantiates his position more carefully and more convincingly, it seems to me, than he did in certain previous works, as, for example, in *Huit-Clos* (*No Exit*). The reader will remember that in that particular play one of the characters uttered a phrase that is now famous: *"L'enfer c'est l'autre."* The impact was dramatically striking, but as a whole less persuasive philosophically. Through such analyses as this one, which probes the question of scarcity and its social implications, Sartre brings his drama off the stage and into a philosophical and sociological work, where we find that the Other is as much a threat as ever.

Since men are often restricted within a certain space and confront common problems of materiality and technology, it is easy to see how these elements of materiality *totalize men into certain groups*. The difficulty arises when groups of a different structure live on the edges of or even actually overlap one another's fields of action, the same unity of environment thus resulting in a contradictory totalization. Sartre gives the example of a group of Chinese farmers who wish to expand their arable land into the roaming ground of a group of nomads, who are consequently pushed into the desert. The same piece of land totalizes group *A* (the farmers) and group *B* (the nomads), and the individual freedom of the one is bypassed (*dépassé*) by the project of the other. Through matter (the land) man becomes for the other man

---

[28] Sartre coins the word *"contre-homme."* Keeping this meaning in my comment, I use "anti-man."

inert and passive, a mere object among objects, an obstacle to be overcome that is no different from the material obstacles of the environment. It is at this moment that he discovers a new *praxis*—war. War is a work, *"un travail de l'homme sur l'homme,"*[29] whereby the Other becomes an absolute object to the conqueror. The case of the Chinese farmers and the nomads is not an academic one; we are *all* tragically united through our living in a world that is defined by scarcity and in which as a consequence our projects sometimes overlap.

Sartre is of the opinion that Marxists—from Marx himself to Engels and their followers—have not sufficiently appreciated the importance of this concept of scarcity. Thus he criticizes Marx's attempt to give an explanation of the precapitalistic society of the Romans in the "Answer to Nicolas Mikhailovski" (1877). In this text Marx describes the transformation of Roman society from a primitive into a more advanced state, the development of an internal opposition of classes, and finally, the eruption of this class structure into a class struggle. Sartre points out that while this may be a truthful narration of the events themselves, it makes no attempt to explain *why* they happened as they did.[30]

Engels in his *Anti-Dühring* does no better.[31] When he claims that the disaggregation of primitive society, which was composed of small landowners, resulted in a realignment which subsequently developed into opposing and conflicting classes, he gives once more a narration of succession, not one of *human* motivation. Any motivation or "explanation" is merely positivistic; thus he formulates such a law as: the speed with which a primitive society changes into an industrial society depends on the speed of the change of its natural products into industrial ones.[32] Even Engels himself

[29] *CRD*, I, p. 211.

[30] *Ibid.*, p. 215.

[31] Engels, *Anti-Dühring*, ed. Costes (Paris, 1931–33), II, p. 33. This reference is given by Sartre himself.

[32] *CRD*, I, p. 217.

is dissatisfied with this explanation and resorts later on to another. This time it is the division of labor which is considered to be at the origin of the division of classes.[33] This approach is historical but not satisfactory either, for it still does not reveal the *human* adventure in all this. The Sartrian *leitmotiv* appears again—it is acting man and matter which has been acted upon which play their part in the unrolling dialectic, not matter alone. For Sartre, then, the basic questions still remain unanswered. Why does the transformation of society from one level to another result in antagonisms? Why does the division of labor (positive connotation) evolve into class struggle (negative connotation)? It is here that Sartre turns for his answer to the presence in man of an inhuman element based upon *scarcity*. Neither Marx nor Engels ever fully considered the element of negativity, which because of scarcity is built-in in man as *that element by which one is capable of killing or vulnerable to being killed*. Sartre gives Dühring ("otherwise *un imbécile*") the credit of at least having understood the importance of violence.[34] Violence is not merely an exterior act—it can be an act no doubt —but it is also interiorized scarcity, or that by which everyone sees in everyone else the Other and the principle of Evil.[35] It is this *interiorized* aspect which Marx and Engels have overlooked.

There can be no doubt that class differentiation starts where there is less production than is strictly required, where as a consequence some have and others don't have, some produce and others do not produce, some are overfed and others are dying from hunger. It should nevertheless be kept in mind—and that is what Marx and Engels do not do—that a multiple form of interiorization runs all through these multiple strata. So, for example, the rich can gladly accept the status of being Other and better than the rest, or less likely, they could refuse it, and the poor can accept their plight as

[33] Engels, *Anti-Dühring*, III, p. 48.
[34] *CRD*, I, p. 221.
[35] *Ibid.*

inevitable in the order of things, or they can react with passion and violence, and carrying the resentment in their hearts, wait for the moment to rebel. This is what Sartre means by interiorization, or the conscious "taking over" of the external situation.

When man starts manufacturing an object with the purpose of negating a scarcity, this object or *matière ouvrée* should result in a diminution of scarcity and in a consequent relaxation of tensions. In true fact, however, it has not, for the labor of man and its objectification in a product has only resulted in making something which in its very being is a comfort for a few and a frustration for the many. What man has made becomes an anti-social force. This Marx has shown already in *Das Kapital*, where capital constitutes a gigantic bloc of alienation. Sartre will show how through concrete experience materiality as a positive presence conditions human relations. Class formation will not only become more intelligible, but apodictically so, that is, necessary.[36] For when comforts and frustrations are harbored in hearts, and not merely displayed in the market place, opposition is certain to result.

GOLD IS DESTINY, OR MATTER AS OBJECTIFICATION AND ALIENATION

When one studies the problem of scarcity and the means which have been taken to alleviate it, it becomes apparent that in many cases the remedy has been worse than the disease itself. An immense amount of energy and potential power was unleashed through the discovery of the uses of iron and coal, an immense wealth was poured into the Western world through the media of steel and the locomotives and machines which were made out of steel, yet, surprisingly enough, notwithstanding the fabulous enrichment, poverty continued as always, or worse still, increased in certain mi-

[36] *Ibid.*, p. 224.

lieus, as for example, among the farmers. The new inventions revolutionized an old society and provoked a complete reclassification and regrouping. Industrialization, which was to have been a remedy to scarcity, drew the farmer away from the countryside and brought him in immense numbers to cities, which soon became overcrowded with his kind; he was leveled to being merely an inert and easily replaceable instrument of the factory. Industrialization, one more attempt of man to counteract scarcity, exacted an enormous price: a "new man" was brought into being, a man who was to be only a producing, inert figure, with no consuming, acting life of his own. Sartre applies to this succession of events his familiar semantics of negativity. Scarcity, as a negation of me (because you are there), challenges my initiative. This negation lies at the origin of man's *praxis*. That this *praxis* and its result under the form of industrialization in the iron-coal era has failed is all too obvious; the attempt to counteract the negation of man has only resulted in a further negation of man.[37]

Sartre sees a similar phenomenon at work in the problem of slavery, which was an earlier human attempt to counteract scarcity. Its remote origin lay in need, or what one may call *negativity*. This need does not have to be present as an actual and positive fact, it may merely be a lack of gain. The scarcity of that labor which is necessary to produce gain replaces the scarcity of tools. One goes beyond the need, or negativity, in finding cheap labor, and one finds cheap labor in organizing razzias and other means of capturing men, who are subsequently reduced to subhuman beings. (By "subhuman" one understands man as a producing but not as a consuming, or at least only a subconsuming, figure.)

It appears clearly from both examples that thus far, any attempt to go beyond scarcity, to cancel its negation has only resulted in producing the subhuman in greater numbers. Scarcity freely "overcome" has not cured the suffering

[37] *Ibid.*, p. 227.

of mankind. Sartre will attempt to explain this sad state of affairs through revealing the close dialectical interplay of man and machines, or of man and materiality. His detailed analysis in the following pages is one more attempt to make intelligible the complex structure of the human *praxis* and its reverberation upon man.[38] The method which he uses continues to be the observation of historical events and a careful analysis of what he sees in the light of their dialectic, again a combination of Husserl and Hegel, but with a strong Sartrian stamp.

It is strange and fascinating, this interplay of man and matter, matter and man, and if it is in part deadly to man (as we have seen) it is in part "life-giving" to matter, which is invested with the power to hit back at man. In order to show the impact of the circular dialectic of matter and man, Sartre uses the example of the policy of deforestation as it was practiced in China for thousands of years, with as its disastrous sequel floods that raged unchecked over the treeless land. The act of deforestation can be equated with an act of colonization; it was a conquest against Nature and against the nomads, it was systematic (as is a human *praxis*, in contrast to natural destruction) and it reflects a unification of multiple human actions within certain spatial limits. This passive unity blocks the active interference of the individual man, who might have foreseen what was impending. All this results in a massive alienation, an alienation which constitutes a fatality for the worker. "The worker becomes his own material fatality; he produces the inundations which will ruin him."[39] As soon as human labor is crystallized, it escapes its human cause (and control) through its materiality and becomes loaded with meaning. It carries a new danger, in that the *correction of nature by man produces an anti-*

[38] *Ibid.*, pp. 229 ff. Sartre's stress upon the negative as the remote origin of the sequel of events is aimed against Engels, who according to Sartre moves from positive to positive, thereby falling once again into that mechanistic conditioning which Sartre so condemns for its overlooking of *human* intervention.

[39] *CRD*, I, p. 234.

human menace. To the extent that man posits himself as anti-physics, nature itself becomes a negation of man. This revolt of nature is in turn counteracted by new activity, in this example, the construction of dams to combat the floods and bridges to cross the waters.

These links between man and matter are even more stringent in the case of the precious metals. They are, as we shall see, simultaneously "product, merchandise, sign, power" and become also "exigency, tensions, limitations, enterprise, inhuman activity."[40] Here, more than anywhere, the *praxis* of man provokes as a reaction a rigid and fatalistic *anti-praxis* and finality brings its unavoidable counterfinality. Thus Sartre describes how the discovery of gold in Peru resulted ultimately in Spanish decadence. First of all, we must notice that the gold is given *human* quantifications: it has volume, it can be numbered, and it is "contained." The container is Spain. Spain is a natural container geographically, but above all, it is so through human *praxis*, which, through a variety of institutions—its customs, the command of an authoritarian king, etc.—has given it a shape.[41] Human *praxis* is unifying and revealing—it is man who measures and counts and contains, it is man who gives gold its value and its meaning. In so doing, this human *praxis sets itself* in the matter—the gold must be transported, loaded and unloaded, guarded and protected, in all this absorbing the labor of men. As usual, however, the dialectic is at work, and matter in turn conditions human *praxis*. "Man loses himself so that the *human thing* might exist."[42]

Sartre discovers a confirmation of his thesis in Zola's *Bête Humaine*, where man is seen as losing himself in becoming a thing. This "thingification," or the *Pour-soi* sliding into the thingness of the *En-soi*, is an obsession of Sartre's, an obsession which came up again and again in his main speculative work. For example, it is discussed there in connection with

[40] *Ibid.*, p. 235.
[41] *Ibid.*, p. 237.
[42] *Ibid.*, p. 238.

masochism: "The masochist, in letting his partner torture
and beat him, tries to become a thing-in-itself. Masochism,
too, however, is a sin and a failure. It is a sin because the
masochist, in attempting to become 'object,' gives up his freedom. It is a failure because he seeks to have his partner consider him as an 'object,' when he is not one and never can
be one."[43]

In this passage, Sartre shows the reverse of his discovery
of the reification in man and reveals the human element
posited in the thing. The gold is contaminated by the presence and manipulation of men, of many men, but it has its
revenge. It has become vital to Spain, its container, but it
will not be contained: the gold *runs away*. This flight of the
gold has been caught in the metaphor of Braudel: "*L'Es-
pagne est un chateau d'eau.*"[44] The gold fights against its
own accumulation and escapes like water from the container
into other places of the Mediterranean basin. For the accumulation of the whole degrades the value of the part, or
in other words, when there is too much of something, it diminishes in value, and we observe the beginning of a gradual
devaluation. In an attempt to stop devaluation, the employer
diminishes salaries, but in limiting income, he lowers the
standard of living of the working class, which in turn dam-
ages his own industrial enterprise. In its flight, it is the gold
which pursues man.

It appears from all this that matter *retains* its meaning as
if that meaning were written in it.[45] It has been invested
with human qualities, as if these had inherited a physical
weight, and has acquired an inert future, which has the
power to hit back at its living past. Man reaches out and discovers the other man *in* the materiality, as if human consciousness had become imbedded in the matter it handles.
This materiality in which the mind of man is condensed be-

[43] My comment in *The Tragic Finale*, p. 60, on the original passage
in *Being and Nothingness*, pp. 257, 276, 278.

[44] *CRD*, I, p. 241.

[45] *Ibid.*, p. 245.

comes destiny: gold is fatality. Matter, no longer pure matter, is now humanized.[46] The paradox is that though we must be somehow more than matter, we are condemned to hang onto matter. It is a threat to our lives and a limit to our knowledge, in society it is even an inert force which holds us, yet like Antaeus we draw our strength from the earth. Man is not matter, yet man and matter taken together constitute all that there is, and any theological addition is superfluous.[47]

For the reader of earlier Sartrian literature, we are only reformulating the famous dualism of the *Pour-soi* and the *En-soi*. Paraphrasing De Waelhens' comment on Heidegger, Sartre writes, "Man is man through being (matter), which he is not."[48] Man has placed in things "his future, his own *praxis*, his own knowledge."[49] Things, therefore, as in the case of gold, absorb human activity and return it, after having materialized it. The power of negation comes from man himself, but once posited in the matter, it often becomes a power of destruction, *for gold contains the envy of many*. Thus, "matter, through the human contradictions it carries in itself, becomes for and through men the fundamental motor of History."[50] Yet, though matter has been endowed with power only *through* man, it escapes his control and produces counterfinality, which breaks the cycle of repetition. What the *praxis* of man has produced and unified hits back at him; man is indeed produced by his own product.

This not only results in a certain leveling of matter and man, since they are the product of one another, but can also lead to the conclusion that the machine commands its operator, since it constitutes itself as an unconditional imperative: it wants to be operated in this way and in no other way. One can say that all commands reach me through the matter, for

[46] *Ibid.*, p. 247.
[47] *Ibid.*, p. 248.
[48] The reference to De Waelhens comes from his little book: *Phénoménologie et Vérité*, p. 16.
[49] *CRD*, I, pp. 248, 249.
[50] *Ibid.*, p. 250.

it is massive industrialization which commands unconditionally the way I have to act. This can, of course, be reduced to a conditional imperative: "If you want to produce such and such an object, you have to handle this tool in such and such a way . . ." But the hypothesis is an abstract one, for when life is at stake, using the means for survival becomes an unconditional order.

One can turn the argument once more and insist that the command reaches man only through the machine insofar as it reaches the machine through man, so that when we say "steam provokes the construction of great factories," it is ultimately through man that all this happens.[51] Without man, steam and machines would disappear. We come full circle here to the *need* which *dictates* the *invention:* the machine is present in the inventor as the awareness of a lack and as "future objectification of a past *praxis* in its realization, which *through the future* wanted to be realized."[52] The man who prepares and launches rockets, in the factories and at Cape Kennedy, is himself under a higher command, the command of the matter—the weight of the missile, the distance to be achieved, the resistance to be vanquished, etc. He is thus in truth caught between a double materiality, the present, which "orders" him to work in such and such a way, and the future which through his own past achievement he has now to execute. Matter always demands more and more, through me.

At this moment we are encountering a problem called objective contradiction.[53] This is a form of opposition which through human intervention emerges in the matter upon which my labor is at present exercising itself. All progress brings its reaction, which Sartre calls "counterfinality." Finality is in accordance with the purpose of an act, but counterfinality occurs when the act itself results in another end that is indirect and unforeseen, as for example when mass in-

[51] *Ibid.*
[52] *Ibid.,* p. 257.
[53] *Ibid.,* p. 258.

dustry, in drawing farmers from the hinterlands, unwittingly kills agricultural exploitation. This is a contradiction provoked by things themselves. There is once more a way for men to bypass this contradiction: one can import agricultural products from the colonies, and to that effect build cargoes, but this fleet cannot in all safety cross the oceans unless there is also a war fleet to protect it.

The concatenation of finality and counterfinality is no less striking, when the industrialization of a certain region results in air pollution.[54] At first glance it may appear that the finality or the original intention resulting in the deed—I wanted to industrialize this region and make it wealthy—was the only intention. The finality, then, would alone be what was wanted, while the reaction would definitely have been unwanted and must be considered to be a totally indirect result. This approach, however, is an oversimplification. Actually—and this is what in Sartre's terms makes things intelligible—counterfinality, although not the primary intention, often is nevertheless part of our intentions as well; for the pursuer of a cause is also responsible for the results, and one is justified in concluding that the second intentionality may have been surreptitiously accepted, or at the very least, not positively rejected. Air pollution affects everyone, but in particular the poor, who cannot avoid it (even for weekends), yet want the factory, notwithstanding its unhealthy contamination. The worker thus both wants and does not want air pollution. The industrialist, on the other hand, although not positively and willingly causing air pollution, has done little to prevent it, and through this negligence has introduced one more element which sets apart the rich as a class.[55] From this it appears that both finality and counterfinality are inextricably connected and that if every finality implies a counterfinality because of the rebounding of the matter, it is no less true that every counterfinality also implies a finality because of the intervention of man.

[54] *Ibid.*
[55] *Ibid.*, pp. 259–60.

From the same starting point, whereby man is tied up with the matter which surrounds him, Sartre develops a similar idea. When an individual is dependent in his subsistence upon a material entity-outside-himself, he has an *interest*.[56] He discovers *his* own reality in an external reality, and he then tries to enlarge this external reality, which is himself. In so doing, however, he makes it more and more *essential,* with the result that when this object involves other men, the latter naturally become more and more *unessential*.[57] Toward them he becomes more and more *inhuman*. This is clearly the case with the employer (and owner of a factory) who buys new machines. Competition compels him to do so, for it is the *interest* of the other industrialist, hence his as well. The thing-outside-himself, or factory, is the supreme interest and it becomes difficult to say at a certain moment whether it is an *end* or a *means,* but it can be seen with no difficulty that it is *my* interest because it is the interest of the *other* (manufacturers). To the extent that it is the interest of the other man I must deny it to him. There is thus simultaneously a *dependence upon the other and a negation of the other*. Similarly, if I am a writer, my interest lies in a book. That book is my refuge against the course of History, my *interest* lies in defending and completing certain positions against later generations. I am at the same time both dependent upon and fighting against History.[58] Whether in the realm of ideas (as in writing) or in the realm of industry, interest is a "negative relation of man with the practical field or his surroundings through the things which he is, or a relation of the thing itself [e.g., the book] to other things through man."[59]

We must add that while the machine is the *interest* of the employer, it is not and cannot be the interest of the worker,

[56] *Ibid.,* p. 261.
[57] *Ibid.,* p. 263.
[58] *Ibid.,* p. 267.
[59] *Ibid.*

for although his living is attached to the machine, he is none-theless a victim of industrialization, one of the many who, in the manipulation of the machine, become merely standard-ized operators. The machine he manipulates makes him "pra-tico-inert"; he does things, but his performance has no soul and no unicity. For him it is a danger and a menace as well—to his health, through air pollution, and to his job, which may be lost through further automation.

The worker therefore becomes an individual without a particular *interest* and a candidate for a certain class. It is too early to discover as yet the seeds for the unifying totali-zation of that class, but it can be seen already that a trend will grow whereby the worker will attempt to change the machine from machine-as-*destiny* to the machine-as-*interest*. One way to do this would be the socialization of the means of production. This does not exclude the possibility, remote no doubt, of suppressing interest altogether, but this could only be done through the suppression of otherness, or *"al-terité,"* that phenomenon by which the machines are of interest for me because they are of interest for you.

The machine has acquired a personality that is at times more powerful than that of its owner. *"Dans les salons des grands bourgeois, les machines se rendent visite et réalisent leur accord provisoire,"* writes Sartre.[60] If General Motors and Renault play golf together, it is not out of any attach-ment to each other but to the machines which embody their *interest* and might also become their *destiny,* if someday, through the intervention of the worker, the tables are turned. Interest lies in the "worked matter" (*matière ouvrée*) or in any matter insofar as each group or each individual struggles to control it or to pull this control away from the other.[61] Sartre with good reason rejects Mill's utilitarianism as a basis for the intelligibility of social phenomena. On the con-trary, if I want machines, it is not because of the fact that

[60] *Ibid.,* p. 274.
[61] *Ibid.,* p. 278.

they are useful to me, but because they are useful to the Other. Observing the conflict within society, Sartre then claims that division among men results from present-day production, and not the reverse. Division is not cause, but effect. What is necessary, therefore, is a change in the methods of production, in the hope of improving human relations. As long as employers and employees stand at opposite sides of the materiality in which their interest is embodied, the combat among men will continue.

If it is a fact that man builds up a dialectic through his relation with matter, is this fact a necessity? Must the accumulation of gold result in a devaluation which results in lower salaries for the workers, and so on? Was it inevitable that the cutting of trees in China resulted in the construction of dams thousands of years later?

Sartre begins his analysis of this profoundly important question by turning our attention to a simple, everyday situation. When we observe a group of people waiting for a bus and all looking in the same direction to see whether it is coming, we can say that the materiality builds up a certain unity, that the matter *totalizes*. The bus becomes that particular entity which, on its way toward St.-Germain-des-Prés, keeps the people waiting together at that particular "stop." To the extent that men are haunting matter, matter commands men.[62] This grip of matter upon man embraces him only as an *inert* entity. The potential bus passenger is mere object, one of many waiting to be picked up; there is nothing any of them can do to hasten the coming of the bus, much as the craning of necks shows that they would like to. It is through the inorganic in the organic that man comes in contact with the inorganic. In this contact with the inorganic, which results in the exteriorization of man himself—in this case as inert passenger—the idea of necessity appears as soon as we realize that having accomplished a deed, we have actually performed something else as well. There is always

[62] *Ibid.*, p. 280.

an undesired deed that lies beyond the desired deed. Thus, if you want to take the bus, you are compelled to join the group of people who are waiting.

This does not imply that there was a compulsion at the start. There is no compulsion even when the results are a necessity, since the choice of the means toward an end is nevertheless *my* choice and results from *my* project. Once the choice is made, however, the act unavoidably walks in a certain direction, whatever I may wish. Furthermore, in every action there is always the possibility of a failure, of which the least that can be said is that it was certainly not wanted. This is a world of interaction, and any action of mine undergoes a metamorphosis from the outside, a change which I cannot prevent. Gold is indeed a power, yet its control "escapes" me. The bankruptcy of a Genovese business-man may appear to be his own responsibility, but it may actu-ally have crashed upon him through an unforeseen, or at least uncontrollable, dialectic of events, for to return to Braudel, we discover that the Mediterranean basin is a material unity, and any events within its borders affect the private business of the Genovese banker. It seems as if one chooses the means toward some particular end, but once one's act is perpetrated, it escapes and in its objectification leads to ends other than the perpetrator had intended or desired. There is, in short, always a double element at work: "objectification (or man working upon matter) and objectivity (or totalized matter working upon man)."[63] The necessity appears even more stringent when the *praxis* is performed with a clear mind and complete knowledge, for when freedom seems to be complete and the choice made in the light of a full acquaint-ance with the facts, the results are more than ever unavoid-able. Necessity works retroactively from the accomplished deed back into its origin *where it was freely born.* It is natu-ral, therefore, that in the achievement of an *opus,* the creator both recognizes himself and finds there a stranger. For there

[63] *Ibid.,* p. 284.

is an Hegelian alienation at work: man discovers himself as *other* in the objectivity, and in objectivized matter, contemplates with sorrow the *anti-man*.

MAN AS FREE PRISONER OF HIS CLASS, OR SOCIAL BEING AS MATERIALITY

Man discovers—and here Sartre uses more than ever an Hegelian terminology—his being-outside-himself as his truth and his reality. It is, indeed, the pratico-inert or the ponderosity of matter in and around him which catches hold of man and places him in a social class. This inorganic presence, strangely enough, both describes and is man: it is actually his "truthful definition." This ponderosity, or pratico-inert, which is me and places me where I belong, gets hold of everyone, sparing none. It lies in the heart of the employer himself, for competition with other industrialists and the exigencies of his customers weigh heavily upon him. Of course, it pins down the employee even more relentlessly, and he finds himself in an even tighter trap. It is a reality, a strange reality no doubt, yet a reality perceived not "by stones or by gods" but clearly *there* for men to feel and push against, to lift or collapse under. This "weight" of the pratico-inert which defines the individual man also classifies him socially. One can truly say that the working woman who spends eight hours a day in a monotonous and fatiguing job, from which her needs are barely fulfilled, has no other essence outside this frustrated self; she truly is what she does. These conditions are part of her individuality and actually define it. *They make her what she is and hold her where she belongs.*[64]

Yet—and this is a hopeful sign—there is something incomplete in this ontological identification of one's self with the pratico-inert of one's career. No essence is ever completely rigid, and one may very well revolt and attempt to go beyond

[64] *Ibid.*, pp. 289 ff.

it. Although the position of the worker in the society of today is quasi-prefabricated, with his whole behavior molding him into a definite pattern, he nonetheless can attempt to go beyond it. Sartre here draws upon the principles of transcendency of which the *Pour-soi*, according to *L'Etre et le Néant*, is capable.[65] For however strong may be the inertia which holds him down, for man there is always the possibility of going beyond.[66] Of course, the going beyond itself, in a paradoxical way, once more draws the limits of his own status, for he underlines what he is in attempting to go beyond it. In point of fact, the worker is caught by his own work. His salary is a result of that work, and if his expenses are limited and compel him to live within certain limitations, he can do nothing more outside his working hours than "make himself what he is," namely, a worker.[67] Man is a strange combination of transcendency and necessary compulsion, and whatever his freedom may be, he is caught in the pratico-inert of his class. One is forced to concede, "It was waiting for me before I was born."[68] Within this class dimension there is, of course, a certain latitude, the latitude of the individual—Peter does not behave exactly like John— but this individualism is only exercised within certain bonds.

It will appear from the preceding summary that although Sartre desperately wants to believe that man, including the worker, is free, that he himself makes himself what he is, yet he is forced to admit that man must nevertheless make himself within a circumscribed area, that he is a prisoner of his own given. One cannot escape the impression that qualifications have undermined the absolute freedom of the days of *L'Etre et le Néant*, and if it still exists, it is no longer absolute. Although freedom is nowhere denied—on the contrary, the greater the threat, the more stubborn the defense—there

[65] See *Being and Nothingness*, p. 171, and *The Tragic Finale*, pp. 38 ff.
[66] *CRD*, I, p. 292.
[67] *Ibid.*, p. 294.
[68] *Ibid.*

is nonetheless the constant implication that it is severely handicapped, or what Sartre calls *inert*. It almost seems as if he himself is attempting to "go beyond" a certain given and desperately attempting to push back the weight of the pratico-inert, lest it crush all individual freedom. His language emphasizes ponderosity and heaviness, as if the possible admission that freedom is no longer what he once thought it was weighs heavily upon him.

Even within the working class itself, there is a further partitioning or compartmentalization. Once more *la machine organise les hommes*, since the amount of skill of the individual worker will classify him either among the skilled or the unskilled, with the machine doing the selecting.[69] All this "is written in Being," and the inertia and hierarchy of rank cannot be easily broken, however great may be the constant effort to do so. "In deciding what they were, the machine has decided what they could do."[70] An unskilled worker is treated as such by the skilled, and condemned by him to be what he is. We who live in a different society, still capitalistic but slightly more advanced, understand the situation created by the machine a century ago, and "we understand (all this) from *our* invisible walls, that is, we have an understanding of all petrified limits of human relations on the basis of the invisible limit which petrifies ours."[71] The "discovery of Being is frightening" concludes Sartre, although one may attempt to ignore what one is.[72]

The stringent limitations of freedom should not make us forget, however, that the *praxis* of men is free temporization, since it efficiently plans and reorganizes and shapes a future. A unification of the working class was possible and has taken place, against all odds, as we shall see later. For the present we must conclude that the fact of belonging to a class, *l'être*

[69] *Ibid.*, p. 295.
[70] *Ibid.*, p. 299.
[71] *Ibid.*, p. 300.
[72] *Ibid.*, p. 301.

de classe, is a pratico-inert status, the necessary result of the individual and common *praxis.*

THE COLLECTIVE ENTITIES

We have now reached the point where it is possible to explore in greater detail the concept of class, to examine its inorganic quality and the viscuous cohesion of its members, which exists, however much it may be internally divided. Such an exploration will make the dialectic of its members more *intelligible*—and less mechanistic—than traditional Marxism has hitherto been able to show us.

From the start we must distinguish between two social entities: (1) the *group,* which aims at a definite purpose and in an organized way pushes toward the elimination of all inertia within itself, and (2) the *series,* or *sérialité,* which, on the contrary, is characterized by its passive, inert, inorganic quality. The group will be the object of a more exhaustive study in the next chapter, but first it must be distinguished from the second of the two entities, the series, which is made up of a juxtaposition of individuals, all of whom are defined within the collective ensemble as Other, but have no further distinction.[73] In order to show more clearly what he means by *series,* Sartre turns for his example to the crowd of people we have already observed waiting for the autobus at a stop along St.-Germain-des-Prés.

What strikes us first of all in this crowd is the solitude of the individual member. These people neither know one another nor care about one another; as Sartre quotes from Proust, *"Chacun est bien seul."*[74] All this fits into the spirit of the modern metropolis, where the individuals are interchangeable, yet in their solitude somehow protected, as for

[73] The term "series" has been used before in the very penetrating examination of Proudhon in his *La Creation de l'Ordre* (Paris, 1927), pp. 188 ff. All this does not detract from the freshness of the Sartrian approach, but we should be aware of the fact that Sartre has invented neither the term nor its meaning.

[74] *CRD,* I, p. 309.

example, behind their newspapers on the bus. Yet solitude does not cancel the dialectic which ties one to the group. Even the man who turns his back to the others knows that he belongs to the group of waiting people. The local limitation (the *trottoir*, the sign around which they gather) and the similarity of purpose (expectation of the autobus) unifies them in a loose way. Of course, the autobus itself is the central link, what Sartre calls the *collective entity*: as object, it overflows its inert materiality and is full of meaning, with a future and a past in the life of the travelers. In the present, it is also that which will dictate the seriality: through this object, which is the bus, the potential passengers become interchangeable, their internal qualities are negated, and they become simply *other among others*. This negation is carried over to their waiting in line, where, in Paris at least, their positions are impersonally dictated by a number emitted from a machine. The very fact that they take turns implies first, the existence of some totality of which they are all a part and second, the existence of the Other. Consequently, although some form of universality is present—they are all alike as waiting passengers—there is nevertheless also a form of succession—I am first, you are second, etc.—the one is never the other.

The members of a series, then, are human individuals who are made to possess an inorganic character—that aspect by which man is "outside himself as an inert object,"[75]—and who are joined to one another in their status of individual *qua* object or *Other*. That which objectifies them, as Other among Others, and at the same time joins them together or relates them is some object, called a collective entity, in this case, the bus. The collective entity, in summary, may be defined as that material and inorganic entity by virtue of which we exist outside ourselves as a plurality in an indistinct way.[76] It is an inert object which gathers together a

[75] *Ibid.*
[76] *Ibid.*, p. 307.

series of individuals about itself, and holds them there as inert and alienated from themselves.

It becomes apparent that the seriality is not structured; in contrast to the *group,* which within itself is constructed and hierarchical, the Other is never the subordinate or the superior, he is simply the Other. In this series gathered together by the approaching bus, the factory owner is equivalent to the lowest clerk, the duchess to the charwoman. In order to understand this kind of collective, one must see that the material object—the bus—realizes the unity of interpenetration of individuals insofar as they are *beings in the world outside themselves,* and only on this basis, and that it structures their relations according to the rule of seriality. The multiplicity—the waiting crowd—finds in an inert (but man-made) object—the bus—its unity of exteriority—that which makes them Other among Others. The seriality comes from the *pratico-inert* multiplicity of individuals, all of whom are equivalent to one another, yet who are compelled to give in to a certain order of succession, which can be either temporal or spatial.

The seriality implies some form of reciprocity, since my place is determined by *your* presence, yet the reciprocity is not mutually even, since the relation does not go both ways in the same fashion. One could as well say that an *alterity* is present—everyone is Other—but in the series this alterity is in succession, with the differentiation determined according to the order of succession.[77] This differentiation is loose and unstructured, nothing more, really, than a convenience— I get on the bus first, then you—and does not actually affect the individual, beyond, of course, meaning that if you are the second in line and there are only two seats, you will be able to sit, but if you are the third, you will have to stand.

There are two features which should be noted: there is a visible unity resulting from some accidental circumstance —this is a bus stop, around which people gather; and there

[77] *Ibid.,* p. 314.

is a less obvious unity, in the fact that every unit constitutes itself in the *rassemblement* as the objective element of a series[78]—the bus rider has a certain place in the line. This being in line or belonging to a series is a way of being of the individuals (in this particular situation of waiting for a bus their reality is in this inert being-outside-themselves), but the serial unity itself is *"une unité en fuite,"* a *rassemblement* loosely held together and constituted only by way of *not* being a structured group. As soon as it would become organized or structured—as for example, into a union of bus passengers protesting the kind of service (as happened in Montgomery, Alabama, when the Reverend Martin Luther King, Jr., rallied the Negroes to "strike" against the transit company) it would no longer be a seriality; it would be a group.

This serial structure has been described as loose, unorganized, escaping any rigidification; for all this, it is nonetheless not just an ideal, fictive entity or a mere concept, it is something very real. This becomes more apparent in the case of Jewishness. To be a Jew is not a fiction in a society which persecutes Jews; it is a real relation by which the Jew is considered as Other by the others. The plurality of Jews as an object of scorn is on this basis a unity and constitutes a seriality. The individuals exist in solitude to one another and are interchangeable; they belong to the collective only by virtue of their Jewishness, not by virtue of their internal qualities (X persecutes Y because Y is a Jew, not because he is strong or weak, noisy or quiet, a farmer or a banker); there is a reciprocity of a kind—"I am a Jew because you are a Jew, and he is not a Jew and calls us Jews." The collective entity is the inorganic and material entity—the plurality of Jews which is the object of scorn—which in its pratico-inert dimension is the foundation of the serial structure—a collection of people related to each other only through their common Otherness and common state of being an object of scorn to those not in the collection.

[78] *Ibid.*, p. 316.

Sartre, continuing his masterly analysis, makes the distinction that a serial structure may be *direct*, as housewives forming a queue at the bakery shop, or *indirect*, as the listeners who are tuned in to a particular radio station. The indirect seriality is characterized by absence, that is, by the impossibility of any easy intercommunication, as in the case of the radio audience. Any reaction for or against what the speaker says is and must be serial. Unlike in the direct seriality where an appeal might be made in the presence of all (as, for example, by the baker), the listeners must be alerted one by one if there is to be any concerted reaction (that is, if there is to be any organization into a group). As listeners we are all alike, a captive audience, which is to an extent powerless, or at least slow to be moved. The broadcasting station is here the collective entity in a double way, for first it produces me as an inert member of a series and "as Other among the Others" (the multiplicity finds in that object its unity of exteriority), and second, it is itself the result of a series of people already converted to the governmental ideas, acting as a series, and of which the radio is actually the organ.[79] Neither of these forms has the structure of a concerted and organized group. An impact of the Other takes place upon the Other as Other, whatever this impact may be—fascination, anger, revolt, etc.

In this perspective, it is clear that the number of constituents within a series is not limited. Furthermore, although they are members of the same series, the individual qualities of the participants may be entirely different. Whatever the range of their internal qualifications or abilities, however, there is and remains in the seriality some sort of impotency to react collectively. Any concerted reactions must await the formation of a group, as we shall see later.

Up to now we have considered the series, or seriality, only as it is constituted by isolated terms, individual human beings, the unity of whom lay only in their alterity as impo-

[79] This example of a seriality will be explored at great length in Chapter VII where Sartre discusses bureaucracy in government.

tency, or their existence as inert Other among Others. This kind of seriality was exemplified in the bus passengers, the listeners to a radio program, the readers of *Le Figaro*.[80] These examples were chosen, however, only in order to simplify the structure of the collective, that we might lay it bare for examination. Actually the coexistence of man—man living among other men—is defined as much by *human relations of reciprocity* as it is by the more solitary actions of reading, riding, listening that are gathered up into the loose kind of unity we have already analyzed.

Since these human relations of reciprocity constitute complex chains and polyvalent systems, they are hard to isolate and analyze, but we shall attempt to see how each individual relation is conditioned by the others through the environing materiality. Sartre gives the example of the dissatisfaction of the workers in a certain workshop provoked by a certain measure taken by the management.[81] This discontent is manifested in the quasi plurality of human relations between the workers, that is, something is built up or gathered together that vaguely unites the workers in their otherness to the direction, not yet organized or erupting into action, but nevertheless *there, in the air*. The communal unrest in the one shop transmits itself to other *rassemblements*, to other workshops which are also constituted in themselves as Others—they have either felt an opposition to their own management upon a previous occasion, or show a sympathy to the discontented workers upon this one—these transmit it to others, and so on. This communal unrest, or worker solidarity, may be external to the factory, internal to the profession, that is, the workers in another atelier, though having no particular present discontent against their own management, feel as others (of the same profession) the discontent of the first atelier and are affected. There is also a branch of lateral seriality, secondary but very important, by which the unrest is transmitted through individual worries to the families,

[80] *CRD*, I, p. 325.
[81] *Ibid.*, p. 326.

and from them to whole groups of habitations. What Sartre is describing is the existence of a *milieu*, which is a special kind of plurality, a quasi plurality by which the human relations in one workshop are conditioned by the human relations in another workshop, through the environing materiality, which provides a *unity outside itself of these interindividual relations*. The relations in one workshop gather force through the very fact of the existence of other workshops with similar problems; there is an otherness in every living relation, and the human relations in the first workshop would be very different without the existence of the other workshops, also feeling themselves as other to their own managements and related serially to the first workshop through this common feeling of otherness. There is a unity of exteriority; they are together outside themselves. This seriality (of workshops) constitutes an inert *milieu conducteur*, a vague, powerless as yet (in its present state) unity, structured only through the Other as Other. There is no direct communication in an organized way, but the seriality itself as a totality of all the relations exists inside the relations of each workshop.

As in a suburb, a collection has been gathered together, not as spatially locatable, not easily grasped, continually escaping, but nevertheless *there* and very real. Like Jewishness as an object of scorn, which becomes very real in periods of persecution, this milieu (of worker solidarity, communal unrest) becomes very real when organization begins, and there are unions, strikes, etc. A force was gathering, with its strength coming from the multiplicity of others loosely constituted in the plurality; each of these others is related to the plurality or milieu on the basis of all the other totalized relations.

The seriality constitutes, then, a certain *milieu*, whether this be the cohesion of individuals, as Others, working within a certain profession, living within a certain section of a city, or belonging to a particular business collectivity, retail or wholesale. Milieu, as we have seen, is ultimately structured through the *Other*. "Each element is linked to the other elements, but it is linked *from its place in the series* and *through its escaping liaison with all* the intermediate elements."[82] There is a unity—we all live in the sixteenth *arrondissement*, we are all small grocers of Montmartre—but it immediately appears that this unity is of the escaping type. *C'est une unité fuyante*. Sartre comes back to this expression again and again, in an attempt to re-emphasize the idea that the unity made up of our plurality—the inhabitants of a particular section, the grocers of another—is one which has no clear-cut limits, no mathematical circumscription. There is some form of container, in which one finds oneself Other among Others, but no attempt toward any grouping is made. It is the elusiveness of the seriality that makes it so extremely difficult to pin down, to grasp, and it slips through our fingers as a concept because it is indeed continually escaping as a reality.

Although not structured like a group, the seriality can be extremely powerful, notwithstanding its passive, inert, unorganized quality. In determining his sales prices, the grocer must take into account his competitor, his customer and "the fact that the customer comes to the store as other than himself,"[83] that is, he acts in the presence of the grocer not only for what he is but also for what he is not. Every buyer is potentially *Other*. He faces grocer Z, but he must be viewed as potentially confronting grocer X. There is an otherness inside every living relation, as we have already seen. One is Other than oneself, yet Other than the Other.[84] The market is a totality—I am in touch with it by visiting this place, or by telephone or teletype—but it is a *detotalized* totality, since it contains a factor of dispersion. The market is clearly a *rassemblement* of the escaping type, and no individual decision really affects it—I alone cannot make up the price of a particular object. The price imposes itself

[82] *Ibid.*, p. 327.
[83] *Ibid.*
[84] *Ibid.*, p. 332.

upon me as buyer or as salesman precisely because it imposes itself upon my neighbor or competitor and it imposes itself upon my neighbor and competitor because it imposes itself upon his neighbor and competitor, and so on.

What we are seeing here is that the collective object, the market, is characterized not by a consensus, an organized unity, but by a flight, a disunity. I, who am a powerless member of the series gathered around the market, nevertheless help to constitute it, by virtue of my isolation from the others. As Sartre has stated it very clearly in an earlier chapter, ". . . it is not the presence of others but their absence which is at the basis of this constraint (in concrete relations); it is not their union but their separation."[85] Thus when the small grocer sees taxes and wholesale prices rise, without being able to increase his own prices for fear of pricing himself out of the market, he feels trapped. His sense of powerlessness is based upon his isolation from others of his kind and may or may not be the stimulus which will provoke him to move toward them and attempt to form a group. Even in that phase, it may be power, but it will be a power that belongs to no one, for it synchronizes with the fear which is everywhere and nowhere. It is, concludes Sartre, serialized fear.

The result of all this is that Sartre's free man, caught in the seriality, loses much of his zest. Man no longer appears as the arrogant Orestes who walks through *The Flies* with all the self-sufficient ardor of a newly conquered freedom. Seen in the stark light of the seriality, man becomes less powerful, trapped in his own inertness. Even his intellectual acceptances based upon faith are nothing but an acceptance of the transmitted "truth," without any possibility of checking it. The powerful dictator is *par excellence the Other*, the anonymous other; the propagation of news under his regime acts as a contagion, but one has to become *explicitly aware* of the disease in order not to succumb and fall victim.

[85] *Ibid.*, p. 56; Barnes trans., p. 78.

At this moment Sartre's negative attitude comes through. If we have left the theme of *The Flies*, we have not moved far from *No Exit*. The Other is here definitely a burden and a source of disillusion.

We are now in a position to understand what a "class" is, for it, too, is "a collective with a pratico-inert character, while the individual himself as a member of the class is a member of a seriality."[86] Sartre's philosophical analysis of the evolution of the French "proletariat" will incorporate these insights, familiar to us by now, and through them, this evolution will become more intelligible. By "intelligible" Sartre seems to mean that they will be seen not merely in a clearer light but at times in a different light altogether. Thus Marx's assertion in the *Manifesto* that "the combined efforts of men" lie at the start of the inhuman character of production is considered by Sartre to be an "unfortunate" statement, since on the contrary, it is in his view the *atomization* of men which is responsible. There is a "combination of efforts" indeed, but that combination is a unity of the type we have just been reviewing—loose, unorganized, and above all, built around an object. "*C'est l'objet et l'objet seul qui combine les efforts humains dans son unité inhumaine.*"[87] It is the merchandise and its price which regulate the relation of buyer and salesman, not the combined efforts of either. Everything is built around *it*. All the rest is mere rite. Outside this object in a capitalistic regime—merchandise, machine, etc.—(and here Marx and Sartre agree) man is atomized, he is *other*, and *other* only in a world of mere (unorganized) multiplicity. Industrialization brings with it the machine, and the machine, as object, as collective entity, alienates the worker, makes him Other among Others. The worker is the negation of the machine world, just as the machine is the negation of the worker. The negation of this negation is, as we have seen, the salvation of the worker, but this will consist in replacing the *milieu* as mere *rassemblement* and organizing it

[86] *Ibid.*, p. 345.
[87] *Ibid.*, p. 350.

into the group.[88] Multiplicity will be replaced by the ordered *praxis* of the group in order to overcome the link-in-
powerlessness which is mere seriality.

The coming together which takes place does so around an
object. This object is at times under a menace, and it is precisely because of this threat that a growing unity emerges—
as, for example, in the case of the *colons* united in defense of
the old colony. Some stimulus provokes a closer organization
of the ineffective seriality, although in its initial phase, the
unity is still passive and marked by dispersion and impotency. This slow, faltering process can be seen in the evolution of the worker and his class. For a long time the workers
are enemies to one another within their own class. "The class
as collective in this case becomes a material thing, made up
of men, which is a negation of man and also a serial impossibility of negating that negation."[89] Gradually, however, as
the history of the workers' movement in France has shown,
a contact is established between the workers. Certain obstacles are overcome, obstacles such as the vestiges of "Christian ideology" and the distances between different cities,
and communication between the workers is established
through newspapers, meetings, etc. Despite the tempting
alternatives of defeatism, discouragement, and abstention-
ism, "organization" is painfully born in the heart of this
passivity that weighs down the seriality. The working class
is simultaneously *"Destin et négation du Destin"*;[90] it is
Destiny, but destiny fought against and contradicted. The
collective does pull itself out of inertia or, as Sartre puts it,
strain itself *"pour s'arracher a l'Etre,"* to tear itself away
from *l'Etre*.[91] *L'Etre* is here, of course, the torpor of the
En-soi-like seriality, which is attacked by *Le Néant*, with
the hope of transforming the poor standing of the worker as
a thing among other things into the status of a free human

[88] *Ibid.*, p. 351.
[89] *Ibid.*, p. 353.
[90] *Ibid.*, p. 357.
[91] *Ibid.*, p. 358.

being, an active, negating *Pour-soi,* through the gradual organization of the collective. In his enumeration of the different phases of the historical evolution, Sartre admits the presence of a strong trend of "necessity" and appears to be quite fatalistic in his views. Clearly, he has nowhere been confronted with such a power of inertia and such a deeply ingrained resistance of the seriality.

It is the constant purpose of Sartre's book to make intelligible the collective *praxis,* as he now attempts to do through tracing the slow organization of the workers' collective and their plan to reconstruct the social field. In order to understand this process, we must keep in mind that there is a double *praxis:* the individual *praxis,* or the negation coming from the individual toward his product, and the collective *praxis* just mentioned. Between both lies the hard and immobile core of the anti-dialectic, or *pratico-inert.*

This anti-dialectic, through the manipulation of individual activity, bears the stamp of the individual. The product of my hands is my "objectification," it is my freedom reified in my work. How this object in many ways hampers freedom is made clear in the case of merchandise. Merchandise imposes itself upon the buyer: *"c'est la liberté qui limite la liberté."*[92] There is a double freedom at work, the freedom of the maker and the freedom of the buyer, but both are caught by the object, which hits at man from both sides. Materiality alone does not transform anything, but it becomes "haunted" as soon as it hangs, as does the merchandise, between two freedoms. That merchandise, by the very fact that it is bought by the other, retroactively affects the maker and the producer. A whole set of freedoms is orbiting around the object, for it is a "negation of everybody by everybody."[93] Nevertheless, it must not be forgotten—for this ultimately makes the pratico-inert intelligible—that at the start of everything lies the initiative of the individual man. In him originated the object, which later, escaping its

[92] *Ibid.,* p. 361.
[93] *Ibid.,* p. 362.

maker, reaches out with its multiple meaning in all directions, "implicating" the others and robbing them of a part of their freedom. Human activities are not suppressed; in Sartre's view, they are merely conditioned and directed. At this moment Sartre so closely links together the dual structure of *Pour-soi* and *En-soi* that they almost become one. "Looking through my window," writes Sartre, "I see autos which are men and of which the drivers are autos, policemen regulating the circulation at the corner of the street, further still an automatic regulation of the traffic through red and green lights, a *hundred exigencies,* which from the ground climb up to me."[94] Behind all these imperatives hides the other(s), who reaches out at me and at the many others, endlessly, indefinitely, until . . . some day perhaps man revolts. The commands reaching him through the objects will provoke a reaction and the serialized power-of-the-seriality start an upsurge. For it is nevertheless man's "willingness" which "takes it" all. Things in their multiple form get hold of him and *he submits* freely. What if he "takes it" no longer?

But let us not run ahead—later on the group will perform what the seriality is as yet powerless to do—here we wish merely to underline the fact that the individual on this globe, although caught in many ways, is *not unfree.* On the contrary, one has to be man and free to be able to grasp the meanings of things and to execute the commands that they imply. Even the worker freely engages himself, although he knows that the machine will be his prison and his alienation. Freedom in these cases admittedly does not mean the possibility of choice but rather the "necessity of living the restriction under the form of an exigency to be filled by a *praxis.*"[95] Although the individual is aware of all this and knows that as other (in the series) he is powerless, he nevertheless goes beyond his impotency through the consideration that the present condition is *provisional* and *relative.* He is powerless now, but *he will change a world.* Just as these words are

[94] *Ibid.,* p. 363.
[95] *Ibid.,* p. 365.

ringing hope in our ears, however, Sartre's pessimism intrudes once more, and he turns their meaning inside out: the
will to introduce a change, from the very first weak efforts, is
merely an expression of incapacity. He who struggles confesses that he is an exploited man. For the class has a viscos-
ity, indeed, and if the worker by exception breaks the barrier
and steps into the world of the bourgeois, his act is in fact a
proof that a similar effort by the common worker is doomed
to fail.[96]

In these and the following pages, Sartre once more seems
sadly caught between freedom and fatalism and painfully
unable to stress either one. One might answer that this is
indeed life, and Sartre's tortuous dialectic merely reflects
truthfully the immense intricacy of human existence on this
planet. It looks as if Sartre's *Pour-soi*, no less than any other
Pour-soi, is hopelessly trapped in the pratico-inert, the
pratico-inert this time being the most complex of all: How
shall I make the pratico-inert intelligible?

Our author does not give up his attempt. His preceding
analyses have in his opinion shown the dramatic impact of
the concept of *negation* and what it does from the point of
view of the pratico-inert itself, as for example in the case of
the iron-coal complex, with its negation of the worker and,
for that matter, of the greater part of a nation. We know that
in the beginning the labor of man was a negation of matter
and that this matter, once touched, becomes the negation of
man. The result, of course, is the fatigue and even enslave-
ment of man.[97] There is in all this no mutual hatred of men
in and of itself but rather a mutual friction of men through
materiality. Their antagonism is caught in an object, yet
ironically, this matter-negation (Sartre's term) eventually

[96] Sartre has in mind the French worker. It is a well-known fact
that in the New World the class barrier can be broken faster and more
easily than in the Old. It is one feature of American capitalism that it
offers the intelligent laborer (and his children) grants that will enable
him to improve his cultural standing, hence increase his abilities.
Whether this impresses Sartre is very doubtful.

[97] *CRD*, I, p. 371.

results in the series, which when organized into a group, is the unity of those very men who were earlier driven apart.

Even before his unification in a group, moreover, the individual man, prisoner of his class and of his career, has moments of lucidity and becomes aware of his "imprisonment" and of the sort of alienation which this or that pratico-inert holds for him and for the others. There are even occasions when the individual worker becomes clearly aware of the social implications of certain acts, as for example, when a Stakhanov, in his greed for a better salary, intensifies his work, thus challenging his associates and compelling them to increase their output as well. In this way he simply becomes his own enemy and makes common cause with the *patron*. There is always an *otherness* hidden in the act and sooner or later the act will with strict necessity turn against him. Although we fall again and again into anti-human failures, there is nevertheless something to be gained through these very failures, since in a negative way, namely, as common impotency, they have a way of cementing together the unhappy victims within the seriality. One bemedaled Stakhanov can cause countless misery to his fellow workers, but if that misery causes them to unite, he can be a remote cause of their happiness as well. All this is obscure and somewhat indefinite at first, since it is, in Sartre's words, *une expérience fuyante:* it runs away with the other(s), who in an indefinite and obscure way constitute the series.[98] However vague it may be, this self-realization and groping-toward-the-other is real and causes the pain of alienation to flare up in the hearts of the exploited men. There is no general and a priori rule according to which under this stimulus the seriality will break up its ineptitude and constitute the *group*. This differs from one case to another. One thing is certain. At a certain moment the individual dialectic, on the basis of the materiality which it cannot cross, will invent *new* media in a *new* social field against the imperium of the pratico-inert.

[98] *Ibid.,* p. 374.

This new dialectic will imitate the remote and original dialectic of the solitary worker when he was working upon the matter. It will *go beyond itself* and *place itself in the service of a common cause.* This new dimension can be called a *culture-dialectic,* in contrast to the previous one, which might be called the *nature-dialectic.* In the past man has produced through his work the anti-man; in the future he will produce through his union with the other the anti-physis, or the correction of nature. Our eventual unification through and in the group will be the negation of "the impossibility of life which threatens the serial multiplicity."[99]

[99] *Ibid.,* p. 377.

Chapter VI

FROM SERIALITY TO GROUP

The Conquest of the Bastille, or the *groupe en fusion*

In the last chapter our description of the seriality inevitably included its contrast to the group, as well as hints as to how the series eventually becomes a group. Sartre will now examine these matters in greater detail, but before he does so, he makes two background remarks to clear the way for his analysis. First, the assertion that the seriality lies at the beginning of group evolution does not mean that it necessarily has a chronological priority, but it does imply that it has at least a logical priority. The one implies the other, that is, the group presupposes the multitude. We are therefore entitled to speak of an anteriority of the collective (as seriality). History gives innumerable examples of this, but that with which we are concerned is the evolution of the working class from mere *rassemblement* to group.[1]

Secondly, it appears from the start, and it will appear even more clearly later on, that Sartre rejects as mere mythology all comparisons of the group to an organism, or what he calls the "biological" approach. Organicism is a trend toward viewing the group as a biological entity like the body, only larger. Sartre denies this super organism on empirical grounds—the object of our observation shows nothing like this to be true—but also for speculative reasons, since the viewing of the group as organism seems to exclude the in-

[1] *CRD*, I, p. 384.

dividual grandeur and dignity of man. Most important of all, it leaves no room for Sartre's cherished dialectical approach, by which group formation is seen to occur as a result of opposition, or to be born out of negation.

An example will make this clear. During the Middle Ages we observe the existence, if not *de facto* at least *de jure*, of three classes: the noblesse, the bourgeoisie, and the serfs. The continual attempt of the bourgeoisie to hurdle the social barriers and climb into the noblesse resulted in a strengthening of those barriers through the formation, in self-defense, of a *group*, with drastic rules regulating the entrance of outsiders. This decision indirectly affected the serfs as well, since it not only revealed their inferiority and impotency, but also the eventual power which could be theirs through grouping. This is a natural event all through history, as the law of dialectic plays its game; as soon as one collectivity organizes itself into a group, the others begin to look for a way to strengthen their opposition. The action is always reciprocal: your self-defense provokes my organization and your organization results in my self-defense. It is the outsiders who through their impotency point up the strength of those who are grouped, and it is in the minds of these outsiders that the group is, through a unifying synthesis, totalized.[2] This revelation of the strength of the other is my negation, betraying as it does, by contrast, my own lack of strength, or virtual impotency.

All this is only by way of a general introduction and serves in Sartre's mind to prepare us for a much more detailed analysis of the extremely involved dialectic which takes place in group formation. Before his analysis of what constitutes and forms the group, he wants us to be prepared for what it is not, and as these remarks have hinted, it is neither an organism nor a superorganic entity.

Sartre basically accepts dialectic as the infrastructure of sociological growth, but he looks at this dialectical procedure

[2] *Ibid.*, p. 382.

with a critical eye. His book—and this must be kept in mind —is *une critique de la raison dialectique*. The dialectic which moves through history is not merely a deterministic one to which man must blindly submit. At every stage the subject intervenes; even in the seriality man chooses to an extent his prison, and if the walls become too confining, he, in unison with others, is driven to escape and forms a group.[3] In the case of the bus passengers, they chose to take the bus from a certain stop to another; if they wanted to achieve a certain end—the arrival at a particular destination—they were of course compelled to stand and wait for the bus which would take them there. One might say that they were caught, but, on the other hand, there is always the possibility of going beyond. Thus, the Negro riders in Alabama might always have accepted unequal service, which as members of a series they were forced to do, but they did not; they united. There is always the human element; man is caught, yet free. He is not the mere helpless pawn of a dogmatic dialectic, as the Marxists would have us believe. Furthermore, Sartre would have us always be *aware* of the events which are operating, as now when we observe the genesis of the group as a *rational* and *intelligible* procedure. It is the intention of the entire work to lay all this before us, to bring it out of the darkness into the light, but as we have said before, others may—and must—do it also. It has always been a preoccupation of Sartre's to investigate how much a person is conditioned by his class and how far he is self-determined. Even in the early 1930s he was admiring Dos Passos' aesthetic solution of the problem in *The 42nd Parallel*, in which the characters were drawn simultaneously as "detailed individuals *and* as purely social phenomena."[4] Simone de Beauvoir, in her account of Sartre's reactions given in *The Prime of Life*, continues, "Cruelly, he [Dos Passos] observed mankind both in terms of the comedy labeled 'freedom' which they play out inside themselves, and also as the mere helpless projections

---

[3] Man not only chooses his prison; he *makes* it as well.

[4] *The Prime of Life*, p. 113.

of their situation. Sartre and I frequently attempted to observe some third person, or more often ourselves, in this stereoscopic fashion."[5] Apparently this omniscience is not limited to Sartre and Simone de Beauvoir, for they admired Dos Passos' presentation of individuals who "in moments of need, or exhaustion, or labor, or revolt . . . had their flash of fulfillment or their instant of truth: [who] *lived*."[6] The *critique* may not result in a philosophical treatise; it may, indeed, be merely a flashing moment of light in the life of some individual worker.

Relying not upon some momentary insight but upon Sartre's more ordered description of the dialectical process, we come back to his presentation and find another of his recurrent themes, one which is basic to Marxism itself, namely, that at the start of all change lies a *need*. We have seen already that need is the stimulus for all human activity—that man's work itself begins in order to fulfill his basic needs and that his project, engendered by "what is lacking" (above and beyond the means for bare physical survival) carries him always beyond-himself-towards. The need is such that it results in the impossibility of the individual remaining what he is. One *must* change, that is, one must break the ground of what is forbidden. Yet this conquest of that which is forbidden contains a paradox, since upon the basis of scarcity, one thinks of oneself and not of the other. How can it be explained that in a situation where all that matters is the survival of the *self*, the *group* has come into being? In answering this question, let us remember that it is an *object* which brings men together. It was the common object, that which we have called the "collective entity," which resulted in the vague unity of the seriality and in the same way, it is an object which will provoke a closer unification, and ultimately the formation of the group itself. This of course needs to be more fully developed, and Sartre will do so through a

[5] *Ibid.*
[6] *Ibid.*

close observation of some of the most striking events of the French Revolution.

On July 12, 1789, there is a state of insurrection in Paris. We observe several things. The Parisians, still juxtaposed in the manner of the seriality, are hungry and tired. Their pleas for a greater equality and a chance to alleviate their misery have gone unheeded by the government. On the contrary, the king and his ministers are set against them, provoking already an embryonic form of unity-in-misery amid the Parisian seriality. People talk and grumble and begin to move. They discover, furthermore, that the army has encircled Paris; everyone in Paris finds himself "particle of a sealed-off materiality."[7] All of these factors—mutual discomfort, the opposition of the government, and the siege by the army—help to strengthen the cohesion of the people: everyone sees himself as other in the other, and yet as himself.

At this moment, carried forward on this wave of discontent, a crowd loots the arms depot. This is a positive deed against the king.[8] The *rassemblement* has acted, and in this free deed it has suddenly discovered that it was a *group*. This is certain only as far as the past is concerned; the angry crowd unified and accomplished something. As for the future, they still must prove themselves, and gathering together their weapons in self-defense, they posit a new act of free self-assertion *qua* group. Some government officials in alarm attempt to form a militia inside the growing group, with the hope of dividing its strength; but the attempt not only fails but results in a redoubled rallying of the people, whose violent reaction against the militia unifies them more than ever and only serves to accelerate the formation of a group-in-opposition.

The dissolution of the seriality is now apparent to everyone. It is not yet a group, but it can already be called *un groupe en fusion*. Borrowing a term from Malraux, Sartre calls the mystique of the collectivity tumbling into a group

[7] *CRD*, I, p. 387.
[8] *Ibid.*, p. 389.

une apocalypse.[9] He chooses his epithets with great care at this critical moment and also takes over Jaures' beautiful expression to convey a sense of the heightened pressure; it is indeed a time of *haute température historique . . .*[10]

The menace now becomes more precise in one section of the city, in the neighborhood of the Bastille. Its eight immense towers have always dominated the *quartier* St.-Antoine, where they were sullenly hated as a symbol of royal arbitrariness. Now the cannons, pointed outward across the wide and deep moats between prison and people, pose a threat from behind, while at the same time the inhabitants must defend themselves against the enemy in front of them, coming from the outside. More pressed than others, they must act as a *group* if they want to survive, and an elementary form of organization begins.

THE PHILOSOPHY OF THE *groupe en fusion*

Sartre now proceeds to philosophize upon the historical events which we have just observed. He notes first of all that a *groupe en fusion* is triggered into formation by "the transcendent action of one or more groups already constituted."[11] Seriality steps from its loose ineptitude into the following, more forceful phase when under threat; or in dialectical terms, negation is answered by negation. This formulation of the process is somewhat ambiguous, however, and should not be understood as a mere deterministic causation—the outside group threatens, the series as a result organizes, *A* produces *B*—since there must also be present what Sartre calls the "act of autodetermination." In other words, the unification which is definitely not wanted by the outside group is produced from the *inside* of the new *groupe en fusion*. This is an important nuance. Although the causal interference of the outside group cannot be denied its part

[9] *Ibid.,* pp. 391 and 410.
[10] *Ibid.,* p. 395.
[11] *Ibid.,* p. 394.

in integrating the seriality of the *quartier* St.-Antoine or of the entire city of Paris, this birth of the new group cannot be *induced* or artificially provoked, if there is no *interiorized* existence of the newborn. The integration is *wanted* by the individual constituents, and it is precisely this positive intervention of the human individual which gives the unification its human aspect. The members of the newborn group interiorize the integration through their assent.

Sartre, wishing to avoid oversimplification (and to demonstrate the freedom of the individual man, ever his preoccupation), reformulates the question in this way: What makes it possible for a member of a series, as for example, an inhabitant of the *quartier* St.-Antoine, to step into that structural unity which is called a group, and which as a group, can storm a Bastille? How does the impotent individual *decide by himself* to become power? To answer that question, we come back always to the common object, in our case the common danger—the Bastille as a power and a presence, the besieging army—around which the seriality of the *quartier* St.-Antoine is orbiting. There are, furthermore, a certain number of relations which have paved the way for eventual unification, as, for example, the comradeships resulting from living in the same section, being involved in the same labor or belonging to the same class. Since these relations have up to now not excluded the impotency of the multitude *qua* multitude, something further must happen, nevertheless, in the strange phenomenon of group formation.

It is to the individual that we must turn at this stage of *"haute température historique."* The organized totality that threatens (government, army) totalizes the non-group (the citizenry of Paris), drawing everyone from his being merely Other and making him the *third man* in relation to a certain constellation of reciprocities. This "third man" is freed of his inert otherness, as object, and discovers a free interindividual reality as an *immediate* human relation; the Other, passive object of the old series, freely becomes acting subject, who himself totalizes. It was a hundred centers of syntheses which rallied together to take the Bastille. For it is through this third man that the practical unity is revealed and asserted as the negation of an organized *praxis*—the onslaught of the government, the army—which threatens them all. "The third man, structurally speaking, is the human mediation through which *directly* [from you to me, me to you, man to man] the multiplicity of epicenters and ends [individual centers of action, isolated from one another in the seriality] makes itself organized as determined by a synthetic objective."[12] In other words, when the outside group totalizes the multiplicity, the latter totalizes itself; *the objective of the third man becomes the common objective,* and it is felt as such by him, he knows himself to be unified with all the others by a common exigency. His danger is my danger, and vice versa. The inhabitant of the *quartier* St.-Antoine is in grave peril, not as an isolated bandit, whose eccentric behavior needs correction, nor merely as *another* in the vague form of a seriality like that of the market, but as an individual of that section and of that particular political brand: *he is wanted* and *he is object of a planned and totalizing annihilation coming down upon all the Parisians of that* quartier. It is "Versailles" which makes every inhabitant realize himself to be the third man.

At this moment one might still object that Sartre's interpretation is merely a form of positivism, as if it were merely the menace of the danger which links all of us together, event *A* inevitably producing event *B*, but this is not exactly the case. The dialectic is not mechanical but supposes the free intervention of the individual, or what Sartre calls "mediated dialectic." In order to understand this, one must see that while up to now I have always totalized my *quartier* from the outside, now, under the menace of the planned attack from the outside, I am integrated in this totalized totality. I am aware of the menace which threatens the series *qua*

[12] *Ibid.*, p. 398.

impotent series, in which I am included, but this time I positively and freely go beyond the impotency and as a result
unify the totality.

The apparent contradiction between me as an insider of a
passive seriality and me as an outsider who totalizes the
series under menace finds its solution in *action*.[13] The Parisians storm onto the streets and through their act overcome
the psychological malaise. Through action, one is practically
integrated. The third man emerges both as human *organizer*
of a unity and as human part of the unity, but in the very act
of free participation, whether as unifier or unified, he dissolves the seriality. His freedom is, of course, conferred by
the collectivity, or in Sartre's terms, "mediated through the
other." When in a riot he escapes with the others he will at a
certain moment stop with them. This is already the beginning of an organization, where the third man does not exactly decide what to do, but simply does it. He does it freely,
yet he does it mediated through the other. He is still in a way
unifier, but the unity does not depend on his unification, for
it gradually grows beyond him. When I belong to the group
in action, I no longer see the group, and this visual limitation
reflects my position vis-à-vis the group, since I no longer
"dominate" the group through synthesis but make it what it
is through my active participation. I am now no longer the
Other, but like everyone, the *third,* that is, one is not just another in a series, but one is *other through the mediation of
the group.* Actually, "the mediation is double, for the group
mediates between the third men, and each third with the
other third through the group."[14]

An example of the first mediation occurs when during a
manifestation a crowd of manifestants sees itself increased
by several members. Individual X belonging to the original
crowd sees this new addition and joyfully adds himself to
individual Z of the newcomers, but this operation can only
happen through the group as such. Each individual gives

[13] *Ibid.,* p. 400.
[14] *Ibid.,* p. 404.

through the group the power which he himself receives through the group. In the Other, I see myself coming: I discover him not as Other (as in the seriality) but as myself. The multitude is here not a juxtaposition but strictly a *praxis,* that is, an act, as the act of manifesting together or of attacking. There is in all this no magic involved; it is simply my freedom recognizing itself in the common action.[15] I am not just the serial Other, but myself, co-operating in a common action, which reaches its actualization from me to the other through the group. Sartre's analysis of these matters in these particular passages of his book seems to me to be a very shrewd one indeed.

He goes on to develop further the second mediation, that of the *third man between the group and the third man.* This type of mediation is exemplified when the third man, in the midst of a running battle, gives the signal to "Stop" or "Go ahead." These *mots d'ordre* are immediately followed by the third man who did not give the orders. They are not strictly orders, they are simply manifestations coming from the third man, myself or the other. One cannot call these *mots d'ordre* products of the group, for they come from an individual, but in the act of understanding and of executing them, I, who did not give the orders, recognize myself, and my free choice confirms them.[16] There is—as it is easy to recognize—a certain ambiguity present. The individual, who always remains a being which is in part transcendent (as subject) and in part self-contained (as object), can at a certain moment break this circle, if he so desires, and assert his transcendence. The third man somehow behaves both as one who transcends the group and as one who is buried in the group. In shouting the *mot d'ordre,* he regulates my activity, but he is not yet a leader. He is still a common individual, myself or the other, who happens to shout the right command at the right moment because of certain topological data.

Sartre at this point recapitulates and attempts to deepen

---

[15] *Ibid.,* p. 407.
[16] *Ibid.,* p. 409.

two major observations which have already emerged in the
preceding examination of the genesis of the *groupe en fusion*.
These *groupes en fusion* fascinate him both because they
are not merely abstract speculations but actual historical
facts which during the years 1788–89 constituted the core of
the French Revolution and because they offer him an act in
the drama of human history where the subject, the human
individual, stands very clearly on the stage.[17] It is Sartre's
task, almost his mission, to raise the curtain and make intelligible the events which took place and above all, the part
played by the individual in those events.

The first point that he makes concerning the French Revolution is that the unification has taken place on the basis of
certain objectives, all of which could be reduced to one, the
defense of Paris. The objective or purpose to be attained has
pushed the group into formation, although often it afterward
survives its own objective. The group is "totalized" through
its object, but the situation of the group is a living one and
it will keep alive when there is a *continual respecification of
its purpose and a reorganization adapted to its purpose.*
Without being an organism, the group in this respect could
nevertheless be compared to an organic structure, for just as
the body reflects in its attitudes and internal reactions the
physical structure of its surroundings, so also the attitude
of the individuals in the group is commanded by the structure of certain objectives. These objectives can be altered
midway and the original purpose not attained at all, but the
group may still continue, with a change in purpose and a
consequent change in attitude. When for some unexpected
reason the *mot d'ordre* or command within the group is not
followed, a particular action may be dropped. Or some ec-

[17] In the first weeks of the Cuban revolution Sartre similarly saw
fulfilled what he here calls the *"groupe en fusion."* He calls it the
"honeymoon" of the revolution. There was as yet no bureaucracy, no
apparatus, but still a direct contact between the leaders and the
masses. It was around that time that Sartre visited Cuba and saw or
at least thought he saw his description fulfilled. See *La Force des
Choses,* p. 515.

centric individual (in the true sense of the word, "not having the same center," misreading the attitude of the group-in-becoming) may rashly start throwing stones at the police, thrusting himself out of the group in an unpleasant and awkward way.[18] These are only minor deviations; what counts, according to Sartre, is the insight into the impact of the future upon the present growth of the group, and it is this insight which must gradually guide the third man. The fact that some *mots d'ordre* or commands have not been followed is accidental and does not alter the fact that some individuals have seen the purpose and acted to that end. The whole movement of the *groupe en fusion* carries its own intelligibility; in achieving its peculiar purpose, the growth of the group was the most natural and economical gesture. No eccentric has stopped that, although it should be recognized that in a group where everyone is third man, someone will act out of line, just as another will reflect the objective of the group and feel its true center; he will be called the *third man regulator*.[19] The *groupe en fusion,* in short, is a process with a purpose: one must find weapons, one must fight, one must defend Paris. Later other purposes may emerge, and the group in its particular structure may consequently be altered to achieve those new purposes.

Ironically, there is in group formation not only the unity of purpose but also a multiplicity of individual syntheses whereby each individual member totalizes on his own behalf the totality of the group. One may well wonder how unity can be produced by such a plurality of individual syntheses, or in other words, how and why a community of actions and objectives is preserved in and through a multiplicity of individuals and their individual syntheses.

We know that at a certain moment the seriality has been dissolved through the free activity of the individual directing himself and others, all of them as third men, toward a certain common *praxis.* This happens simultaneously in all mem-

---

[18] *CRD,* I, p. 413.
[19] *Ibid.,* p. 415.

bers of the collectivity. The *mots d'ordre* are shouted here and there, but they are not the cause of the movement. What does count is the realization that my *praxis* comes back to me through the other as supported and accepted by the totality of the group. "If the *mots d'ordre* are followed, it is because they have all given them."[20] In the *groupe en fusion* there are hundreds of individual syntheses, yet they are, *as multiplicity*, dialectically negated in the very act of constituting the group. Each act can be said to be a free individual development, yet it is such only through the group. The group alone makes the act efficient and is instrumental in its success. Although it can be said in all truth that the individual freely joins the group, it is no less certain that if he wants to survive, he *must* join, for salvation lies where the group is. While the seriality was always elsewhere, or as Sartre put it *"en fuite,"* it can be said now that salvation is *here*. The *we* expresses the ubiquity of the *me* as interiorized by the others, which is not at all the case in the seriality.

Although there is at this stage of the game no leader, there is nevertheless a strong solidarity and common action, which, although internally diversified—I do this, you do that—keeps all of us subordinated to the common purpose. Once the victory is achieved—in our example, the capture of the Bastille—some form of frustration may follow, but this comes only later, as a counterfinality. As the reader will remember from the last chapter, the *praxis* of man always provokes as a reaction its *anti-praxis*, finality always produces a counter-finality. The free act of man sets itself in the matter, and in so doing, escapes his control and is endowed with the power to hit back at him. The dialectic is a living one; it is man who acts upon the matter, it is man, not some superorganism, who took the Bastille, but now it will be the Bastille which takes man, for fear sets in as part of the counterfinality. The group settles down at night around the ruins, but the old chateau, although tamed, is still a menace. As if to conceal

[20] *Ibid.*, p. 418.

that menace, they decorate the site with festooned lamps and pasteboard trees and erect a sign, *"Ici l'on danse"*—it is almost as if they must dance away their fear.[21]

One should not see in all this any *hypersynthesis* transcending the individual act, for there is only the *individual* synthesis which knows itself to be identical "with" any other individual synthesis. This synthesis—and Sartre is insistent —happens "from within" in freedom. It is from the "within," through the individual choice, that the plurality becomes unity. The group is of course not indifferent to its numbers, since this factor can become instrumentally effective, but the number does not in itself constitute the group. It is merely instrumental in the usual manner of the inorganic; man must work through the matter.

This ubiquitous presence of the individual synthesis through and in the other is practical, and by this Sartre means it is an *act*, not a state of mind: it is a *praxis* which through the object or group results in a common act. Yet the common act itself, this ubiquitous presence, is an ubiquity in freedom. A *groupe en fusion* is a revolt in freedom, and a conquest against alienation.[22] My freedom recognizes itself in my own action and simultaneously in the action of the Other. No one is imposed upon.

This is a crucial point for Sartre, and here more than ever he asserts himself against a Leninist interpretation of Marxism, which is squarely materialistic and mechanistic. For Sartre, there is a mutual recognition in reciprocity, not an abstract recognition, but one manifested in the common act. This does not imply that there are no conflicts, for there are indeed. The liquidation of the seriality goes more slowly here, faster elsewhere. The individuals, being free, are not homogeneous, and there are orders and counterorders. All this is, nevertheless, accidental in the essential process, the gradual changing over, in freedom, from *seriality* to *group*.

[21] The descriptive detail is from Thomas Carlyle's *The French Revolution*, p. 281.

[22] *CRD*, I, p. 426.

The nuance between freedom and compulsion at this point is a subtle one; I join, that is, I give myself in freedom, but there is immediately a self-imposed limitation upon my freedom. My choice is actually a dependence *here* within the group rather than death *elsewhere* in complete independence. Facing the alternative of all or nothing, the group is born, and it is only on the basis of an impossibility of living any longer as a human being that one unites. If the individual loses himself in the group, it is nevertheless only in order to find himself.

Once united, the individual may face hardship and even violence. Here Sartre obviously has in mind the days of the *Terreur*, where the freedom given up to the group gave way to violence, and some of the very revolutionaries who had helped to form the group themselves became its victims when they dared to retract the freedom they had once so eagerly bestowed upon it and now wished to wield again as individuals. They became victims of their own alienated freedom, for "There is only a dialectical contradiction between . . . Liberty . . . and Violence exercised against the Other whether outside or inside the group."[23] John Ford has given a masterly presentation of this form of repression of the group against the individual member in his classic film *The Informer*, where Victor McLaglen, playing the informer, was summarily eliminated, after having "taken back" the freedom he had earlier so enthusiastically dedicated to the Sinn Fein.

All this is looking ahead, however, and will be the consequence of the fact which concerns us at present, that the totalization of the group going out from the individual and embracing the plurality of the group also englobes, on the rebound, the individual himself; he is both unifier and unified. The act of individual interiorization pulls the group together, but it is not mere immanent activity, remaining within the subject. It transcends him, and in so doing, imposes a control upon his freedom from the outside. If this

[23] *Ibid.*, p. 429.

whole activity were merely immanent in each individual, without the outward manifestation and its consequent restriction upon him, one would then have to call upon some form of hyperorganic structure to identify and tie together the group. On the other hand, it would be falling into the opposite extreme if one were to consider the action from the outside to be all-powerful, since then we would have in the group nothing more than a molecular ensemble, without any intervention of the subject.[24] Neither supposition actually takes place. What does happen is that I am a unifier, as is every subject, and this unifying activity results not in an ontological and organic unity, but in a unified and common *praxis*, which curbs my own unlimited freedom. Yet this common *praxis* is to the advantage of all, for unlike an organism, such as the human body, which is both means and end, the group is merely means, and its end is the salvation of the individual. Group, then, is not an organism or hyperorganism—Sartre is adamant in rejecting these epithets—it is, rather, a common *praxis*, resulting from a multiple interiorization accomplished in freedom, together with the unavoidable yet freely accepted mortification which such a common *praxis* implies.

As we conclude this section, let us keep in mind that we are still in the phase called the *groupe en fusion*, and have not yet reached the phase of strict *organization*, or still less, that of institution. Although there was a differentiation of functions during the capture of the Bastille, this had only a provisional aspect, often dictated by the place where one found oneself—since I happened to be in the front ranks of the group, I was the one who had to climb over the wall. Although there is undoubtedly some co-ordination, it is not yet organization; the group needs to be unified only enough to undertake a particular action and it does not feel the need to reflect upon its status. It is only after it has done what it had to do that it becomes more conscious of itself. It was only after the Bastille had been taken and the heat of the

[24] *Ibid.*, p. 431.

battle over that the need for a new form of integration became urgent. Once the tension is over, the menace of seriality appears once more. The group *qua* group survives through the legacy of its past action, but a problem arises concerning its permanent character, which must somehow solidify that inheritance. It is important for the survival of the group that I, who am now a guardian during the night after the capture of the Bastille, keep the awareness of the group as a common reality alive. The interiorization must survive, but it will have to struggle against the encroachment of solitude and fragmentation.

The Oath and *Terreur*

This menace of atomization is met by means of the *oath*, whereby the individual freedom previously given over to the group is frozen there. More technically, the oath is the "affirmation by the third man of the permanence of the group as a negation of its exterior negation," that is, the third man recognizes the necessity of the group to combat any further threats of extermination and thereby emerges permanently, he hopes, from his former inert seriality.[25] The oath itself imposes a new form of inertia, since it eliminates all out freedom on the part of the individual members of the group taking that oath. The group thus becomes its own inertia, as a protection against slipping back once more into mere seriality after its immediate objectives have been achieved. The oath is, furthermore, a form of reciprocity, in the sense that through the oath I protect myself and the third man, the one being protected through the other. This reciprocity must be mediated through the whole group, since my oath is only a guarantee when taken for granted by the others as well. This definitely modifies the status of the group, for the clear implication is that from now on I could become a traitor. My oath is a protection against any such deflection. All this does

[25] *Ibid.*, p. 440.

not destroy my freedom, which is actually *"une liberté qui jure . . . ,"*[26] yet this freedom is undoubtedly restrained through the oath itself, once it has been taken. Here freedom is limited from the inside and it is juxtaposed to the freedom of the Other, who likewise limits himself from within.[27] As a result, the taking of an oath brings with it as an unavoidable concomitant a state of affairs where the third man once more becomes *Other*. Although he is not yet the *Other* of the seriality, there admittedly enters an element of the pratico-inert, since the agents themselves become pratico-inert through the oath. This conformity contrasts with the flexible dialectic of the *groupe en fusion;* the future has become more rigid.[28]

Even though it has been at a certain cost, there is nevertheless the compensation that less labor is involved at the stage of the oath than in the earlier phase of combat and conquest. The group arose in a spirit of sacrifice. Its unity was the enemy. This object pressing toward unification no longer pushes them. All these differences between the phase of the oath and the previous phase should not make us forget that fundamentally they have the same motivation, and that motivation is *fear*. The danger is still present, although now it lies within rather than exterior to the group, for the fear is now that of seeing the group itself dissolve into seriality. In order to avoid that danger, the group itself exerts pressure on its members, and they themselves are thus in danger *within* the group. Violence threatens them not from the outside but from the inside, that is, from the group itself. The oath protects my freedom at the risk of my own life. This results in what Sartre calls a state of *terreur*. The deeper intelligibility of the oath is seen to be the "affirmation of violence as the diffused structure of the *groupe en fusion*."[29] This *terreur* appears, however, only when there is a danger

[26] *Ibid.,* p. 442.
[27] *Ibid.,* p. 443.
[28] *Ibid.,* p. 445.
[29] *Ibid.,* p. 449.

of dissolution.[30] It is of no consequence whether the oath is invoked through a transcendent object (God, the Bible) or whether it comes from within, and is more immanent. The intervention of God does not really matter in Sartre's conception, for the oath really implies the possibility and admission of violence by man upon man, and it is thus man who asserts himself to be absolute. In a religious group, God is in charge of the punishment, but even there, men sometimes act as his surrogate, or more precisely, the group acts "before" God and in his place. In any case, I, the victim, have freely accepted to be such through the oath. My oath implies death as a possible destiny.

Since the group is not an organism, it has to act in the manner described or it would disintegrate. It lives under *Terreur*, but that *terreur* is one which unites, not one which separates. There is in each of the members a solicitude for the other, but it is a "mortal solicitude."[31] All this is concrete and practical, not merely abstract, and it results in a totalization *here* and *now*, which is quite different from the "flight" that was characteristic of the seriality. Sartre calls this new situation *"le commencement de l'humanité."*[32] If he waxes somewhat rhetorical, it is because for the first time man finds himself to be powerful through a *common* freedom which is able to conquer the helpless seriality. This common freedom is not, of course, based upon any common human nature—as we all know, Sartre will have none of that—but it stems from a recognition of the other as an accomplice in the act "which pulled us out of the earth."[33] We are brethren, not because of a received similarity of nature, like that of peas in a can,

---

[30] *Terreur* is presented here principally as a potential physical punishment to the traitor, as for example, when a member of the underground movement during the war did not submit to the order given by the group, he was under the threat of a severe penalty that might even be death. *Terreur* does not always have to be in the form of physical harm. It can very well, in the opinion of this writer, exert its power through the menace of excommunication or of the Index, or any other form of moral ostracism.

[31] *CRD*, I, p. 453.

[32] *Ibid.*

[33] *Ibid.*

but because we are the sons of our own common free choice.[34] Unity comes from free choice.

This is a striking passage in Sartre's text, but the reader's admiration is tempered by a certain malaise when he notices a continual insistence upon a "common" freedom, which as a result of a common oath in the past is entitled to be protected by violence in the future. For it clearly appears now that the *groupe en fusion* has become a *groupe en contrainte*. The traitor is not dismissed: he is simply eliminated. Sartre shows little tenderness, although I am not certain that he would be as heartless in reality as he is in his dialectical description. According to him, the violence inflicted upon the traitor implies a bond of love among the executers. The danger of the outside enemy, observed at the origin of the *groupe en fusion,* is now replaced by *terreur*. Perhaps we cannot yet call this right of violence a *right* in the strict sense of the word, since we have not yet an *institution,* but we can call it a *jurisdiction* in a vague way. It is not an individual right, or a social contract, or habit or custom. It is a sort of jurisdiction which Sartre is at pains to explain, and so eager is he to pay it his respect that he even calls it something "sacred." Thus, something is sacred when freedom comes back to the individual through some sacred media as an imposition and as an "absolute" limitation. The group under oath has this sacred character, and ceremonies are quite often the material form through which the sacred character reaches its members.[35] However, it should be added that the oath does not have to be an explicit act, but may very well be implicitly present without any external performance or ceremonies. Above all, it is a necessity, whether explicit or implicit, exterior or immanent, when the group is no longer gathered together in one *place* or in one *building*.[36]

[34] "Introduction to *Les Temps Modernes,*" in *Paths to the Present,* p. 436.

[35] *CRD,* I, p. 458.

[36] At the close of the "March for Freedom and Jobs," a manifestation which drew thousands of Negroes and sympathizers together in Washington, D.C., in August 1963, the leaders asked all present to take an oath, an oath that after they had disbanded and returned to

THE ORGANIZATION

The evolution of the group continues, and we approach a new phase which is called *organization*. Organization implies that there is a distribution of tasks, and it is again the common aim—"common interest, common danger, common need, which is at the origin of this distribution of tasks."[37] This division may be imposed without taking the individual into account at all, or it may respect his talents and capacities. Whichever manner may be chosen, it is an activity of the group upon itself and results from the needs of the group at this particular moment. Once the oath has cemented its unity, a differentiation within that unity arises through the distribution of jobs designed to meet different needs.

Up to now we have seen the individual as the one who freely interiorized the multiplicity into a group and who subsequently through the oath that cemented the group saw his function reduced to one of mere membership or otherness in inert freedom. The unity of the group-under-oath has remained abstract, abstract in the Hegelian sense of "incomplete," but now through the distribution of functions it takes on a concrete character. The function or particular job differentiates the individual and gives him a meaning in addition to mere alterity-under-oath. The *terreur* which we have described was efficient but remained remote, since it appeared only when there was a deflection from the group. It was a menace but not a mission. Now the individual will have a particular function for which to train himself.

their homes throughout the country, they would continue the fight for civil rights and the protest against inequality. The Bastille had in a sense been taken—the March had been an enormous success—but now night was setting in, and with it, the fear that the participants might be lost to one another in the darkness of separation. The oath, though it involved no threat of *terreur* beyond the price of a renewed apathy, was an attempt to cement the gains of the day.

[37] *CRD*, I, p. 460.

In order to make this new ordering clear, let us turn to the example of a soccer team. One player is chosen to be the goalkeeper and subsequently prepares himself for that position by acquiring various skills. It is his duty to be a skillful goalkeeper, to keep the ball from going between the posts, and it is his right as well, since the position carries with it certain privileges. If I belong to the group, I want the goalkeeper to be treated in a certain way and I expect him to expect from me that special consideration. Duty and right are correlative coming from every individual toward every third man, as part of the *praxis* of the group. This function also restricts the freedom of the goalkeeper in a new way, since to be a goalkeeper is to be a goalkeeper only and not something else. The function is a determining limitation—he must function as a goalkeeper and train himself for that position—but it is also a release from mere alterity, since it confers on him a sovereignty over a particular portion of the world, the area of the goal posts. The individual caught in the *praxis* of the group is confined by his oath and reduced to being a "common" individual—it is the team which matters above all —yet his individual possibilities are still great—he can become the best goalkeeper of the league. He sacrifices the eccentric—he cannot leave his post—but he exerts the common function in a singular way.[38] Similarly, we find that a tool, in providing contact with the world, is a limited approach which restricts that world, but at the same time it makes possible a sovereignty upon a portion of it, as, for example, does St.-Exupery's airplane in *Wind, Sand, and Stars*. To be a pilot is to be a pilot only, yet the possibilities within this function are various and splendid.

We see a common denominator in our two examples, the soccer team and a group of revolutionaries: they both contain a variety of jobs, each of which looks to a future to be fulfilled, and this future can only be fulfilled through organization. Each individual movement conditions the movement

[38] *Ibid.*, p. 466.

of the others, and each attempt receives its justification in the future. Its truth is its fulfillment, states Sartre, echoing Hegel. My individual action is both annulled and fulfilled in the accomplishment of all individual action. Thus, each individual act contains both a right and a duty, and all acts end up and are absolved in the objective attained. "Individual *praxis* is a mediation which cancels itself."[39]

All common purpose is achieved through individual and differentiated actions. So, for example, in the soccer game, the center forward who has the ball at this moment must execute a very personal action—*he* and he alone must outmaneuver his opponent—before this can become part of a more extensive strategy to a common end. Yet it is equally true that individual freedom here is for the present discarded, for its assertion in and for itself would eliminate the team.[40] When a single player in a game lacks team spirit, he jeopardizes the accomplishments of the team. This emphasis upon a common purpose above all personal ends does not mean to minimize individual initiative, which in certain circumstances (in the soccer game: bad weather, much wind, excellent opponents) may require an unusual effort from the individual. Within their specific functions some members of the team are better than others. Indeed, individual achievements and skills may count for much in the gradual execution of a victory; an element of creative freedom most certainly belongs to each individual, even though he be a member of the team.

We now see what the organization means; it is both a distribution of functions, with the consequent possibility for individual initiative, and a subordination of individual ends to the common purpose. "The function is a task to be executed . . . and a relation between every common individual and all the others."[41] It is, in short, a regulated heterogene-

39 *Ibid.,* p. 470.
40 *Ibid.,* p. 472.
41 *Ibid.,* p. 474.

ity. The oath was already an abstract preparation for this internal differentiation, through its reintroduction of alterity —under oath, we are all equal, all members of the group. It is only afterward that we can afford to be different. It is only after the leveling that organization steps in with its differentiation, and with limits drawn to that differentiation. Each individual function creates a situation with the group and through the group, with each one of its members. We members of the group are all brothers tied together by this complex dialectic of each toward each through the group. One can only specify the functions of X with an eye upon Y, or point at the functions of Y with an eye upon X. There is a brotherhood at work, but it should never be forgotten that the brotherhood is *Une Fraternité-Terreur*. The group may be a large one, almost indefinite and vague, but the oath binds together its absent members and the *Fraternité-Terreur* persists.[42] When we speak of the organized group, we do not imply that everyone is indispensable, although the function is. Sometimes the "indispensable" member is eliminated or exiled in a purge, or at other times he is kept on as a mere number, thereby proving that he was not indispensable.[43] Sometimes in the midst of some action, as in a soccer game for example, there may be a reorganization within the global organization on the basis of the game, for the change of situation within the spatial ambit of one part results in a reciprocal modification for all. Within the group there is a continual movement and fluidity of reciprocities.

After having stated his basic principles, Sartre steps into a detailed analysis of some very complex groups, of which there are many examples in our modern society. He considers, for example, the intricate relation within one city of the adult worker who produces with the children who do not yet produce, and the older and retired people who no longer produce. The reciprocity of the producer goes in a double

[42] *Ibid.*, p. 478.
[43] *Ibid.*, p. 481.

direction: it goes toward the past when he takes care of the retired, and into the future when he provides for the child. Everything is reciprocal and everything is fluid, for the reciprocity will change when secondary reciprocities are at work, as, for example, when the proportion of old and young varies.

At times these reciprocities explode in violence, as in the revolt of Budapest in 1956. In Sartre's interpretation, a rectification of that which he proposed earlier in his article "Le Fantôme de Staline," one of the causes of the revolution must be sought in an internal strain within the working class itself. With the coming of the Communist regime, this class was swelled to include not only the workers of the old days but also an entirely new group of people, the former *petite bourgeoisie*. The Hungarian Communist Rakosi joined hands with the Russians to liquidate the *petite bourgeoisie* as a class, and they had never forgiven him or the regime their downgrading. Consequently, it was a revolt of this minor group of malcontents within the working class which erupted into a nationwide revolution. If Sartre admitted a correction in his views, however, this did not change his fundamental judgment: he disapproved then, and continues to disapprove of the Russian intervention.[44]

What the Communist regime missed in our example and what any regime often does not find is the way to reconcile the dissident individual elements and to set them to working toward a common objective. *Terreur* arises when for one reason or another the regime fails to integrate the minor groups into a new whole, and when secondary reciprocities begin to take the place of the primary ones, as in Hungary, where the *petite bourgeoisie* refused to recognize themselves as workers working for the liberation of the working class and fought against the new role and the leaders who had imposed it. Since modern society is pluridimensional, the art consists in keeping its complex structure in balance. Ac-

[44] *Ibid.*, p. 485.

cording to Sartre, a mathematical logistic could be made up of these mutual reactions, of their growths and corrections, but the task does not tempt him, and he gladly abandons it to the mathematicians.[45]

[45] *Ibid.*, p. 486.

Chapter VII

FROM GROUP TO AUTHORITY

We have come a long way from the looseness of the seriality. The individual in the series, as Other among Others, had no power with which to combat impositions upon his freedom, yet after he has united, first lightly in the heat of the battle or opposition, later more strongly in a group held together by an oath, and still later in a more tightly organized collection of individuals, each with his different function, is he not caught in a structure which makes him more a prisoner than ever? It looks as if, at the end of the last chapter, Sartre left himself open to a rather difficult question. For if a mathematician or a specialist in cybernetics can put these matters into statistics, are we not fully immersed in the inorganic and have we not given up the life of the dialectic within the group?

Sartre's answer to this menace of the inorganic is to admit that its intervention cannot, in truth, be overlooked and that there is indeed a skeleton of the inorganic and the quantifiable within life. He makes a heavy qualification, however, in adding that what is skeletic is not so much the individuals as the *relations* of these individuals. Any one of them is free to step out of the scheme at will, and what will remain will be the relations and what at this point Sartre calls structures, in imitation of Lévi-Strauss's *"Structures élémentaires de la parenté."*[1] These structures are the empty schemes in which family relations—to take an example—fulfill themselves. Con-

[1] *CRD*, I, p. 487; Claude Lévi-Strauss, *Les Structures élémentaires de la parenté* (Paris, 1949).

sidered aside from the living dialectic, they are susceptible to mathematical calculations, but they are nevertheless originally dependent upon a free choice. They are built upon rights and duties, oaths and engagements freely taken and freely fulfilled by the candidates. Only when *A wants* to marry *B* does the complicated scheme of relations between cousins, nieces, parents, aunts, and uncles begin. The possibility of using mathematics can only follow upon a free decision.[2] The structure of the group is an ambiguous entity, one which has a mechanical element and yet is the expression of a living integration and *praxis* of unification. As a consequence, it implies a "contradictory tension: it is both freedom and inertia."[3]

This pre-existence of a scheme of relations and a free acceptance (or rejection) of those relations later is seen when a child is born into an existing group. Sartre launches here into an extremely provocative discussion of the emergence of a child into a group. Every child that is born is heir to a ready-made scheme; as he emerges into a milieu under oath, for example, he is himself bound by that oath, which has been taken for him by his parents. Even before his birth, he is a "*determined* possibility of the father and mother"; his limit is *their* limit as long as he is only a possibility, but it becomes *his* limit as well as their limit as soon as he is born.[4] The purpose of such ceremonies as baptisms and initiations is to make available the possibility of a later interiorization of an oath on the part of an individual as a free common agent. The oath must first be an external link of the individual with the group in order to qualify him as a *common* agent (one choosing from within the group); without the oath, as an individual agent, he cannot lift himself as easily to the level of the group and must therefore choose as an outsider, from without the group. The power of the group is never his, and a decision made from outside the group

[2] *CRD*, I, p. 491.
[3] *Ibid.*, p. 487.
[4] *Ibid.*, p. 491.

(whether to join it) is very different from one made within it (whether to remain or leave). In incorporating him within the group, the parents open both possibilities to him, whereas the unbaptized, the uninitiated have only one possibility, unless through a greater effort, they are able to lift themselves to the level of the group, there to know and decide.

The word "common" has occurred again and again in these pages, gathering a weight of meaning at each recurrence. We saw it used first to describe an objective that united all men in its pursuance and that in so doing, drew them out of their mere alterity into a new relationship of being "third man." In this relationship, a freedom was conferred by the collectivity, "mediated through the Other," that released a new power to man. This freedom was called a *common* freedom, and in enabling man to conquer the helplessness that was inevitable in the seriality, it lifted him to a new level of efficiency, so much so that Sartre called it "the beginning of humanity."[5] Unity was seen to be the result of *common* free choice. It will be Sartre's constant worry to qualify the two terms *common* and *free* and to distinguish between the inertia imposed by the group and the free acceptance of the individual, who is *free common* agent. Wherever the terms are encountered, they should be read with a sense of their real depth of meaning, of their ambiguity and reciprocity, for if freedom is conferred by the collective, the collective can only exist through free choice.

This digression on the terms *common* and *free* has been made so that as we return to Sartre's discussion of the emergence of the child into the group, we will be certain to give both words their full weight. Sartre goes on to discuss—although it is as a footnote—the often-questioned attitude of the French Catholic who, although lukewarm or even freethinking himself, nevertheless has his children baptized and even educated as Catholics.[6] The Catholics whom Sartre

[5] *Ibid.*, p. 453. On the *common* individual and his inert freedom see also a very interesting passage in *CRD*, I, p. 493.

[6] *CRD*, I, p. 491, footnote.

has in mind are those who are themselves Catholic by origin, no longer by faith, and who through their respect—and perhaps by virtue of a cousin who is a seminarian, or a maternal aunt who is pious—may still be considered and consider themselves to be members of the group. These are the parents who say of their children, "They must be free; they will choose when they are twenty," and rather than make total indetermination the basis of this later choice (actually an impossibility, since this already implies a choice for the child on the part of the parents), they put him in possession of his common freedom, which he interiorizes "as the real power of his individual freedom."[7] From this superior level, from an inside knowledge of the group, where he has a function and a reciprocal relation with everyone in the group, he can decide whether he wants to remain within it fervently or in a lukewarm way, or whether he wants to reject it entirely. This is a choice in freedom which is not open to the "atheist by birth," who is only an individual and has never known the power of faith as a common freedom, his to choose or criticize. Thomas Aquinas may seem a strange companion to Jean-Paul Sartre, but here he joins hands (however loosely!) in recognizing the power of the group as a whole in the dialectic of the individual decision—"The small children are baptized in the faith of the *whole church*" (italics mine), and in pointing out the weight of the parental decision—"Natural order requires that the child who has not yet reached the age of reason be directed to God through the reason of its parents. It is therefore in the faith of the parents that the children are saved."[8] It is only the believer who has the experience both of the power of religion in the Christian community and, if he has doubts, of the inferiority of the state of solitude.[9]

In truth, whatever the parents do, they inevitably create prejudices, for the atheists are also a group, and the child

[7] *Ibid.*
[8] *Summa* III, Q. 68, art. 9 ad 2; *ibid.* art. 10, resp. and ad 3.
[9] *CRD*, I, p. 492 (in footnote continued from p. 491).

undergoes either the implicit baptism of atheism (or indifference, agnosticism, etc.) or the explicit Christian baptism; in any case, he bears the weight of the parental decision all his life.[10] The liberals, whatever they say, must also make decisions for their children without being able to consult them in advance. It is equally true, of course, that these decisions will actually mark the child only as the child freely interiorizes them later. The born Catholic must nevertheless make himself Catholic, the born atheist must choose atheism. As Sartre wrote earlier of the worker, "Man is only a situation: a worker is not *free* to think or to feel like a bourgeois; but in order that this situation should become *a man*, a whole man, it should be lived and left behind on the way towards a particular aim. In itself, it remains indifferent as long as a human freedom does not give it a meaning: it is neither tolerable nor unbearable as long as a freedom does not accept it, does not rebel against it, that is to say as long as a man does not choose himself in it, by choosing its significance. Then only, within this free choice, it becomes determinant . . ."[11] The schemes are there, the structures are pressing to be filled, but it can be only a *man* who fills them, in all his limited freedom. In every group there is some inorganic inertia for the individual, but this obtains value and significance later on, as the child-grown-adult interiorizes the decision concerning his future taken by his parents.[12]

Sartre has been attempting in these pages to discover and describe the structure of the group, and his probing has led him to an ambiguity which couples the freedom of the individual with a certain qualification of that freedom which he calls *la necessité de la liberté*.[13] This *necessité de la liberté* does not refer to his celebrated "one cannot not be free"—that unavoidable obligation of the *Pour-soi* to be free,

---

[10] *Ibid.*; on the solitude of the atheist, see my book *The Planetary Man*, I, Ch. VIII.

[11] End of Sartre's "Introduction to *Les Temps Modernes*," first issue, 1945, quoted in the anthology *Paths to the Present*, p. 441.

[12] *CRD*, I, p. 492.

[13] *Ibid.*, p. 494.

by which a refusal to make a choice is in itself a choice;[14] it points, rather, to the unavoidable incorporation of the individual in some collectivity, which brings with it an inert element which is part of any free decision on the part of that individual—"one cannot not be in a group," and being in a group, one is necessarily weighed down by a certain ponderosity. This inert element that enters into the freedom of the individual in the group, or the "common individual," has been described through the example of the child born into the group and initiated into and subsequently educated in its rites. Through his description of collective realities, in which man is *situated,* it seems that Sartre has been laboring to supply that "synthetic psychology" that he has earlier declared was lacking in Marxism.[15]

Another example of this *necessité de la liberté* can be seen in the domain of military subordination. When in the midst of a battle a lieutenant gives an order to a soldier in his command and the soldier executes that order, he is, in his very obedience, accepting and interiorizing it as his own. Nevertheless, this *praxis* presumes the silent presence of the *liberté-terreur* and a whole complex of rights and duties.[16] The soldier is obliged to execute the order, under threat of court martial, so that there is a certain weight bearing down upon his freedom. This possibility of betrayal and subsequent punishment presumes the existence of an organized group, with a hierarchical structure of ranks of command and subordination and the ensuing relations of soldiers with officers. These structures constitute a skeleton of the inert, which is quantifiable, but there is at the same time always an "unforeseen area which stands out of the social field."[17]

[14] See *Being and Nothingness,* pp. 478 ff.; *The Tragic Finale,* p. 106.

[15] "Marxism has not yet at its disposal a synthetic psychology fit for its totalitarian conception of the class." "Introduction to *Les Temps Modernes,*" in *Paths to the Present,* p. 440.

[16] *CRD,* I, p. 495.

[17] "Introduction to *Les Temps Modernes,*" in *Paths to the Present,* p. 440.

The soldier is not a stone or a tree or a number: he may disobey, however unlikely, and accept the consequences not only of court martial but also of breaking up the unity of the group which is his freedom.

The structure of the group, then, includes both analytical and synthetic elements, both inertia and freedom. It is obvious that in the groups we have mentioned, as for example in the army, analytical necessity exists, and in that domain, things can be counted, calculated and predicted—so many men have to be nourished, the food has to be carried to the front line over such and such a distance, etc.[18] In addition to this *analytical* skeleton, however, the structure of the group also implies the subjective synthesis or totalization, in other words, the interiorization and acceptance by individuals of the total activity. The group has no separate organic status; Sartre once more wants it to be clearly understood that its very existence is made possible only through the integrating process of each individual. He even goes so far as to say that for the individual the group is a means, an instrument for his security, even an object, an object which he can manipulate to an extent.[19] Perhaps the term *quasi object* would actually be better here, for since I am myself part of the group and through the oath caught in the group, I cannot confront the group as an extrinsic and distinct *object*. I am in it myself. The ambiguity which we discover is not unlike that which we have earlier remarked in the act of reflection.[20] The individual act of reflection, as has been sufficiently shown in our speculative analysis, is never entirely *one*, nor is it entirely *dual*. Reflection has both oneness and duality, since in the act of reflecting, one tears oneself away from oneself, yet not entirely so. In the same way, the group in its reflective attitude, that is, when it faces itself, never constructs a double entity. It can never

[18] *CRD*, I, p. 486.
[19] *Ibid.*, p. 498.
[20] *Being and Nothingness*, p. 150; *The Tragic Finale*, pp. 43 and 73.

entirely confront itself as one confronts a distinct object.
Yet when I claim that the group is my quasi object, it should
be understood as follows—and here we introduce a nuance
which brings us very much in the line of previous dialectic
—I cannot in confronting the group divorce myself from the
Other, since as *common individual* (that is, individual
caught in the group through the oath) I am the *same* as the
Other. I interiorize what he desires (as far as the group is
concerned) and he interiorizes what I wish. This "sameness"
reaches even into the functional differentiation. The organizer (or leader) is really the *same* as the one who is organized (or subordinate) and both respectively in their function
of leader and subordinate approve, by way of interiorization,
the order to give and the order to be accepted.

As a result of the confrontation of the group with itself,
or of the reflective attitude of the group upon itself, the
group gets into action, that is, it modifies its purpose or perhaps reinforces and accelerates its current course. Its action now requires a structure, which was not yet the case
with the *groupe en fusion*, which acted under the immediate
pressure of some common danger or need. In the aftermath
we need organization, with its leaders, propagandists, spe-
cialists, ordinary members, etc. This structure, constituting an
unavoidable inorganic skeleton, is the necessary expression
of the totalization of the group. A function develops itself
naturally in the group, as a means to fulfill some end or
action, and as such, is one of its vital expressions. This function, and all functions, provides the structure of the group.
They are wanted by the group, since, as member, everyone
is the same as everyone else; all of us, as members of the
group, want that particular objective, that form of propaganda, that sort of activism. These activists (the name reserved by Sartre for the more active members of the group)
have a certain autonomy, and the way in which they fulfill
their function may very well be unique. Their relative autonomy does not prevent them from being, in fact, the expression of the interiorized acceptance and approval of the other

members of the group; their activism is actually the remolding of the group by itself, and this reshaping requires a structure, a structure according to which a certain power is recognized in some and executed by one or another. All these things were not yet present in their specific, clear-cut way in the *groupe en fusion*—the "leader," we will remember, was only the "third man regulator" who rose spontaneously from the crowd because of some topological or psychological advantage—but they inevitably appear as soon as the group is beyond that elementary stage and begins to consolidate itself as a group.[21]

The reflective attitude of the group expressed through *action* has also a noetic character, that is, the individual members of the group have an "idea" of the group, an idea which the group produces of itself. This idea is pervasive and shapes a whole way of thinking and of viewing the world, as well as of judging other people and events. A Marxist, a Catholic, a Frenchman views things in a certain way by virtue of his Marxism, his Catholicism, his French nationality. It is in fact the judgment of the "common individual" of that particular group. Although there is a certain inertia involved, the "idea" of the group does not have the stability and fixity of a piece of gold; being human, it is elastic and within certain limits evolves, and the "common judgments" of a Marxist, a Catholic, or a Frenchman may very well change over the years.

We have seen that the structure of the group is twofold, with an inorganic skeleton and a more spontaneous or synthetic element. We can discover this same dualism in the idea which the group forms of itself. Since it is a result of individual totalization, from the inside, this "idea" is something felt in common by the group and is quite often totally unknown to the outsider. One has to be a Marxist to know what it means to be a Marxist, since only those who belong to the group can know what it truly means. Since "being"

[21] *CRD*, I, p. 502.

is a part of knowing, this "silent knowledge which the group has of itself" often eludes the anthropologist.[22] This is, I believe, a very acute observation on the part of Sartre. To an extent, it explains to the outsider why members of the group behave in such and such a way; their membership and internal acceptance of certain views and ideals has revealed to them a world which he can never understand or penetrate.[23] Even the primitive tribes have their "principles," perhaps not abstracted into a written or even a spoken code, but nevertheless universally lived and practiced within the tribe. Their matrimonial ceremonies, for example, may consist of rites which reflect the ethical positions of the group. The anthropologist can enumerate the events which take place and interpret them in his own light, but he can never quite grasp the inner common convictions which give them such a wealth of meaning to the participants, for whom these convictions serve as absolutes and are ethically normative. Their ceremonies are a form of showing fidelity to the oath,[24] but the *exact* nature of that fidelity and of the unwritten oath itself never finds its way into the anthropologist's dissertation. Literature gives us abundant examples of this in-

[22] *Ibid.*, p. 503.
[23] Edward T. Hall has written a book entitled *The Silent Language* (Garden City, New York, 1959), in which he attempts to pursue some of the ways in which people communicate silently with one another. The approach to time, for example, differs greatly in different groups; the American businessman feels insulted when he has to wait for forty-five minutes for an appointment with a Latin businessman, whereas for the Latin, this is perfectly natural. This is because the "duration scales" are different: for a businessman of the eastern United States, meeting an equal in the daytime, Hall gives "eight time sets in regard to punctuality and length of appointments: on time, five, ten, twenty, thirty, forty-five minutes, and one hour early or late, each with a different meaning." Both Latin and North American would find it difficult to cope with the Afghan who made an appointment with his brother but failed to mention the year (paperback ed. [1961], pp. 29, 136). This handling of time, although quantifiable in the example, rests upon something unquantifiable and ineffable.
[24] *CRD*, I, p. 504.

ability of the outsider to understand in all its innuendoes
and nuances the idea which a group has of itself.[25]

This also explains why conversion is usually a slow process, for it involves, beyond the intellectual or abstract
knowledge of a new faith, a whole new way of looking at
things, of judging persons and events, which must be internally accepted and felt. From the point of view of his
philosophy, Sartre could not be more right. Yet earlier he
has written that conversion was a matter of "the instant,"
a sudden break in the individual's way of living and thinking.[26] However paradoxical this may seem, the two statements do not really conflict. There may indeed come an "instant" in which the individual has a sudden insight into the
futility of an old point of view and the possibilities and beau-
ties of a new one, as when an atheist becomes a Christian.
The insight may be instantaneous, as also its acceptance,
but the subsequent adaptation to the new *group*, with all its
inner and felt common convictions and outlooks, may be
painful and long.

In addition to this internal interpretation of the idea, usually ineffable, there is also that self-knowledge of the group
that is concerned with the mechanical or skeletal structure.
This is, of course, communicable, since it refers not so much
to the internal way of living of the group as to its rules and
laws, which are readily open to observation from the outside. It is the inert and quantifiable element, such as the
rules which regulate family relations. We add once more that
even in this area, however subject to mathematical calculation it may be, the dialectical reason is nevertheless still
supreme and keeps the analytical reason always in its place.
Graphs, tables, predictions can be made, but the person is

[25] E. M. Forster, whose novels all dramatize the impossibility of
total *comprehension* between people of different countries or social
classes or sensibilities, introduces his *Howards End* (1910) with the
motto, "Only connect . . ."

[26] *Being and Nothingness*, p. 465; *The Tragic Finale*, pp. 104–5.

always free to step out of the statistic. For History ultimately belongs to the dialectic.

ORGANISM OR ORGANIZATION

In the pages that follow, Sartre comes back once more to the problem of what type of being to ascribe to the activity of the group insofar as this activity is common and constituted. There is an admitted unity which is somehow preserved, but is this unity *organic* or simply *organized?* Does it resemble the unity of the individual himself, or is it something different?[27]

Sartre emphatically rejects any magical or mystical interpretation that would give the group a Gestalt or some sort of collective consciousness and insists that its unity lies only in the common *praxis* and the common purpose, as interiorized by each of the members. The group is not a totality. It always strives toward the unrealizable totality, hence is continually in motion. Its freedom lies in the freedom of its free members, and it keeps alive through their continual internal inventiveness. As we have already seen, it is in order to achieve a common purpose that the members of a group undertake a common action, and this common action presupposes organization. The group to Sartre is nothing more than this organized activity, held together first by the oath, later by institutionalism and authority, directed toward common ends; it is not some hyperorganism which exists outside of this common activity. It is not a totality, but simply perpetual totalization. Sartre will now attempt to corroborate this position, with some extremely complex arguments, all of which constitute a desperate struggle to keep the individual organism (or human reality) at the center of everything and to reject any overarching "entity."

He first observes that the historian or the sociologist who begins a study of the group himself belongs to a group, what-

[27] *CRD*, I, pp. 505, 507.

ever group this may be, and by virtue of his own membership, he is able to understand and comprehend the group
wherever he sees it. He is himself an organism which can
interiorize an organization, and is thus able to understand
the process in others. If he, Sartre, is a Frenchman and a
member of the *petite bourgeoisie intellectuelle,* he can then
realize what it is to be an African, an American, a worker,
and this is not a mere speculative understanding but one
through his own *praxis,* from the inside. This leads to the
interesting conclusion that the group lies *within* reach of the
individual organism, or within the immediate experience of
the human individual and is not some hyperorganic entity
—like God or Gestalt—out of reach for the human reality.[28]

It remains true, however, that the group is not the individual. It runs along some different, more efficient level,
where the seriality is overcome and where the oath, *terreur,*
organization are possible. At the start of all this, whatever it
is, stands the individual: he *posits* the group through his
totalization, and constitutes it in the race to the Bastille.
(Actually the race and totalization are synonymous, since
one totalizes in one's action.) In the light of these reserva-
tions, the homogeneity between the *praxis* of the group and
that of the individual becomes all the more striking. This
similarity can be observed without difficulty whether one
observes the group as object or whether one looks at the
praxis of a group as subject. In either case, that which is
not an organism is acting strangely like one.

We see this, for example, in the activity of the group-
object. In the hands of the individual, the group can become
means and object, as in the Praetorian Guard in the retinue
of the emperor. They do for him what he cannot do all by
himself, since they can be stationed at every gate and if necessary, even cover every window, but it is he who totalizes
their intention, that of guarding his person. He encompasses
their *praxis* in the way he grasps his own *praxis.*[29] They are

[28] *Ibid.,* p. 509.
[29] *Ibid.,* p. 512.

nothing more than instruments within his field. Thus he uses the men who make up the Praetorian Guard somewhat in the way he might use certain tools. *"Tel qui peut s'abriter derrière des rochers, peut aussi s'abriter derrière des autres masses, des hommes."*[30] Through the oath men become rocks, to be manipulated, moved, used as a shelter against some danger or against the failure to achieve some end which requires their united efforts. In this use of the group—of many men, many rocks—there is something similar to the use of the machine by an organism, which uses the machine to do more than it can do alone. Behind the machine, however, stands the man, who invents it, runs it, gives it its purpose. So also the group is tool, and it stands between me, the individual member-sovereign and the purpose to be achieved, as a tool stands between the individual worker and his work. One can even say that the structure of the group is not unlike that of the workshop; just as tools are disposed in a variety of ways, each with a different usefulness, so also the inner structure of the group, with its hierarchy, presumes the existence of various functions with a variety of purposes. In its most primitive forms, the group as utensil can almost be said to be an inert tool.[31] Both tool and group nonetheless echo an individual *praxis*. The shoe factory turns out many more thousands of shoes than the individual cobbler, but it follows his procedure; so also the Praetorian Guard can be in many more places and exert a greater combined strength than the emperor all by himself, but it does what he would do himself, protect him against the enemy.

We discover this same imitation of the individual *praxis* in the case of the group-subject, as, for example, when a group is pursuing a fugitive. The Mexican priest in Graham Greene's *The Power and the Glory* realizes very well that it is a careful, planned pursuit which is after him. That pursuit is like the project of an individual, and the group like a living organism, only larger, more powerful. The fugitive knows

[30] *Ibid.*, p. 513.
[31] *Ibid.*, p. 514.

that the police are everywhere—on the mountain and in the valley, in the houses and on the roads. The group of the policemen is a ubiquity—they are everywhere—yet it is a unity as well. One could say that the priest himself is their unity, for it is a unity all out to catch him: it is organized freedom for his extermination. Here it acts very much like an individual organism, but frighteningly more efficient. Although all this may not make us conclude that the group is an organism, the individual observer cannot help noticing that there is a striking resemblance between the two. The group has power, it is directed toward the future, as in the case of the individual working by himself, and this future comes down toward the present as a unifying force.[32]

Some of the villagers in Greene's novel were not "for" the revolution, however, and refused to turn in the priest. Had they all interiorized its aims as fervently as the revolutionaries themselves did, the pursuit by the police would have been greatly simplified and, of course, there would have been no drama to put into a novel. From all this we can see that no unifying impact can reach the group from the future unless there is individual interiorization. This is of supreme importance for Sartre. As a revolution gets under way, with a *groupe en fusion* gathering together the formerly disparate elements into a common, consenting force, we are unable to discover any organic synthesis or *Gestalt*. The initiative may come from the top (authoritarian form) or from the bottom (democratic approach), but in either case, it comes through and to man, without the intervention of some hyperorganism. Instead, what we observe is a form of reciprocity, a mutual acknowledgment of the participants, "a practical recognition in the act on the tacit basis of the oath."[33] Everyone sees himself in the Other, in a common project and a common purpose, and the individual loses himself in the *us* in order to find himself a stronger *I*. Sometimes, as in the uprising of 1917 in Petrograd, this feeling of solidarity expresses

[32] *Ibid.*, p. 516.
[33] *Ibid.*, p. 520.

itself in a slogan. Thus the stunned cry, "The army is with us!" circulated like wildfire among the revolutionaries, who, ordinarily accustomed to opposition from the military, now included the soldiers themselves within their mutual recognition.[34] The "us feeling" was all the more striking in that a traditional opponent was now interiorizing and interiorized *with them.*

This dialectic of reciprocity—I am the same as the Other—does not, of course, exclude a heterogeneous structure. There is always some form of organization at work. Even when there is not yet a leader or an official authority, there will be an agitator who keeps things going. In so doing, he is only expressing the common purpose. A diversity of functions is necessary. Since the individual soldier lacks eyes in the back of his head, the square structure of the legion must supply them for him. Similarly, he cannot fight night and day, but must be replaced by another team while he regathers his strength. The diversity does not seek to emulate the living organism, but merely to complete through human inventiveness and the strength of the many what was lacking in each participant acting alone.[35] Even if we concede that the group does remotely imitate the unity of the organism, we can still say that it nevertheless merely imitates life, but is not itself life. In truth, it is life which uses the group and gives it the necessary diversification, for behind the organization stands always the individual organizing.

In emphasizing the unity of the group and its organization, we do not want to deny that there is a plurality, or to assert that the individuals within this plurality are always in perfect agreement. On the contrary, they conflict, from their first heated proposals on the street to their more considered decisions made in meetings and committees. The deeper reason for their conflict is that every solution which is proposed is necessarily a limited one. The conflict, then, will

[34] *Ibid.*, p. 519. Sartre also cites in this context a similar instance, when the Navy joined the uprising in Kronstadt in 1918.
[35] *CRD*, I, p. 521.

have to be solved, either through concession or through absorption or even through the elimination of one of the parties concerned. Whatever may happen, whatever the means used, the solution that will be adopted will be an individual solution, that is, one that comes from one individual, although it may eventually be corrected and amended by another individual. The result has sometimes been called "an agreement of minds," although actually there are no minds, "no more than there are souls."[36] There is not even agreement. There is no reason why Peter and John must *agree* in the same way two scientists agree; to make such a claim is to reduce history to an analytical procedure. Agreement is accidental, for concurrence in the same action even if it means the limiting or even eliminating of some proposals is all that matters. The solution that, in fact, will be reached is more than an agreement; it is a solution that makes the member of the group *un homme engagé* through and through. The idea that will prevail and upon which we "agree" (or concur) may very well result in the cry, "*A la Bastille!*" The acceptance of this "order" means the liquidation of other solutions and directions—or other ideologies—and the realization that a new practical field has been indicated. My view is at present your view and vice versa because of our participation *in* the group. It is a reinteriorization of the multiplicity. This process does not require any hyperorganism, but is nothing more than the common acceptance of the same solution, according to which a solution is mine to the extent that it is the solution of my neighbor. The same solution is *everywhere* among us members of the group, the solution of one having become the solution of all.[37] "*L'invention de la solution est un moment individuel qui trouve partout son ici en se déterminant réciproquement par sa présence réciproque dans tous les ici.*"[38]

The strange phenomenon of the group, however, is that what has been accepted in freedom deteriorates into inertia.

[36] *Ibid.*, p. 527.
[37] *Ibid.*, p. 530.
[38] *Ibid.*

What is accepted by all and obtains a common character is also by this very fact frozen. This does not mean that all growth is excluded, but it is considerably slowed down, and once a change is accomplished, it too becomes inertia. This is a characteristic feature of the group. The group grows and evolves like an organism, with this notable difference: while the organism starts from inertia and grows into living freedom, the group starts from freedom and grows into inertia. This inertia must always characterize the group, for it is part of any common work and is precisely that which makes the group possible as common activity. The solution or view which has been accepted must carry with it a certain rigidity and be imposed, if necessary, upon all, with dissensions either eliminated or absorbed into the unity of the group.

Once more, the group is not an organism; it merely acts *as if* it were an organism, which distributes the jobs in order to achieve the common end. That common end comes from the future down toward the present and constitutes the unifying power of the group. It is under the pressure of a need that the group was founded by the individual participants, and in that sense can be called a *product,* a product of the individual dialectic. Thus Sartre has called the individual interiorization *une rationalité constituante* and the group *une rationalité constituée.* As such, it is not a totality in the way an organism is a totality; although it strives to be a totality and is continually in motion, it never reaches the limits of an organic totality. The group, born from the organic, remains always haunted by the organic. Sartre seems to emphasize here the *contingent* character of the human organism in a way that bears some resemblance to a Thomistic approach. Thus the contingent is unable to create what is similar to itself, but can only procreate; man can make a group, but he cannot make an organism. The *rationalité constituée,* product of the organic, is doomed never to attain the organic status itself, which remains ever an ideal toward which it strives.

We can now understand why the common *praxis* does not

have the translucid intelligibility of the "individual" *praxis*. As individual *in* the group, I encounter certain limitations and restrictions which I cannot overcome. This inertia contains an obscurity which I can never entirely clarify, never make understood in the way I can make understood an act which is entirely individual. The interiorization of the multiple activity must be undertaken again and again by each individual because of the unpredictable element introduced by the others.

Similarly, it is difficult to confine the group spatially, as one can the individual, for it has *la profondeur du monde*. The individual has also his spatial extension, but unlike the group, he carries with him, wherever he goes, a strong internal unity. This biological unity, called organism, has also its internal "communications," just as the group has its "liaisons," but while these communications in the living body are organic, those within the group are inorganic. There is a lot of "non-group" between the members of the group.[39] In addition to the dispersion imposed by space, time also plays a role. When the group attempts to accomplish something, it takes a certain time, and there are many deviations. Both space and time, then, are great creators of inertia and argue against the group as a biological unit.

The group is no more a machine than it is an organism, but just as we saw that it had "organic" characteristics, so also we see that it will run efficiently to the extent that it is "*machinale.*" It is organization, or as Sartre now puts it, in line with his previous expressions, it is *une dialectique constituée,* and this must be understood in the sense that "it is not a dialectical *praxis,* realizing a unity of individuals, but that there are individual and constituting dialectics (*des dialectiques individuelles et constituantes*) that invent and produce through their work a dialectical apparatus in which they lock themselves up with their instruments and which specifies itself through the purpose."[40] As we have seen, this

[39] *Ibid.*, p. 536.
[40] *Ibid.*, p. 539.

internal, self-isolated apparatus fails in its attempt to become an organism, and its perpetual totalization never becomes totality.[41] It is in constant need of repair, and this repair can be made only through the addition of new members. In its plurality and far-reaching ubiquity, it can never be frozen. On the contrary, the incessant addition of new members results in a certain orientation or *processus* which cannot be stopped, cannot be mathematically pinned down so that one can ever say definitively, "This *is* the group, once and forever."

Process, unlike *praxis*, requires an intervention which repeats itself and yet results in a being different because its originators (individuals) are different. There is no determinism involved in either of the two, *praxis* or process, since the evolution is wanted and oriented and defined on the basis of a certain future, yet there is a different intelligibility.[42]

In the *praxis* of the group, I, as a common individual, understand the other (common) individual, since he is the same as myself. There is a limit, however, to my complete understanding of him, and this limit is his individuality. Although common, he is individual, and as such, produces a blind spot in my comprehension. Under the skin of the common hides the unique. Except for that limitation, the intelligibility of the *praxis* poses no problem and requires no super individual entity, but merely the individual act of interiorization of the ensemble and its striving toward the common purpose.[43]

When I observe the group as a *process*, however, it appears as something which slips away from the control and sometimes even from the comprehension of the individual group member. Process is something which he somehow undergoes, and as we have seen, alters, slowly and subtly but irrevocably, his "common" judgments. It results from the incessant addition of new members, who, although free synthe-

[41] *Ibid.*
[42] *Ibid.*, p. 542.
[43] *Ibid.*

sizers of the totality, through their very number and novelty give a certain irrevocable orientation to the group. This phenomenon has been studied by such scholars as Lewin, Kardiner, and Moreno, to whom it appears to be plainly unintelligible.[44] Although Sartre agrees with the findings of these men, that the group does have some inner orientation over the years, he does not share their puzzlement over its intelligibility, since for him the obscure and inert aspect of the group as process constitutes only one moment in the intelligibility of the group as a whole. It is also in the light of this unavoidable evolution that some symptoms of the group can be understood, as, for example, that aging which takes place when the recruiting of new members is slow and the leadership becomes too rigid. Growth and rejuvenation form part of the process of the group. All these aspects deserve attention, for it is obvious that process and *praxis* are not synonymous and that if one wants to judge and to estimate the value of a group, it is not enough to consider its present activity or *praxis*. One must also keep an eye upon its process, that is, its change or lack of change, in short, its direction.

In conclusion, we may say that the group is a *dialectique constituée,* that is, it is the result of the free intervention of man and as such, it is intelligible. We have seen both how it is born out of the free and creative will of man and how nevertheless it unavoidably carries along with it the weight of the inert. There is freedom, of course, but this freedom is limited from the start, since it is a guided and restricted freedom, *une liberté jurée.* Its success lies in its achievement: it did take the Bastille but it can never omit the individual, who is the *dialectique constituante.* Behind the group, just as behind the machine, stands the organic, individual man.

The analytical reason has impressed a great many people

[44] Lewin and Kardiner have been mentioned before. J. L. Moreno is a Roumanian-born sociologist and M.D., at present living and working in the United States. He is a specialist in social research, mostly concerned with the pattern of relations among people within a group.

through its amazing achievements. Taylorism, for example, in teaching us that any activity can be broken up into its components, in the way an automobile is made upon the assembly line, has pointed the way to a use and economy of time that considerably increases man's output.[45] The electronic computer is an even more amazing feat, since it can break up very complex problems and "count" their parts. This division and calculation of the quantifiable is the work of the analytical reason. On this Sartre would agree. Yet he would add that there is no organization à la Taylor, nor is there any electronic brain that can operate outside the dialectical reason. Within the dialectic we discover some phases of the analytical, for the free and creative intervention of man results, through its very *praxis*, in producing some zones which are analyzable and quantifiable, divisible and enumerable. The man was there first, however, before the time study and before the IBM machine.

For present-day automation is only one more invention which in its analytical structure is a product of the mind of man. It is more than a product, it is an imitation of the human model, or organism. Automation is in its "passive," inert structure a complex attempt to imitate the skill of man and thus save his labor. It is not too much to say that man as organism serves as a model for both the *machine* and the *group*. Although neither groups nor machines are organic in their structure, they nevertheless constantly are driven to imitate the organic category. Their limitation is at times striking but never complete, for they never become organic.[46] We must look still elsewhere to discover the sort of being we can attribute to the group.

STRUCTURE OF THE GROUP THROUGH THE NON-GROUP

It is to the relation of those who are grouped with those who are not grouped that Sartre turns in order to pin down

[45] *CRD*, I, p. 549.
[46] *Ibid.*, p. 552.

that "existence" of the group that has hitherto eluded him. His attempt here is reminiscent of the line of thought in *L'Etre et le Néant* where he denies a real nature to human reality but accepts in its stead a categorization of men by and through the other. Thus the Jew becomes a Jew only because he is considered as such by the non-Jew. Indeed, all character cannot exist in and for itself, but only for-the-Other. "Character is the result of a classification born out of a comparison with Others."[47]

Coming back to our present study, we see that the group has an impact upon the seriality of those who are not in the group. This impact may be negligible, as, for example, the reaction that a group of stamp collectors provokes among those outside their group, but it may also be considerable, as seen in the much stronger reactions produced by such a group as a militia. It is easy to see that this group, as a negation of the seriality, would affect the neighboring seriality which is still powerless, but what is important is that this effect produces, in turn, a reaction.

This reaction implies a totalization coming from each of the non-grouped individuals toward the group. It is the outsider who *posits* the group as a group and as a unit under oath. Thus when I deliver my airmail letter to the postal employee through his narrow office window, I am making an act of trust in the whole group of people concerned with the mail service. "The whole mail system in France is affected by the *praxis* under oath which carries a letter from Lille to Nice."[48] When I come to the post office in Lille, I confront each function as part of the whole group and although I may know the individual employee, I do not treat him as such, or at least only incidentally, but in this context, merely as an employee.

The group becomes through the customer a sort of *inertia under oath*. This is the *being* of the group. For the customer the postal service is an entity, with an interior structure,

---

[47] *Being and Nothingness*, p. 350; *The Tragic Finale*, p. 82.
[48] *CRD*, I, p. 556.

various tensions, a spatiotemporal spreading out. This *is* the postal service here, and nowhere do we find any collective consciousness that could place it elsewhere. As for the member of the group himself, he confronts the rest of humanity as *une forêt humaine* which surrounds him and posits him as a member of the group. They know him, respect him, hate him as such, regardless of his personal qualities, for whatever he may be as an individual, he will first of all be treated as a "member." The individual becomes in these relations "un-essential." He may still have importance in another context, but in this one, all that counts for the outsider is his "membership."[49] One considers in this one person the whole group. As the incarnation of the group, he is the "being-accused" as group by the entourage. An irate customer who has waited far too long in line may very well vent his anger upon the man who, standing behind the window, stands there for the group. This identification, even though made by the entourage, is of course not the fault of the entourage, but of the group itself. The *forêt humaine*, or entourage, is interiorized by the group member. The *parti* or group is normative and is knowingly so, to both the outsider and the insider. Even so, Sartre continually insists that the objective totality of the group comes to the group through the Other. From the inside, as we have repeated again and again, there is always the interiorization of the individuals which results in a totalization, but this interiorization is caught only on the rebound against the background of the non-grouped Others. If I understand Sartre correctly at this point, it looks as if the group member needs the background of the non-group member to execute his totalization.

Sartre next turns to other matters but comes back again to this topic a few pages later.[50] It is as if he wants to make it absolutely clear that however important the individual and his power of totalization are, however efficacious the oath is as a cementing together of the group, it remains true that

[49] *Ibid.*, p. 559.
[50] *Ibid.*, p. 567.

the group gets an ontological status and its force of synthesis only through the non-member. Deep interiority, then, is actually the other side of abstract exteriority. Sartre could not be more Hegelian at this point.[51] This *being X* of the group which we reach, that is, the compression of its structures and tensions, past and future, is still possible only through the Other, the non-grouped one, even though the latter ignores them. Indeed, I can say that the *being X* of the group (the term is Sartre's) *is* through the Other's ignorance.

These views seem to be a logical development of those briefly sketched in *L'Etre et le Néant,* where community life was not a focus of study and thus was mentioned only in passing. Even so, Sartre was already making a distinction between the "us-object," when I and the Other become equivalent and unified through being the object in the world of a third person, and the "we-subject," when I do something in concert with others.[52] At that time, he considered the "we-subject" to be a very loose kind of organization, with the "I" emphasized much more than the "we" ("I am with somebody"); it was "merely a psychological structure, however, and certainly not an ontological one."[53] On the other hand, the "us-object" was considered to be "a real dimension, depending upon the existence of the third man and resulting from Being-for-the-Other."[54] It looks as if here Sartre is bringing together the "we-subject" and the "us-object," which had no strict correlation in the earlier work.[55] Now, though you and I and another interiorize a common objective, we are still not a group unless there is someone else who does not interiorize that project and is thus outside the group.

It is also interesting to recall that in *L'Etre et le Néant* Sartre denied the possibility of the existence of any form of

[51] *Ibid.,* p. 562.
[52] *Being and Nothingness,* pp. 413 ff.; *The Tragic Finale,* p. 92.
[53] *The Tragic Finale,* p. 94.
[54] *Ibid.,* p. 95.
[55] *Ibid.*

human totality, any *we humanist*, any human intersubjectivity, since in order for this to be so, there would have to be some new third being looking at us, that is, God, and for Sartre there is no God.[56] In the light of the preceding pages on *La Critique de la Raison Dialectique*, we could say that Sartre has not changed his views; the human totality still can have no ontological status as a group, since there is no one outside it.

THE INSTITUTION

There is a certain paradox in the fact that it is the outsider, the non-member who, in his viewing of the group, is necessary to constitute it, to give it its ontological status, yet it is the insider, the member, who, through his act of totalization and mediated reciprocity, gives it its practical, functional character, but can never confer its ontological character. Indeed, the practical and the ontological are in conflict. This is because, as it will appear, the member is *in* the group but never completely *one* with it.

We see this in the situation of the players ranged on the soccer field. When we consider two individuals, *A* and *B*, we see that it is through *A* that *B* knows what his own future gestures will be. In that sense we can say that there is something sovereign in the attitude of *A*, since he regulates the future of the group or of the team. Yet he is himself a member of the group, hence "his sovereignty is limited by reciprocity."[57] The same thing can be said of the others: they are each and all sovereign, and simultaneously, everyone is quasi object of the Other's regulation. There is a permanent totalization (I am sovereign), but at the same time a continual detotalization (I am quasi object). For the time being, *B*, within the activity of the team, recognizes the sovereignty of *A*, but this means also that *B* is recognized by *A*. *B* is someone who cannot be overlooked. Everyone is thus

[56] *Ibid.*
[57] *CRD*, I, p. 564.

both essential and unessential, and there is a continual tension between *immanence* and *transcendence.* "My sovereignty is never a transcendent sovereignty,"[58] but on the other hand, my dependence is never completely immanent either. The resulting conflict is obvious: to be *in* the group means that you are unable to get outside and at the same time unable to identify yourself *completely* with the group. There is a practical unity which is necessarily a contradiction with the ontological one. It is this conflict between the common and the individual which results in a new transformation: the group becomes *institution.*

We have seen that the *terreur* resulted from an awareness that the newly formed group possessed no inner cohesion, no independent status, since it was only the product of a multiple totalization, which, when dispersed, carried always the danger of disintegration. The introduction of *terreur* was therefore the necessary price for the cohesion of the group, but it was the individual who paid that price, since if the group is essential, he becomes unessential. On the other hand, there is nevertheless still something essential in him, something which cannot be taken away, for there is always "the moment of *praxis,*" which is his moment and must belong to the free individual dialectic. The group cannot *act* as a "multiple interiorization," it can only act through the individual, here and now, and this very execution of his duty brings the individual out of the group and perhaps, paradoxically, into his own exile. Against this menace, the oath can be merely a negative protection, a defense against what the group itself *induces him to do.* Thus the individual may have to travel abroad, in an act of obedience and in accordance with the oath, but the consequent contact with the outsider, which might prove to be a danger for his convictions, is a result which cannot be entirely prevented. In order to serve the group, the individual must sometimes step out of it.

Although the group is in a certain place *un contenant,*

58 *Ibid.,* p. 566.

the members cannot always be strictly limited as content within that spatial container. One does not really live spatially *within* the group; after the Bastille has been taken, the streets clear and the rebels return to their homes. In an even more important dispersion, the unity of the group depends upon its organization, with a differentiation of functions, and these functions, to be most effectively fulfilled, often require the autonomy of the individual, with his expenditure of initiative and sometimes even his physical isolation. It is indeed an irony that the future efficacy of the group depends upon "my individual freedom—that is, upon that movement which releases for me as real possibles the dangers of exclusion, physical liquidation, and betrayal."[59] This is a strange yet unavoidable paradox, implying as it does the contradiction that the practical unity of the group—its unity for action—requires and yet at the same time makes impossible an ontological unity that is close-knit.

A typical example is the movement of the "working priests" in France, the whole purpose of which was to bring the workers back to the Faith and to protect them against a Marxist materialism. In order to do so, the priests decided to live as closely as possible with the workers, to enter into their world by working side by side with them in factories, yards, and ships, and by living on the same wages, which often meant in slums and overcrowded rooms. They were to be workers in every way save one; they were in addition priests, whose function was to bring the word of God into an indifferent world, to introduce spiritual values into a materialistic milieu. The intentions of the group were clear, and so were the means. The most immediate result was, of course, that the "spatial container" of the priests was no longer the rectory or the convent and that their habitual associations were no longer with their sacerdotal colleagues. The working priest spent most of his time out of the group, even though his withdrawal was only in order to serve the group. It was,

[59] *Ibid.*, p. 570.

of course, to be anticipated that for some of them the dangers of "exile" proved to be too great and they lost their equilibrium as priests; some gave up their vows of celibacy and married, others gave in to the materialistic atmosphere and themselves became Communists. In a highly controversial decision, the Church ended the nine-year-old "experiment" in 1954, on the grounds that it carried with it too great a risk to the priests involved, and substituted a "Workers' Mission," which was to "co-ordinate" a lay apostolate with the ministry of *parish* priests in their efforts among the workers. In effect, the exiles were being called back into the group, however great the benefits of their work outside it had been.

In introducing this example, I want merely to illustrate Sartre's theory with a particularly apt case. Sartre's thoughts were certainly far from the missionary efforts of the Church, but his conclusion—"The group makes itself for action and dissolves in the action"[60]—has a particularly pertinent application in that area. Every act on the part of a member of a group could be a refusal of the oath, but such must be the fluidity and freedom of *human* individual participation. For "the individual is never entirely in the group, nor is he entirely outside it."[61]

The group reacts to this state of affairs through the introduction of a new safeguard, the *institution*, and the common individual becomes the *institutional* individual. Even if it does not constitute progress in the full sense of the word, this evolution seems to be a necessary one, for as the group goes forward, it does so at a certain price to the individual. We notice that each time a purge takes place within a group, the purpose may be to "re-establish the interior homogeneity, actually they replace the quasi-structured heterogeneity (function and power of the opposition) by a vague (or diffused) heterogeneity."[62] A purge does not change the

[60] *Ibid.*, p. 573.
[61] *Ibid.*
[62] *Ibid.*, p. 576.

minds themselves, it merely changes an outward behavior. I am in the group without being in the group as *myself*, or rather, we are all in the group and no one is outside the group, since the transcendent dimensions (by "transcendent" we mean the tendency to go outside the group) are cut out —by force. The attempt to reintroduce conformity by force constitutes a *terreur*. The *terreur*, however, is not a final solution, since one can never get hold of the Other in his otherness. Commenting on the *Terreur* of the French Revolution, Sartre considered it to be an unavoidable reaction not so much against individual freedom per se as against the menace of seriality. The historical threats of those days— invasion, counterrevolution, etc.—were such that the *Terreur* was necessary to prevent the dispersion of the Other, to keep the group itself together. In truth, the *terreur* is actually a natural development of a group, any group. It is not a minority dictating its will through violence, but it is my- self and all of us involved in a mutual distrust and a mutual hope, the hope of consolidating the group through consolidating the inert within us. The oath provides one basis of the inert, but this basis is insufficient. The *terreur* is an attempt (however vain) to produce in the group an ontologi- cal unity instead of a mere practical unity. Everyone now becomes an inorganic thing through which the purpose will be accomplished, and the freedom which is left is the free- dom of the group, not of the individual, except as he finds it through the group. When individual freedom is alienated, or entrusted to the group, and only the "function" is left, we are on our way to what we call an institution.[63] This implies two main transformations: the introduction of a certain de- sired inertia, and the appearance of authority.

As an immediate result, the institution has a greater sta- bility and a greater rigidity, but it has also by the same token a strong power of *inertia*, since it considers the ultimate purpose and the immediate function as *essential* and the in-

[63] *Ibid.*, p. 580.

dividuals as *unessential*. In this situation, any individual who proposes a change is suspect, for that is by itself a revelation of his individual freedom.[64] A *group* becomes *institution* when there is an impotency toward alteration. It remains directed upon a common objective, but it is frozen through the internal alterity, which is, as we know, characteristic of the seriality. Yet it works. There is still not an "entity" in the idealistic sense of the word, but there is a unity of alterity from now on replacing the absent unity of the group. In an interesting development, the individual is "recognized" through certain institutional prerogatives, for example, the uniform of the lieutenant or the decorations of a hero. "Command and powerlessness become reciprocal, and so they become *terreur* and inertia."[65] The *praxis* of everyone becomes reified, but the climax of degradation is reached when the individual himself wants to become a thing. One is actually destined for such an eventuality before one's birth, especially when the victim of certain military and civic categories. The fact is that when the individual is born into a certain society, he cannot escape being included in certain groups as well. Not without reason do we speak of a prefabricated inertia.[66] Here, however, we are only returning to the problem of the freedom of the individual born into a group, which was considered at the beginning of the chapter; if the accent then was upon his freedom, notwithstanding the inertia of the group, it is now upon the inertia of the group, which nevertheless limits the freedom of the individual.

A second innovation is the appearance of *authority*. The remote foundation of authority lies in the sovereignty which started with the *groupe en fusion*. At that time the "third man regulator" could be anybody. In further evolution we saw how *Fraternité-Terreur* took over as an essential determination. This approach appears to be a necessary qualification and is a form of authority, but real and stable authority

[64] *Ibid.*, pp. 581 ff.
[65] *Ibid.*, p. 585.
[66] *Ibid.*, p. 586.

comes only with the institution. Authority rests upon seriality and inertia, yet its efficiency consists, paradoxically
enough, in fighting against dispersion. In certain circumstances, as when the group is dispersed, the power of individual synthesis and totalization breaks down, and at that
moment *authority* takes over and exercises its power of
synthesis.

It does not make sense to claim that authority comes from
God, as a "divine right," or that it is an expression of the
totality, incarnating some form of collective sovereignty.
Both interpretations must be rejected according to Sartre,
since (1) there is no God and (2) there is no ontological
unity of the group as such. Actually we should not look for
any "metaphysical" foundation of authority, for there is
none. It arises naturally from within the group, from the
concession of its members, for in fact, "every man is sovereign,"[67] but as we have seen, in practice there are limitations, and these limitations come from other men. We are
all quasi sovereign within the group, but we cede a certain
measure of our sovereignty to the group in return for the
greater possibilities of unified action. It is now our task to
explore what makes one of us capable of blocking the circularity of the third man and of becoming *the* sovereign.

Before turning to this, let us insist once more that the
sovereign does not incarnate some form of collective sovereignty. That sort of "mystical" thing does not exist in the
group; in its stead, there is only a multitude of quasi sovereigns. Among them, the sovereign is regulator. His presence results in the impossibility of every third man becoming
regulator, for he (*the* sovereign) is mediator of communications, a function he has obtained through explicit or implicit
concessions. One mediates now through certain offices—"*des
bureaux*"—and the sovereign himself becomes the "*indépassable*" entity.[68] One cannot go around him; he stops the
flow of circularity. The common imperative ordering the

[67] *Ibid.*, p. 588.
[68] *Ibid.*, pp. 591, 592.

group to strive toward a common purpose reaches me or returns to me through the sovereign. This is what is commonly called an order. Through the oath I am obliged to be obedient, and if I want to protect the group, I cannot not be obedient. From now on my freedom is alienated, or rather my freedom is in the sovereign because I want it to be there. Of course, this transferal suffers a limitation in the individual, who, however obedient he may be, is nevertheless the one who is going to execute the order and who exercises therein a certain freedom of action. If he is a soldier, he is the one who calculates the distance, pulls the trigger at the right moment, etc.—the immediate decisions are still his.

The ultimate freedom of decision of what to do and not to do nevertheless belongs to the sovereign. He reinteriorizes the multiplicity of institutions, and mediates between them; through him, military organization, finance, law, education, etc., are kept together. He is the ultimate regulator and the one beyond whom no one else can go, as we have said, the "*indépassable*."[69] This does not prevent him from being a "common" individual and from losing himself in that "common" aspect, so that it makes sense to shout, "*Le roi est mort, vive le roi!*" King, president, pope in their function, however exalted, merely temporalize the eternal.

The act of obedience is actually a presence of the authority in the individual and somehow it brings him nearer to the other individuals, for in the act of obedience he becomes the same as the others.[70] The institutional Other is not, however, the serial Other. The presence of authority testifies to an institutional monolithism, which was not the case in the seriality and true to the origin of the word, the monolith as a single block of stone *shaped* into a monument, the institution is a kind of monument, with the institutional others as its stones. For all that, Sartre still energetically rejects the implication that authority gives the institution an ontological status as one being or entity. It does not *con-*

[69] *Ibid.*, p. 596.
[70] *Ibid.*, p. 597.

stitute an incarnation of the group, but merely *acts* as an organ of integration and in this sense, the metaphor of the monument is misleading. The institution resists change and rests upon a certain inertness on the part of its members, but it is not shaped once and for all; the verb must be kept in the present progressive tense of *shaping*.

Institutional monolithism keeps persons and things together through a variety of means, and among these may be included that of the *terreur*. This is not always true, but we do find that the group that is in a process of institutionalization indeed lives under *une autorité terreur*. "*Produit par la terreur, le souverain doit devenir l'agent responsable de la terreur*."[71] The sovereign wants unity and gets it, but his method follows a biological pattern, that is, the "unity of the organism: his right hand trusts his left hand and no other hand.[72] This beautiful quotation expresses the less beautiful spirit of suspicion which is present in the institutionalized group. Paradoxically enough, the leader wants a sort of unity which the common individual cannot easily accept, for the latter is, in fact, not part of an "organism" and to consider him as such is to force him into an alien mold. The result is that the individual becomes a sort of quasi-inorganic entity whose inertia carries and executes the orders of the sovereign.[73] Indeed, he must empty himself of his own individuality and submit mechanically, *perinde ac cadaver* (Sartre himself here quotes the Ignatian motto). Although in some circumstances there can be a mystification or provisional enthusiasm, it can only be provisional and as soon as the emotion passes, the masses return to their molecular dispersion.

At the origin of the practical, necessary introduction of a certain individual as sovereign, there lies a double element: his own qualities of power and the lack of power among other individuals. Sartre cites as an example of power in a

[71] *Ibid.*, p. 600.
[72] *Ibid.*
[73] *Ibid.*, p. 601.

potential sovereign the medieval chevalier, who had a horse while the others fought on foot. One must remember, indeed, that in all or at least most cases, there was first a *de facto* exercise of power and afterward a legalization or an attempt to excuse it *de jure*.[74] All this is an intrinsic part of the gradual institutionalization of the group. In and through the institution, everyone frees himself of his freedom and finds it again on the summit, that is, in the hands of the sovereign. It is in the hands of one person, but he *has* the authority now because he *had* it then.

Sartre seems to imply here that all sovereignty is a *pis-aller*, that is, one follows one man blindly, for fear of worse adventures. Yet it always remains difficult to say whether in the relation between the sovereign and "his" people, he belongs to the people or the people belong to him. No a priori solution can be given here, and the concrete circumstances of sovereign and people must reveal whether or not the sovereign incarnates the end and wishes of the people or whether they are merely his instrument. In the belief of this writer these passages strongly echo Hegel in their concept of freedom. It is not necessary to go into Hegel's very complex notions on the subject, but we might recall here one form, his "subjective freedom," which is a self-curtailed freedom, according to which the individual grants obedience and devotion to a rationally organized State.[75] It is an attitude based not upon fear and habit but upon conviction. It implies allegiance not exactly to a group but to a State, which, according to Hegel, is an entity based upon reason and not upon instinct, as would be the case, for instance, with the family. Not all of this applies to Sartre's freedom in the group, but it is obvious that a parallel can be made, since some form of self-discipline and self-restraint seems to

[74] *Ibid.*, p. 602. This applies not only to medieval chevaliers but also, in the opinion of this writer, to our own reactions as well. First we throw the bomb on Hiroshima and afterward look for legal and moral justifications.

[75] See Hegel, *The Philosophy of History*, trans. J. Sibree (New York, 1956), p. 39.

be attached to both forms of freedom. That any parallel at all can be made is striking when one considers how Sartre's concept of freedom, purely speculative and unrestrained in *L'Etre et le Néant*, has become more limited when viewed in the concrete.

Returning to the medieval chevalier and his rise to power because he literally towered above his contemporaries who were on foot, we can discover an analogy, claims Sartre, with various modern situations, where certain groups and their leaders range their power against the helplessness of the non-grouped serialities.[76] For example, we can point to the powerful publisher William Randolph Hearst, who dictatorially governed a chain of newspapers (his group) and in this way inflicted *his* opinion upon the public opinion, that is, upon the mind of the seriality, or non-grouped multitude of readers. His power, since it was organized and put into print, was great, and it became even greater because of the very powerlessness of the others, who were less vocal. In short, he rode while the others walked, and Hearst himself became in a way a unity of his readers, an abstract unity that is. The Hearst Empire reigned over a Hearst mentality, and although there were unorganized protests, no real legitimation was necessary, for here too, to exist was to be legal.

STATE AND SOCIETY

The intention of the preceding remarks was not so much to give the historical origin of sovereignty as to show that it is dialectically intelligible. The chevalier has ridden and continues to ride through history, with power pitted dialectically against powerlessness and becoming more and more concentrated in the hands of fewer and fewer persons. The conclusion was that the group in its gradual process of institutionalization comes more and more to be under the control of a sovereign.

This sovereignty becomes a more complex concept when

[76] *CRD*, I, p. 605.

it is viewed not solely as a phenomenon of the group, of all groups, but when it is seen as operating in society at large. "Society" is itself not strictly a group, as "group" has been defined, but rather a plurality of groups and of their relations to the serialities outside them, all of these—groups and serialities—within some container or limited space.[77] This ensemble also has a sovereign, and this sovereign is called the "State." The State is power, and this is so because one group, called the State, is conceded authority by the impotent seriality of the other groups. The State does not express the wishes of the multitude, according to Sartre; this would be mere mystification. It is, more coldly, merely a *processus* of institutionalization and an inevitable result of a society of groups protecting itself, which, once established, calls itself "the *legitimate* government." There is nothing legitimate or illegitimate about it; it merely *is*. It is a factual *processus*. "I am obedient because I can do nothing else and that gives pseudolegitimacy . . . to the sovereign."[78] Thus Sartre once more sees in the concept of State something fatalistic and in the submission of the individual (and of his group) something inevitable. The State is authority and can be defined, in the terms of Mascolo, as the unity of all the impossibilities which define the exploited individual negatively.[79] The State has started as a group which gradually, from its need for unity of command, deposited the sovereignty in the hands of one man. This sovereign group manipulates the underlying collectives and groups as a series, and its own authority is nothing but power wielded by virtue of the powerlessness of the outside seriality. This and this only makes the sovereignty of the State intelligible.

It is in this light that we can understand how the State identifies itself with the dominating class in a society (in case the society is not a classless society) and keeps the op-

[77] *Ibid.*, p. 608.
[78] *Ibid.*, p. 609.
[79] *Ibid.*, p. 610.

pressed class what it is, through force if necessary.[80] A revolution can alter the situation and a new class become the dominating class, but of course the State does not want its equilibrium disturbed, since it may find itself replaced by another group, which then becomes the State. Sartre thus finds Marx to be completely consistent in his assertion that the State is maintained at all costs by the bourgeoisie.[81] Since the State is, in fact, synonymous with the dominating class, the bourgeoisie, it will strive ever to preserve things as they are and keep class struggle to a minimum. This brings, then, a strange contradiction, since the State claims to be a sovereign unity of all classes, yet actually identifies itself with one of them. Although it claims to be national, it favors the dominating class. Even within this one class, an internal crisis remains always a threat, and the State may meet its downfall not only from the outside—as in a rebellion of the oppressed class—but also from the inside, that is, from a split in its own group. Thus, the 9th Thermidor, which marked the end of the *Terreur* and of Robespierre, did not originate among outsiders but arose from within, as a crisis of authority within the governing group. The constant threat of annihilation causes the governing group ever to strengthen its power and concentrate its authority in the hands of one person or a restricted group. In order to do so, it must ensure the permanent powerlessness of the others, and this it does through keeping them in serialities, which it may manipulate for its own purposes and preservation.

GROUPS, SERIALITY, AND EXTERO-CONDITIONING

The analysis of this manipulation of the serialities by these sovereign groups includes some of Sartre's most perceptive

[80] *Ibid.*

[81] On this idea in Marx, see *The Communist Manifesto* (New York, 1948), p. 11, and *The German Ideology* (New York, 1939) in the section on Feuerbach. The same idea is less explicit but nonetheless present in *The Eighteenth Brumaire of Louis Bonaparte* (New York, no date), pp. 57 ff.

passages. The helplessness of the individual in the face of an increasingly organized and institutionalized society about him has been explored by many in recent years, but Sartre's pages shed a new light upon the phenomena that have been observed, through their attempt to give a philosophical explanation, from a point of view with which we are already familiar. Thus, in Sartrian terms, groups work upon serialities, that is, upon ungrouped individuals, exerting an exterior control upon the decision of the individual that has been called by "some American sociologists" *extero-conditioning* (Sartre approves of the term and takes it over), as opposed to *intero-conditioning,* which also implies a limitation of freedom, but is a limitation which comes from the inside of man, from the individual's own decision, as when he freely takes an oath.[82] In intero-conditioning, the individual interiorizes the common purpose and accepts his function and the functions of others as the necessary structure of the group; in this sense, and in this sense only, is he "the same as" the others; his inertia comes from the oath. The manipulated seriality, on the contrary, has no common purpose, and the sovereign group tries to see that it doesn't acquire one, since its metamorphosis into a group is the first step toward rebellion or revolution. The inertia of the series comes from its impotency, and everyone is in it only to the extent that his action and his thoughts come to him from the others. The object of the sovereign group, then, is to condition everyone through making him Other among Others, in other words, through keeping him inert and passive. It is not enough, however, for the group to *extero-condition* the series merely through its impotency and passivity. A more active co-operation of the serial member must be enlisted, and this is done through "fascinating" the Other, every Other, with a deception, the deception of believing that in acting like the Other, he is acting like the totality.[83] This is the trap of extero-conditioning: the sovereign plans to act upon the

[82] *CRD*, I, p. 614. Sartre does not specify who these sociologists are.
[83] *Ibid.*, p. 615.

series in such a way that it feels as if it is totalizing itself. Says the sovereign group, for example, American funeral directors, "Everyone owes this respect to his Loved One, that he ride in a Cadillac (for the first time) to his grave"; echoes the member of the series, "Everyone else gives this kind of funeral, therefore I must, too, or I will not be respecting my Loved One." In following the tradition, set by the funeral directors themselves, he feels himself to be part of a practical totality, those who in their mourning pay their respects to the dead. It is important for the Funeral Industry to keep in the public image certain material accompaniments equated with dignity, respect, and love. The series must act as a totality, the others do it and I, as Other, do it, but the unity of that totality must be of the escaping type, everywhere and nowhere, for if it were to assemble and discuss the expensiveness of the modern funeral, its possible incompatibilities with religious or philosophical beliefs, that is, if it were to organize, to totalize itself as a group with the common purpose of objecting to the extero-conditioning of the funeral directors, it would make possible a rebellion against that sovereign group.

Sartre found a simple example of extero-conditioning during his trip to the United States in 1946, when he was struck by the weekly announcement on the radio of a list of "ten best-selling records."[84] The implication, of course, was, "Buy this record, for it is a best seller," in total disregard of any independent value judgment of the eventual buyer. Sometimes another argument was used, the judgment of a group of experts, as when a "board" makes the selections for a "record club." In both cases, the outside opinion, whether determined by the "people" through their purchases or by the "experts" chosen for the panel, does not necessarily reflect my view, but merely the view of the Other. The same techniques are used by book publishers, who have made "best seller" a household word; Sartre turns for his example

[84] *Ibid.*

in this field to a French one, the Prix Goncourt, where once more we find the *actio in distans* of a group upon the series through the intermediacy of a jury, the authority of which is not contested, even though it is self-bestowed.[85] (Actually the judges might be competent, but they are still imposing their views, however well-founded, upon others.) We see in these examples that the members of a series, facing the record companies and the book publishers, are powerless.

It should be noticed also how, through the announcement of the sale of a certain record, a "best seller," there is a mutation of quantity into quality. The supposition is that this must be a good record, since many have been sold. The series through its directed choice has built up a hierarchy of values. Yet, however truthful all this may appear, there is a lie underneath, if it be only the fact that the number of copies of a certain book or record sold is never given in proportion to the total sales of books or records. In addition, there is a deception involved in taking the week as a chronological limit: the purchases have to be made in *this* week, and the whole "psychology" consists in showing the person who has not bought the record what he has missed during that span of time. He is an accused man, a defendant! Fortunately, he can still repair his mistake, for there is another week coming; it is characteristic of the advertising in this field to speak always of the future, of "the record you *will* love." The group wants constantly to indoctrinate in him that he must act like the Other, but ironically, the Other is no one but himself, for every Other is leaning upon the Other in a series, and he listens to the record which has been chosen by the Other and by himself *as Other*. Ultimately what he is doing when he buys is what the group wants him to do.[86]

The purpose of the sovereign group is clear: to sell as many records as possible, through making it appear that the totality buys. This is extero-conditioning. It gives the individual the illusion that he is a member of a totality. In fact, it

[85] *Ibid.*, p. 617.
[86] *Ibid.*, p. 619.

"pushes the alterity into the extreme, since it determines the
serial individual to do as the others do in order to be as they
are."[87] If he continues, the buyer will finally have the same
collection as the Other's, which is actually no one's. For the
totality of which he feels himself a part is a false totality,
directed from the outside, as a determination of everyone
by the others, and of no one by himself. The "everyone" of
whom the transcending group speaks—"they are all buying
this record"—is in fact no one; paradoxically, each one, in
trying to be like the illusory everyone, contributes to and
constitutes the illusion, but it nevertheless remains without
foundation—each one tries to be everyone, but everyone is
no one.

Sartre sees this principle of extero-conditioning to be most
pervasive in the more advanced capitalistic countries, where
it is to the interest of industry and commerce, whatever
may be their rivalries, to be united in extero-conditioning
the masses to buy more and to adapt their budgets not to
their personal needs and tastes but to the requirements of
the national economy. Full production and a "healthy" national economy depend upon the consumer, who must be
convinced that he needs more and more things. The frantic
buying at the Christmas season represents a united effort of
the transcending group—including bankers, who sponsor
Christmas clubs; department stores, which enthrone Santa
Claus in the midst of seductive displays in their toy depart-
ments; municipal governments, which decorate the streets
of the city to create an "atmosphere" (for buying); etc.—
and if there is an individual protest here and there, to the
effect that this may possibly not incarnate the "true spirit"
of Christmas, it must be drowned out by the noise of carols
over the loud-speaker and more performances of Mr. Scrooge.
For the sales statistics calculated in the more sober month of
January are a crucial index to the state of the national economy, and in order that they may reflect a flourishing condition, the consumer who is accustomed to a certain degree

[87] *Ibid.*, p. 620.

of prudence and thrift, who in other words is intero-conditioned, must be wooed away from his independent thinking and choices and buy like the Others. He must be made to feel he is a Mr. Scrooge if there are not piles of presents heaped about his Christmas tree, as there are under all the other Christmas trees.

It is not really possible to extero-condition the adult unless he has been habituated to this conditioning as a child. In other words, he must be conditioned to being conditioned, and Sartre finds that this is indeed the case in the American schools. There everyone is taught "to be the expression of all the Others" and the one who is most perfectly Other among all the Others is the most rewarded.[88]

Sartre holds that a knowledge of these structures of extero-conditioning is of vital importance in understanding certain historical events which in the past have been interpreted as the result of a spontaneous movement of the masses. One discovers that in actuality they were a result of a systematic manipulation of the serialities by certain sovereign groups. The active anti-Semitism of the German *petite bourgeoisie* under Hitler, for example, was not a spontaneous movement but rather a systematic extero-conditioning by a group upon the series. The sovereign group, in this case the Nazis, made it appear that "everyone" (who was no one) hated the Jews —there were signs of this hatred everywhere, on the radio, in the newspapers, on the walls, in caricatures, definitions repeated a hundred times, etc.[89] The Jewish mannequin was draped with such hateful characteristics that it was not considered out of order to smash the store window to destroy the image. The propaganda of the sovereign group served two purposes: that of supplying a concrete designation—"the Jew" is this kind of person, hence worthy of your hatred; and that of supplying an attitude for the seriality—everyone feels this way, hence I must. The hatred of "the Jew" was in each member of the series the hatred felt by the Other, not

[88] *Ibid.*, p. 621.
[89] *Ibid.*, p. 622.

by himself; the Others all hate the Jews, it is the climate of opinion, against which I dare not rebel. The government, then, set up this feeling that the Other was anti-Jewish, and all these Others together had a kind of unity, nourished by the mass media. Some gave in to the hatred incited by the propaganda of the sovereign group and became themselves the pratico-inert agents of a directed pogrom; these were the name-callers and the window smashers. Everyone else became involved as well, however, if only that when a Jew was arrested or executed by order of the government, the lack of protest was a passive assent to the action of the Other. Everyone was an extero-conditioned criminal, to the extent that he assumed the crime of the government insofar as it was committed in another place and by the Other.[90]

The acceptance by all the others of the violence of the sovereign group produces only a false unity, however, a unity which rests on two false bases. First, the "acceptance" is only the impotency of resisting it, not a genuine acceptance, so the active persecutor is not actually acting in the name of any real totality. The practice of the sovereign group is to intensify the separations through fear, distrust, propaganda, so that there is an illusion of unity in accepting the pogrom, when actually it is impossible to realize any other unity than that one. The separation of members is immense. Second, the serial acceptance of the persecutions increases the separation of its own members, one from another, since each one accepts as Other, not as himself. At the moment of the pillage or execution, each one realizes that nothing can stop his passive participation, since he and the others are not themselves in danger and there is no possibility of the series totalizing itself into a group with a common objective. Even were there some more noble objective than self-defense, say "love of humanity" to totalize the series, the sovereign group introduces distrust as a supplementary factor to keep them separated. Thus no one acts against, and in not acting

[90] *Ibid.*, pp. 622–23.

against, all are tacitly helping to perpetrate the crime. Everyone is made, *from the outside*, the Other responsible for the violence committed by the Other.[91] Where "collective responsibility" is serial responsibility, it doesn't matter whether one inwardly assents or refuses.

Furthermore, the fact that there is no opposition to the pillaging keeps the persecutors in a series, not pushing them toward any organized effort. The pillaging is allowed by the government only as a series of isolated, dispersed incidents, with the agents acting always in the milieu of the Other, never as an organized group. The sovereign group wants to prevent organization at all costs, and the trick is to draw from the masses the desired manifestations of anti-Semitism while at the same time keeping them in a series. Indeed, it is characteristic of any sovereign group which wants to exterocondition the outsider in the series to oppose any organized reaction. The funeral directors who urge costly funerals, the merchants who begin to decorate their store windows with Christmas trees before Thanksgiving do not mind scattered criticism too much, but they are upset by any attempt at organized opposition, which would transform the series upon which they work into an opposing group. For the sovereign group cannot tolerate any *organization* of the series that would give it the power to fight back.

EXTERO-CONDITIONING AND THE GOVERNMENT

This *"monde de l'Autre"* is the world of government as well as of business;[92] we have already seen the tragic consequences of this in the case of the Hitlerian regime. We do not have to look to such extreme examples as a Fascist dictatorship, however, to discover that the action of the State toward its subordinates consists of a gigantic extero-conditioning. Even in the democratic countries, the electoral system is based upon an elective body that is viewed as an

[91] *Ibid.*, p. 623.
[92] *Ibid.*, p. 625.

immense and passive multitude, "and the list of the elected candidates does not better express the *will* of the nation than the list of best-selling records expresses the taste of the customers."[93] According to Sartre, the only means by which that will could be truly expressed would be by a revolutionary regrouping that would combat the inertia of the institutions, but this the government in power of course wants to prevent.

We have already seen earlier in the chapter how the group which was organized in freedom becomes increasingly institutionalized and that what was accepted in freedom deteriorates into inertia. The individual is in the group not as himself but as Other, and anyone who proposes a change is suspect, since this is a revelation of his individual freedom. The unity of the institutional group is a unity of alterity, and the freedom which is left is the freedom of the group, not of the individual. It is the group, its immediate functions and ultimate purposes which are essential, at the cost of the individual, who becomes unessential. Furthermore, the freedom of the group is in the hands of a sovereign (person or restricted group) and in the act of obedience to that sovereign, each individual becomes the same as the others. The institution keeps its members together through a variety of means, among which are *terreur* and extero-conditioning; at this point, we have reached a new constitution of the group, the stage of bureaucracy.

Bureaucracy is a complex hierarchical system of levels, the lowest of which is supposed to have a direct contact with the masses, the needs and wishes of whom it conveys to the next level, and so on, up to the summit. What actually happens, however, is that the lowest rank is only an inert, inorganic instrument of the rank above it; the role of each rank, manipulated by the groups superior to it, is to exterocondition the others. Surrounded by series, based on the passivity of the masses at the bottom, each level is itself serialized and passive, for the sovereign group at the top encourages the inertia of all the collectives below. The sub-

[93] *Ibid.*, p. 624, footnote.

ordinate groups seem to be actual mediators, but they act only as Others, never as themselves; though they are themselves sovereigns (over those below), they are so only in the "milieu of the Other."[94] From one end of the hierarchy to the other, the objects governed by the laws of exteriority govern other objects under them. "The paralyzation of the system climbs necessarily to the summit, where the sovereign alone is untouched."[95]

We can see an example of these mechanisms in operation in the approach of the conservative South toward the problem of desegregation. The Negro population had for years had its needs and desires established, if possible, from the outside; thus, "they're all right if they keep their place" was the extero-conditioned white feeling, and the colored maid who devotedly served the family was often devotedly loved back, but as the maid. When the maids and gardeners wanted to work in offices and factories, teach school, become lawyers and doctors, and realized that their segregated schools were inadequate for their aspirations, some "enlightened" whites conceded that they might indeed expect facilities that were "equal but separate." The real feeling and need of the Negroes, the anguished cry for a recognition of their dignity as human beings was smothered in seriality and went unheard. At each level of the hierarchy of the white society in which they lived, the people were extero-conditioned to think of the Negro as inferior, or at least as different. If an official were to believe otherwise, on his own, he would still be held back from voicing or acting on his opinion through the mistrust of his equals, who might not invite his daughter to their parties, or fear of his superiors, who might relieve him of his position. The superior who dismisses the anti-segregationist, the neighbor who shuns him, may not want to do so, but they do so as Other, because the Others want it. Thus no one dares to protest effectively, and the voice of the governor, reinforced by some scattered demon-

[94] *Ibid.*, p. 624.
[95] *Ibid.*, p. 626.

strations of segregationists against the Negro, is the voice of a silent state. There may be many who deplore his policy, but they are paralyzed by their serial isolation, one from another.

In short, "the difference between the local director and those he directs is not great . . . both live, act, and think serially."[96] Each director is for his superior simply a piece of inorganic matter, an inert and passive entity, albeit "a superior instance of the seriality"[97] of those he represents. If he were to exercise his autonomy and individual initiative, if he really did act as "sovereign" over those in his command, he would be suspect. He is held back by distrust of his equals, or "serial *terreur*," by his own extero-conditioning, and by fear of his superiors. Sometimes there are rebellions and protests, but the one who rebels or protests or innovates is always "Other, stranger, suspect, leader."[98] His equals and superiors maintain that they govern in the general interest, while the *"meneur,"* the rebel, is an anti-sovereign who would govern on the basis of his own personal interest. His cry is an isolated, serial cry that cannot reach the ears of those who are extero-conditioned not to listen. When it is heard, it is often too late. General Billy Mitchell, the leader who early saw the importance of air power, was court-martialed for his initiative, and it remained for a later generation to see his plea reach the summit. In the days before the French Revolution, the king and his counselors were not really aware of the extent of the seething discontent of the populace. The deep and real needs of living and suffering people never traveled up the ladder of bureaucracy to the king, and when they did, it was too late, for they had by then formed the basis of a group, a group which refused all mediation because it wanted to constitute its own sovereignty. It was too late for any concessions, however great, for revolution had come.

Bureaucracy is, in summary, "the extero-conditioning of

[96] *Ibid.*, p. 625.
[97] *Ibid.*, p. 626.
[98] *Ibid.*, p. 625.

the inferior multiplicity; distrust and serial *terreur* at the level of one's equals; the annihilation of organisms in obedience to a superior organism (each dissolves in himself his organic individuality as an uncontrollable factor of multiplicity and bases himself with his peers in an organic unity of the superior)."[99]

Curiously enough, Sartre maintains that bureaucracy and red tape are worse in the "socialistic" states (his euphemism for any communistic regime) since, all things considered, there are still more open tensions and complaints in the bourgeois democracies. The socialistic regimes are immobilized by their policies, while the parliamentary regimes remain in ebullition, or as Lévi-Strauss puts it, they are "*à chaud*."[100] As a consequence, the sovereign is more aware of what happens, and has to consult the dominating class which brought him into power, while in a socialistic state, the sovereign or the sovereign group turns on top, in a vacuum. Having no struggle or control through other groups, it has only itself to control itself. The result is an increase in bureaucracy and an eventual evolution into a police state, which tolerates no control outside itself.

This is one of the weaknesses of the socialistic world, and notwithstanding its accomplishments, there is still a great need for "debureaucratization, decentralization, and democratization."[101] Whatever may be Sartre's sympathy for socialism and leftist movements, he shows little enthusiasm for their realization in the "socialistic state," as, in the prime example history has given us, Russia and her satellites. There the "dictatorship of the proletariat" has never come about; indeed, it could not come about because the idea itself is absurd and contradictory to the laws of dialectical reason. At first it is too early to install a dictatorship of the proletariat; we see this in the Revolution of 1917, when a group of only a few, not particularly representative of the proletariat, took

[99] *Ibid.*, p. 626.
[100] *Ibid.*, p. 627.
[101] *Ibid.*, p. 629.

over. The sovereignty of this group "was from the point of view of the masses neither legitimate nor illegitimate," it simply was, and adds Sartre sarcastically, "Its practical legality results from the fact that the sovereign has built up his illegality through his faults and through his crimes; so History has judged."[102] At present it is too late to install a dictatorship of the proletariat, in the sense of a real exercise of power by a working class which has totalized itself. The exercise of power by a combination of an active and sovereign group together with the passive seriality of workers makes no sense whatever. Indeed, as we have already said, the whole concept of a "dictatorship of the proletariat" is an impossible one, since the group can never become, in any form, a hyperorganism.[103]

Sartre's solution, then, does not consist in any hope for the future establishment of an impossibility. He sees the sins of Russian socialism—bureaucracy, *terreur*, and the personality cultus—and admits that in the era of Stalin, the sovereign, through these means, became the *indépassable*, the one beyond which no one could go, to the extent that state, party, and personality were, for all practical purposes, one. He would like to see, on the contrary, the relinquishing by the sovereign of his monopoly of the group ("democratization") and the "progressive wilting of the State in favor of a regrouping of the different extero-conditioned serialities"[104] (decentralization and debureaucratization). In the era of Stalinism, Stalin himself took over the function of the multiplicity, and the individual interiorization of a multiple activity was rendered impossible; there was no multiplicity to interiorize, *praxis* was *processus*, inert and inevitable. This was extreme centralization and bureaucracy.

On the contrary, the constituting dialectic must develop as free organic *praxis* and as a human relation of reciprocity, but in so doing, it also decides the possibilities and impossi-

[102] *Ibid.*, pp. 629 ff.
[103] *Ibid.*, p. 630.
[104] *Ibid.*

bilities of the common *praxis* and introduces its own inertia. The critical experience makes possible, however, the maintenance of the double character of *praxis* and *processus,* *praxis* as activity, *processus* as inertia, with both the possibilities that are opened up and the limitations which are the inevitable concomitant.

Sartre concludes with a summary that emphasizes once more the increasing institutionalization of the group as an inevitable phenomenon. The same air of fatalism which we have observed earlier hangs heavily over this passage, with only the previous plea for "the critical experience" to lift the oppressive weight of inertia. Thus the unity of the group is seen to lie in its object, in the groups exterior to it, in each of its members as excluded third, ultimately, in the activity of the sovereign, to whom power is delegated. The power is never really *in* the group itself, except through the powerlessness of its members, a powerlessness which gives the material functions a greater power and inertia. The true efficiency of the group lies in its immersion in the matter, but where this happens completely, where *praxis* becomes *processus* and action becomes inert and passive, the common ends are no longer controllable. Without ceasing to be the common ends of the group, they become destinies.[105]

[105] *Ibid.,* p. 631.

Chapter VIII

THE GROUP IN THE WORLD OF
THE CONCRETE

Sartre at this point begins to slow down the progress of his dialectical examination in order to summarize what has been said before and to "locate" his present position. We will remember that in the very beginning of his *Critique* he emphasized the concrete character of every event in history and the fact that the event was made by the man, as well as the man by the event. The idea of reciprocity was early introduced, whereby a group in action is reacted upon and itself reacts to the reactions it has itself provoked. Life was seen as movement, a mutual involvement of man and his universe, reacting and interacting upon each other. Every group as a totality may have a status, its rules and administration, but that status is an open, detotalized one, subject to further growth or eventual death, according to the members within it and its interactions in the world. In this earlier statement of what was to follow, Sartre was opposing to the rigidity and dogmatism of Marxism wrongly interpreted the insights of existentialism, which would correct the dogmatic dialectic of Marxism with a critical dialectic that would follow the movement of history itself. He is thus in line with the objectives stated at the beginning of his study when he attempts to place the "group" in the world of the concrete.

This "localization," however, does not make these passages any easier to read; indeed, they are as difficult as ever. One of the most frequent criticisms of Sartre's book is that he has shown an utter disregard for his reader, from the Table of

Contents, which, with its four uninformative entries, might better have been omitted, to the carelessness of his text—repeated sentences, uncompleted subdivisions (*A*'s with no *B*'s, 1's with no 2's), parentheses that are opened but not closed.[1] This lack of regard for the reader, interpreted even more strongly by some as actual contempt, is ironic in view of the fact that the author calls upon one to do so much. Thus everyone is expected to totalize the dialectic on one's own behalf and to perform a critical rethinking of history, not to accept blindly such rigid interpretations as those of some Marxists. The dialectic which moves through history is not merely deterministic; at every stage—individual, serial, group —the free individual intervenes. If he cannot control, he can at least be *aware* of the events that are operating. This is actually the purpose of the *Critique*—to make the operations of history intelligible; others should also make the same attempt, even if the moment of intelligibility be only for an instant. Sartre struggles to see man not as a hopeless pawn of a dogmatic dialectic, of the "forces of History," but as a man who, if not in charge of his own destiny, is at least aware of it.

More important than the technical details but in the same spirit, the text itself is needlessly difficult and disorganized so that the reader must struggle to find his way. That way, notwithstanding its detours, has led the reader, by means of the critical experience, or the "*critique de la raison dialectique*," to see that there is at all levels an indissoluble unity of the organic and inorganic, on the level of the individual, of the series, of the group, and of history itself. It is now Sartre's purpose to show this once more, in a more concrete way, and the emphasis of these pages is upon the relation between the group, which we are now prepared to understand, and other collectives, as they operate in the world. Sartre attempts to keep all his arguments in line and feels

[1] The Table of Contents is as follows: Questions of method—page 13. Critique of dialectical reason—page 113: Book I—page 163; Book II—page 379.

the need to bring in once more the problem of scarcity as
the remote cause of the genesis of the group. The reader has
the feeling that the combination of the different elements
within his dialectic at times gets a little out of hand. It is
our task—when Sartre has forgotten it—to keep in mind the
general trend of the argument, and when necessary, to close
the parenthesis for him.

THE GROUP AND ITS RELATION WITH THE COLLECTIVE AND WITH THE *matiére ouvrée*

As we have already seen, the *praxis* of the group takes
place not in a vacuum but in a world of matter, where it
objectifies itself outside itself and thus somewhat escapes the
control of its originators. This objectification, or impact of
the group, has three consequences. First, it can be said that
it directly affects the environmental field and produces definite changes in the other groups and serialities of that field.
Once a group comes into existence within a certain milieu,
it asserts itself dialectically. Sartre here remains faithful to
a position with which the reader has become amply familiar.
He does not believe that philosophical exploration has done
all that it can when it merely enumerates a certain number
of entities and presents each of them in a static way, totally
ignoring their mutual relations. "Essential analysis" is not
sufficient; truthful investigation must be undertaken in the
awareness that there exists a flowing life between the multiple human situations, such as groups and other collectives.[2]

It is to be expected, then, that the group will not only
have an impact upon the environing materiality, but that it
will itself feel the rebounding of that impact, as the second
consequence of its *praxis*. Thus the impact of the group
upon its environment may very well appear to be a success
in its *immediate* field—Sartre gives as an example the occu-

[2] The term "essential analysis" as opposed to "existential analysis"
was used by Professor P. Fransen in his article "Three Ways of Dogmatic Thought," *Cross Currents* (Spring 1963), pp. 142 ff.

pation of a country by a victorious army, where the conquest seems to be complete and the goals of the victor obtained. Yet one must look beyond the initial victory to see that by virtue of the omnipresent dialectic, the effect of the all-powerful, conquering group is somehow robbed of its apparent strength and inevitably results in some form of alienation for the victor himself. The solitude of the victor is never an unchallenged one. What this may produce in the future we cannot say, and it doesn't really matter in our present examination; the important point is that things have to be understood in an historical progression. One cannot, furthermore, consider mankind as *one* man. There is, on the contrary, a continual growth based upon the plurality of men, upon the action and reaction of the groups themselves.[3] Thus the dispersion is one not only in time but also of a multiple interiorization. It is for this reason that the objectification of the group—the impact or result of its *praxis*—often escapes the group. Coming back to our example, we see that it is extremely difficult for the occupation forces to foresee not only where and when and how underground movements of resistance will emerge, but also what will be its own reaction to them. Any prophetic insight is obscured by the fact that in addition to the *synchronic* effect of the group, the immediate or simultaneously produced effect, one must also take into account what Sartre calls the *diachronic* effect, the element of duration. He is stressing here a new emphasis which has become fashionable in modern philosophy, that things happen in time, and thus, that what does not happen now may very well come to pass later. All this becomes even more stringent when action and reaction stretch over more than one generation. The accomplishments of the "original" group, that is, the group in its first phase, are often transformed by the children, who "steal" the intentions of their fathers and gradually replace them with other goals. The long-range results of a group *praxis* can be seen in the after-

3 *CRD*, I, p. 634.

math of the first World War, contrasting France and Germany, where the "expensive victory" resulted in a strong pacifist movement in France, while in Germany it produced feelings of revenge which crystallized in the world of Nazism and renewed dreams of conquest. Such are the diachronic effects of the group *praxis* that today's victor becomes tomorrow's victim.

Sartre's third point underlines the fact that the group itself undergoes the counterfinality of its actions through a slow but irrevocable ossification. We have already described in detail the sad decline of the group as it becomes organization and institution, and the accompanying "petrification" of the individual group member. Here Sartre pushes his description still further in maintaining not only that institutionalism is the previously designated *"pratique petrifiée"*—ossified action—but also that the action is no longer even its own action but originates from outside the group.[4] Studies by American sociologists of sales techniques used in the United States have shown, according to Sartre, that the salesman must first *manipulate himself*, that is, interiorize goals which are not his own, before he is able to manipulate others.[5] In other words, in order to persuade the customer that he must buy what the Other is buying, he must himself become Other. ("I have one myself and could not do without it.") This "world of the Other" in which each group member lives has already been amply described in the previous chapter. The nuance which Sartre wishes to introduce here is that the techniques which are developed to extero-condition the series outside the group horizontally end by exteroconditioning the group members themselves vertically. The only difference between the manipulated series and the manipulating group is that the former submits in unorganized exteriority, as exteriorized Other, whereas the group members have an organized action which has been interiorized but is nevertheless entirely determined by its object, and is

[4] *Ibid.*, p. 636.
[5] *Ibid.*

thus a false unity; they have interiorized Otherness.[6] At this point the group has returned to the serial status from which it came, this time with its "practical unity the inert seal of pure exteriority."[7] Unorganized powerlessness has become organized powerlessness, and the series that was no more than a helpless pawn in the hands of others is replaced by the group that is no more than a machine.

The mass of people surging toward the Bastille had a far different future in mind. Sartre chooses a Marxist terminology to characterize the noble origin and purpose of the group. Thus it was to have released man from the status of otherness, of alterity, that makes him "the product of his own product" and to have made him instead "the product of the group, which means—insofar as the group is freedom— his own product."[8] Through the group, before ossification sets in, each Other is given the possibility of liquidating in himself the Other of the powerless series. It could be the "free milieu of free human relations," producing the free common individual; the group could be "the most efficacious means of governing the environing materiality" and "of liberating man from his alterity."[9]

That is to say, the group *could* be freedom, but this seems to be but Sartre's beatific vision, and in the concrete, on earth, things turn out differently. Fatalism once more intrudes, and the group as seen above is contrasted with its less glorious endings in institutionalism and otherness, in passivity and inertia. This evolution seems to be an inevitable one, although every group doesn't have to go through all the different phases. (The *groupe en fusion* may dissolve then and there, or it may undergo a long development; a sovereignty may arise directly from the collective.) What does seem always to be true is the fundamental reciprocity between group and collective. The group constitutes itself

[6] *Ibid.*
[7] *Ibid.*, p. 638.
[8] *Ibid.*, p. 639.
[9] *Ibid.*

from the Others of the collective and bears always, as birth-marks of its origin, the submissive and exterior character-istics of the collective from which it issues. There is a mutual action and reaction between the group and the seriality from which it comes, just as in the reverse, the purpose of the group affects the surrounding series, who could perhaps join, but refusing membership, assume their alterity as if it were the result of a free common *praxis*. (In other words, they achieve a totalization by virtue of non-membership in the group.) Between both, the dialectical exchange is compara-ble to an osmosis.[10] The series infects the group with its passivity, and the group causes the series to reflect upon its status and perhaps eventually even to form itself into its own group. Sartre calls the influence upon the group of the col-lective the "first circularity" and the falling back of the group once more into collective the "second circularity"; this con-stitutes for him the movement of History. This double cir-cularity from the collective to the group and back into collective embodies "the terminal moment of the dialectical experience and also by the same fact the very structure of social life."[11] All of history is shown to be a "perpetual dou-ble movement of regrouping and petrification."[12]

In summary, both the organic and the inorganic are op-erating at all levels. At the start of everything is, of course, the individual, but he is not a Robinson Crusoe, who con-fronts matter alone on a solitary island. Notwithstanding his dependence upon others, however, the group member is *in-dépassable,* for beyond the *raison constituée* there lies al-ways the *raison constituante,* that is, the mind of the individual man, with its function of totalizing or of mentally encompassing the multiplicity of the group. All groups come from the series, however, and as we have seen, eventually go back to them, for "the group carries a destiny of seriality

10 *Ibid.,* p. 640.
11 *Ibid.,* p. 642.
12 *Ibid.,* p. 643.

from the moment of its practical totalization."[13] If matter is humanized, the organism is likewise contaminated. It is Sartre's continual worry to show the intelligibility of this successive dialectic, as he now proceeds to do with the notion of *class*.

THE WORKING CLASS

Sartre has earlier discussed the concept of class in conjunction with his presentation of the notion of seriality. At that time, the members of a class, as of the working class, were seen to be powerless members of a series. The working class was a collective, built around an object, the machinery and merchandise of industrialization, and the worker himself was alienated, a mere Other among Others. This meant that his truth and his reality lay in his being-outside-himself, in the pratico-inert weight of the matter in and around him. In this earlier chapter we described the fatigue which overwhelms the working woman, who emerges from the monotony of her working hours into a gray world of unfulfilled needs. Following Sartre, we stated that she has no "essence" other than this frustrated self, that what she does (and can never do) constitutes her being.

It looks as if man's freedom is truly doomed. Yet Sartre, in his earlier presentation, insisted upon a means of salvation, for if man was forced to live within certain given limitations, he was, on the other hand, always free to revolt against them. The weight of inertia was seen to be almost crushing to the individual worker, but the sheer weight of his misery might also cause him to unite with others and to form a group, with its new possibilities of freedom.

We are prepared, at this new meeting with the concept of class, to deepen still further our understanding of it and to place it in the world of the concrete. Sartre still sees "class" as made up, above all, of the powerlessness within

[13] *Ibid.*

the seriality. The *being-of-a-class*, as of the working class, is determined by the pratico-inert only by virtue of this serial dispersion. The worker is exploited because he is isolated, and it appears as if he is locked up forever in this world of the Other, helpless to escape and become truly himself. It is at this point that Sartre comes to the rescue and adds that no class struggle would ever be possible unless "there existed the permanent possibility of dissolving the series."[14] The class is, then, not only a present status—the pratico-inert which catches hold of man and keeps him where he is, man's destiny—but also a possible status—the potentiality of transcending the present condition and of forming a group, the negation by man of his destiny. The group itself is, in relation to the class, this possible status, that to which eventually the working class can tend; it stands *"comme un statut possible en permanence."*[15] In moments of social unrest, of conflicts and strikes, the class exists in fact as practical totalization, as if it were a group, and even though the movement later falters, the very fact that it took place at all shows the possibility of the class-as-unity.[16]

Still, the class as a whole is not transformed into a group, even in periods of revolution. The series lives on, surrounded by groups of action which have varying degrees of development—they may be random strikes in one village alone, or unions so highly institutionalized that they are almost bureaucracies—and which pursue varying immediate objectives. There is, indeed, a triple element within the concept of class, the real unity of which is thus "a liaison of interiority between *common* multiplicities and *serial multiplicities.*"[17] What really makes you belong to a class is your behavior. If you act as a worker, if you have interiorized the aims and objectives of the worker, you belong to the working class, no matter to which of the elements you be-

[14] *CRD*, I, p. 644.
[15] *Ibid.*, p. 647.
[16] *Ibid.*
[17] *Ibid.*, pp. 643–44.

long. Outside of this fundamental unity in behavior and general objectives, in *praxis*, Sartre sees the class as divided into three parts: (1) the inert series, powerless, but nevertheless profoundly affected by the groups outside itself; (2) the *groupes en fusion*, or under oath, rising up among the workers themselves in moments of social unrest; and (3) the institutional and organized group of the unions.[18] The second two elements are drawn from the seriality and carry its marks; their subsequent relationship to this series from which they have come is so complex that Sartre will later feel compelled to defend its very intelligibility. The three have no ontological unity (beyond "seriality past, present, and future,") but, as we have seen, they do have a practical unity through their common behavior as workers.[19] They cannot be considered to constitute a group, since there is no fraternal interiorization on the part of all the workers. Sartre exemplifies this in his detailed examination of the origin and organization of the French syndicates, or unions.

[18] *Ibid.*, p. 647.

[19] Sartre sees the *being of a class* as pratico-inert, determined by the seriality. The *groupe en fusion* and the organization and institution have their being-outside-themselves in the series from which they come and which still sustains them. In other words, the group has its *being of a class* outside itself in the series, while the series finds both the affirmation and the negation of its being in the formation and actions of the group. The worker carries upon himself and in his being the sentence of the exploiting class, but in the common actions which arise, he finds both the affirmation of his class as worker, determined by his salary and his job, and the freedom to overcome it, to change through common action his present dissatisfactions. The *being of class* is, thus, not only present seriality, but might be defined more fully as seriality past, present and future—past in the *groupes en fusion* and the unions, present in the unorganized masses, future in the eventual dissolution of the groups. The seriality is overcome when the workers group to undertake some action, and returns when they take up their work again, whether as victors or vanquished. This is the ontological status of the worker. The *praxis* of the group, as the dissolution of the serial being, is either the present and practical reality of the common individual or his future possibility. The permanent dissolution of the seriality, the actualization of the class-as-unity would bring with it a new ontological status.

Although these syndicates claimed to *incarnate* the workers, they were actually a group composed only of the elite, which excluded the workers who were in the outside series. We see once again the medieval chevalier riding to power while the others, in this case, went on working. In forming the syndicate-group, the syndicalists asserted that they, and they alone, were the workers, and they imposed their decisions upon the majority outside the union-organization. There is a certain irony in the fact that these aggressive elements, in forming a group out of the seriality, were asserting their membership in the working class (one asserts what one is in attempting to go beyond it), yet once the group was formed, it escaped the workers and became a group strange to the working class.[20] The union official is no longer a worker because he no longer works like a worker, and the union is the working class "objectified, exteriorized, institutionalized, sometimes bureaucratized."[21] The union is of the class, but the entire class is not present within it.[22] It is the *authority* of this class, but cut off from it; it is a group by the very virtue of its separation, that is, by virtue of the serial dispersion of the non-members. The latter now have a double seriality—a seriality exploited by the employers, and a seriality manipulated by the unions, in that the obedience and confidence of other workers in and to their unions elsewhere conditions the obedience and confidence of the workers here.[23] We can find no better example of this state of affairs than in the Teamsters' Union in the United States, where James Hoffa and those around him claim to represent the workers, yet impose their decisions, made on the higher level, upon the vast majority below. The individual worker may not agree with the "bosses," but he is rendered powerless by his serial impotency to protest, by the *Fraternité-*

[20] *CRD*, I, p. 646.
[21] *Ibid.*
[22] *Ibid.*, p. 644.
[23] *Ibid.*, p. 645.

Terreur wielded by the union, and by the absence of any more effective means of opposing the employer.

The union stands always as the external guarantee of a possible interiorization of all the working class, as the "abstract skeleton of a united class, a permanent invitation to unite."[24] It represents practically the possibility of unity in its permanence, but it is still not itself this unity. The work of its members is to maintain across the separation and by their centralized unity this possible unity as sovereignty and to bring about the local conditions that will permit it to come about.[25] Its own members have only a serial, inert being, on the level of the institution, which, as we have seen in the last chapter, makes the function essential and the individual unessential, the actions of the individual inorganic (or performed as Other) in contrast to the organic (performed on his own initiative). "The tension which determines one by the other, the serialized Sovereign, and the series inertly receiving the inert sign of its unity, renders always possible, under the action of definite circumstances, the liquidation of the seriality."[26] In other words, the series, with the example before it in the unions of the unity that is possible, will dissolve and unite in a common action, constituting as it does so its own sovereignty, from within.

These *groupes en fusion* thus exercise their own sovereignty and throw off the inertia of the other two elements. They fill in with skin and bones the abstract skeleton of the institutionalized group. Ontologically, they belong to all, since they are the "being of class transcended and conserved"; practically, they are defined "dialectically against the series as resistance passed or still to pass, against the unions as exterior and objective mandates which are either to be refused, interiorized, or ignored."[27] This is to say that

[24] *Ibid.*, p. 647.
[25] *Ibid.*, p. 651.
[26] *Ibid.*, p. 652.
[27] *Ibid.*

the group which rises from the series may pursue the same objectives as the unions, or it may repudiate them and with them, the sovereignty itself of the unions. The *groupe en fusion* agitates for the common interest of a local group of workers and in so doing, acts for the entire class; it is the *classe agissante*,[28] the *action of the series*. Although it dissolves the series locally in its very formation, it is the action for the *entire series* (the whole class) but in a *particular situation*.[29] This is what the Marxists call "the emancipation of the proletariat by itself."[30] It is unthinkable that any of these local actions would clash with the interests of the working class (as was the case with the unions) and the syndicate member should affirm them. This he doesn't always do, however, and there is a certain contradiction. The local group may contest the sovereignty of the union member as being only intermediate and passive, whereas theirs is free and fraternal. He, on the other hand, will say that their actions are only a "particular determination of the class," hence limited and finite, and that only he can regulate them through the sovereignty of the syndical institution, which guards the general interests of the class itself.[31] It is true that attempts by the *groupes en fusion* to go beyond the seriality that is the working class produce still another seriality, in that each group, with its limited goals, determines all other groups as Other and that this milieu of seriality is that in which the union thrives.

The conflict of sovereignties shows that the *praxis* of each level may not only differ but actually may conflict and contradict, so that there will be conflicts between diverse forms of the same action. The end objective is the same for both —the mobilization of the working class—but the immediate means may differ. The *groupe en fusion* supports the institutional group as an inertia, as its own inert exteriority, and

[28] *Ibid.*, p. 654.
[29] *Ibid.*, p. 649.
[30] *Ibid.*, p. 654.
[31] *Ibid.*

where the immediate objectives coincide, it even interiorizes it as its own. This can only be done, however, as a determination in reciprocity, since the group is defined always by its mediated reciprocities. Where they do interiorize the same objectives, the *groupe en fusion* acts as a subsidiary to the union, and may even relinquish its claim to action and deteriorate into a series again.

What happens specifically actually belongs to history, but what can happen in general, all the possibles, are nevertheless intelligible, not by the analytical reason, but by the dialectical reason. In the past, considerations of "class" have been oversimplified, in tending to view the working class either as unified and fighting *en bloc* against the exploiters or as entirely serialized and impotent. In reality, in the process of history, the class is not an "either-or" but a combination of the three elements we have been viewing, with various ones coming to the surface at various times. Any understanding of the "working class" must take into consideration all three levels and the state they are in in relation to each other, and in order to do so, one must *comprehend* the individuals involved at the various levels.

INTELLIGIBILITY OF CLASS BEHAVIOR

It becomes clear from the preceding pages that the "working class" cannot be studied merely as an object which can be conceptualized and the "action of the working class" as a causal sequence, as some anthropologists would have us do. As an alternative, Sartre applies concretely the principles which he has set forth in his "Question of Method," discussed in our Chapter III. In accordance with those principles, the working class is seen as a totalization in course, a movement from certain given conditions toward certain objectives, with each level acting reciprocally in relation to the reactions of the two others, to whom, in turn, his own reaction may be the object of a guess. It is the task of the historian who is himself situated to reproduce this totalizing movement, or in Sartrian terms, to "comprehend" it. This he can do because he is a human being, and as a human being, he can *exist* the *praxis* and the project of the human beings who are in particular, concrete situations other than his own. From this point of view, he will see that the action at one level of the class is understandable only if one considers it in relation to all the other levels, since a totalization is operating in the working class, by which it carries on the same action (interiorization and *dépassement* of material conditions imposed by the other) at its different levels, with secondary conflicts subordinated to a fundamental accord.[32] At each level one must totalize the entire class, which implies an awareness of the other levels. "Comprehension" is necessary not only for the historian who would understand the process which is in the making but also for the agents themselves who are making that history. The syndicate, for example, must measure the combativity of the series, for a series which is too passive will not easily follow the union directive to strike, while a series which is too active may very well take things into its own hands and become what Sartre colorfully calls *le groupe sauvage*.[33] The *praxis* at any level is at the same time *its own and other*. "The class is both *praxis* and inertia, both the otherness that is the result of separation and a field that is common to all."[34] In the growth of any one of the elements, one must presume a totalization that is already there, for this growth would not take place unless there were some form of totalization. New groups arise under need, but in their birth, they "comprehend" the class by way of totalization. It is their field of action, a "totality to totalize."[35] (By the same token, it is not a totality already totalized.)

The observer who is situated—Sartre here emphasizes, as he has throughout his book, the point that it is *man* who is

[32] *Ibid.*, p. 669.
[33] *Ibid.*, p. 660.
[34] *Ibid.*, pp. 661–62.
[35] *Ibid.*, p. 662.

studying *man*—can grasp the unity of the different levels of action in a common project. For example, if the price of transport is raised in a certain locality, it is reacted to commonly but differently on the various levels. It is *"lived as powerlessness 'to conquer' in the series, as a provocation* to action in the group, as a *particular and local objective* to be viewed in the light of more general and fundamental objectives on the level of the union."[36] Sometimes the conflicting and contradictory actions of the different levels work against each other, and in provoking still more repressive actions on the part of government or industry, seem to make no sense whatsoever. This is because the plurality of systems, each with its meaningful (*signifiants*) actions, produces results that belong to no system. Thus a manifestation will have neither the violence that the rebelling group had hoped for nor the calm deliberation that the syndicate had counseled.[37] The end result—the objectification of the *praxis*, or the *processus*—seems to be a mere *thing*. Working hours have been lost, the workers have become discouraged and disheartened, and all seems to have been for nothing. The positivist would see this as an irreversible series of events in a physico-chemical system, signifying nothing. What he overlooks, however, is that the very senselessness of the movement makes a great deal of sense if it is followed long enough and if it is viewed from the inside. Viewed *in the light of the totality*, the resulting *processus*, though a failure, can tell us what state the working class is in, that is, the degree of self-consciousness it has, the relationship of one level to another, etc. As we have observed in an earlier chapter, one must watch not only the *praxis* of a group but its *processus* as well. The non-significant objectification is thus seen to be a synthesis of the various levels, each with significant but broken actions. The *raison dialectique constituée* has as its negative limit its ending in the non-dialectic.

The difficulties in comprehension come not from the com-

[36] *Ibid.*
[37] *Ibid.*, p. 659.

plexity of the object but from the *situation* of the observer, or of the agent.[38] Thus if the action is taken on one level, one may ask in desperation, "What are they waiting for?" or, "Why do they let us disperse?" but the answers become less elusive when all the levels are taken into consideration. It is only then that one comprehends the circularity of conditioning and control and understands the perpetual readaptation each level must make toward the common action in the light of the other levels. The class is still a *totality to totalize*, still in perpetual, circular, dialectical movement. Were it a totality, it would have to have one totalizer who would be able to block the circularity, but it is not, and the ultimate totalization lies in the individual, or as Sartre calls him "the free organism," who is immersed in the different levels of the class.[39] This "free organism" totalizes in an individual, free act, on every level, yet mediated through the other levels. Sartre calls this activity of the free individual comprehending the totality the *dialectique constituante*, and without it, there would be no history to comprehend. In order to make clearer both this circularity of control and the importance of the individual, Sartre gives as an example the mediation of the series in the conflict between the local syndicate and the groups which are "spontaneously" formed. The final action is a *processus* of all three dimensions, each finding its sense in relation to the other two, and this *processus* is comprehensible, whether it gives the final appearance of a well-ordered action or of hopeless chaos. If the workers' movement is able to be stamped out by the union, this is possible only because the class as a whole is in such a state of dispersion that the union is able to wield more authority and power. Or on the other hand, it may be impossible for the local workers' movement to be held back because it has too great a significance for the class as a whole. In either case, the actions are not isolated, self-sufficient monologues but must play out their dramas in dialogue with the rest of

[38] *Ibid.*, p. 657.
[39] *Ibid.*, p. 665.

the class. The union officials and the strikers *comprehend* their situation in the class in order to determine the possibilities which are open or closed to them. These possibilities or impossibilities do not come from the outside, in the words of Sartre, "like a phantom"; they are, rather, the result of the individual freely totalizing his serial alienation, which he is free to accept or reject.[40] The class assumes *in action* its being-of-class.[41]

Comprehension, in conclusion, is possible because ultimately it is we ourselves who produce the actions of the class. Where these escape the agents, who are perpetually totalizing and in so doing, making history, and the witnesses, who attempt to understand that history-in-the-making, it can be grasped only as *processus*.[42] This *processus* cannot be conceptualized into an abstract notion, since the class is not some hyperorganism where all the contradictions of experience are suppressed and resolved. On the contrary, the *processus*, though escaping the control and direct comprehension of man, is tied to the human situation. It is impossible (though paradoxically, necessary), to grasp the class as total objectivity; for that to be possible, the class would have to be seen as a totalized totality viewed from outside the human condition, an impossibility for anyone but God. This means of course, that the only dimension of the class which Sartre will allow is that performed by way of integration by the individual mind. The class is continually making itself, and Sartre will not grant it any exteriority other than that of the abstract limit of our comprehension, that point beyond which we cannot go.[43] The most that the viewer, himself totally

[40] *Ibid.*

[41] Action may of course mean "inaction." Thus Martin Luther King, Jr., has written of and to the Negro in America, "Moreover, we must learn that passively to accept an unjust system is to co-operate with that system, and thereby to become a participant in its evil." *Strength to Love* (New York, 1963), p. 6.

[42] *CRD*, I, p. 667.

[43] We are reminded here of Sartre's refusal in *L'Etre et le Néant* to allow any conceptualization of a human being, since he, too, is continually making himself.

immersed in a class, can hope to achieve in dealing with a social multiplicity is to comprehend the various individual projects, as they are mediated through one another, and to follow the *praxis* of all from their given conditions to their objectification. One must study them *in their becoming,* and when that becoming ends in objectification, in alienation, or for the group, in a return to the series, in short, in the pratico-inert or the anti-dialectic, the limits of comprehension are reached. Still the "witness"—be he anthropologist, sociologist, Marxist, etc.—must supplement intellection with comprehension, or he will run the risks of dogmatism or of relativism.[44]

THE CLASS STRUGGLE AND COLONIALISM

Up to this point, for purposes of simplification, we have been considering the working class as if it existed in isolation from other classes, but we must now admit a new complexity to our study in introducing the impact of the opposing class. It becomes necessary to explore the problem of how and when (and whether) one can synthesize a diversity of classes in a larger unifying totality.

The first point to establish is the nature of the opposition between classes. Sartre brings up once more the conflict between Dühring, who reduced that opposition to sheer oppression, and Engels, who equated it with economism, in terming it an unavoidable conflict of molecular forces based upon changes in the mode of production.[45] As would be expected, Sartre brings man back into the equation (with Engels, man was no more than a variable quantitative) and insists that any social modifications and consequent conflicts are based upon their interiorization and the resulting free *praxis* of the individual. We have already seen how it is the attitude of the individual man which unifies and to-

[44] *CRD,* I, p. 668.
[45] Sartre's disagreement with Engels on this point has already been discussed in Chapter IV.

talizes the surrounding plurality as future possibility, and how the objectification of his *praxis* may escape him and constitute a passive and inert totality which turns around to negate him. In other words, it is the dialectic itself which gives birth to the anti-dialectic of the collectivity, or what Sartre here calls *l'ensablement de la dialectique* (the gradual blocking of the dialectic).[46] There is a perpetual circularity between *praxis* and pratico-inert, between the constitution of a group and its dissolution back into a series. If man creates through his own *praxis* his own inertia (the anti-dialectic, the pratico-inert) it is also man who lets himself become victim of that pratico-inert, through his acceptance of it in constituting (by his passive action, or his inaction) a false unity (as we have seen in the case of exteroconditioning), an alienated working force, or a seriality.[47] The *processus*, as pratico-inert, as the inexorable, relentless direction of a group is thus continually upheld by man's action (or *in*action), a very different conception from that of the "economists," who would consider what are really the negations of interiority to be external determinations, and the man-made, though uncontrollable *processus* to be a physico-chemical phenomenon. Sartre's entire text has been a detailed development and demonstration of the thesis that all changes and conflicts discovered by economism must be supported by the concrete movement of a human and historic dialectic.

Sartre would thus qualify Engels' assertion that "the mode of production in human history is the infrastructure of society" with the addition that this is so only because "labor, as free activity . . . is the infrastructure of the praticoinert."[48] One cannot deny that labor loses itself in the inert; this is indeed the destiny of everything which comes from man. Nevertheless, these objects of man, even in their inertness, point back to an originating mind, for machines and

[46] *CRD*, I, p. 671.
[47] *Ibid.*
[48] *Ibid.*

tools are the thought of man written in the matter. Further-more, if man is a prisoner of the pratico-inert which he has himself made, he is so freely, since it is his choice to pick up the tool or to stand behind the machine. All of these points should be abundantly clear by now, but Sartre wishes to refresh our memories before transposing them to the more concrete arena of colonial struggles.

There he insists that one cannot merely say that the various groups which are involved are the expression of the interests of their class. They may be indeed, the colonial system did indeed respond to the objective needs of French capitalists generally, but nevertheless it was originally built by *particular* interests (of *this* banker, *this* shipper, *this* manufacturer, *this* French settler) united and organized by a common activity and a common intention (through pressure groups, government statesmen, the army, etc.). The colonial struggle is not an unavoidable evolution of molecular forces, or the result of the encounter between a highly developed civilization and a backward one, as economism would have it; colonialism was originally built by living men, who pursued an organized program that included the liquidation of a certain number of natives, the dissolution of their traditional institutions, the deprivation of their property, and the forging of an economic tie with the "mother" country, to the disadvantage of the natives.[49] These practices all served to make of the Moslem, for example, a serial being, powerless to react since his own "group" had been destroyed, powerless to live as other than a "*sous-homme*," since he had been dispossessed and was considered in the new milieu to be unemployable, or employable only at the rates the conqueror set. Sartre mercilessly attacks the inhuman violence of the colonial, in asking what more could be expected of men who in their factories at home made of their employees mere subhumans and in cynically adding, "If he so considers his own compatriots, what then is the Algerian [to him], a

[49] *Ibid.,* p. 675.

dog?"[50] The colonialist has inherited the attitude of violence and exploitation, as the rapport of his class, the bourgeoisie, with the dominated class, the proletariat, but if it is undergone as pratico-inert at home, he reinvents it abroad, and his own *praxis* now finds a new form of violence in colonialism. This is the evolution of violence: an inherited structure of alienation in the pratico-inert, its actualization as *praxis* in colonialism, its objectification in a new pratico-inert system defining the relations of colonizers and colonized.[51] It is the dialectic of living men who produce the anti-dialectic of exploitation, and who continue to control it.

For it is not only the colonialist who comes under Sartre's fire; the son, also, is responsible for the violence of the system. Even if it has produced him and is lived in part as inertia, the struggle must nevertheless be continually reinvented and confirmed by living men, and it is the son who freely accepts to continue the attitude of the original exploiter. We will recall that this problem of the amount of freedom available to the child born into a group has been discussed in an earlier chapter; at that time, Sartre admitted the presence of some inorganic inertia, but nevertheless insisted that the pre-existing structures and schemes, here "colonialist" and "colonialism," could be filled only by living men and that the child-grown-adult must himself interiorize the decision already made for him. If racism is a product of the colonial system of exploitation and conquest, which made the Moslem the Other, the Enemy, it must still be maintained and reinvented in the daily conduct of the present generation.[52] "Son of the colonial and son of the Moslem are equally children of the objective violence which defines the system itself as a pratico-inert infernum. But if the violence-object produces them, if they undergo it in part as their own inertia, it is because it was (first) violence-*praxis*

50 *Ibid.*
51 *Ibid.*, p. 676.
52 *Ibid.*, p. 671.

. . . it is man who has written his violence in the thing."[53]
The son is both victim and perpetrator, for Sartre adds, in
phrases reminiscent of those in *L'Etre et le Néant*, that violence can only be maintained when reinvented.[54] In the
earlier work the emotion of sadness was compared to a cup
that continually loses its contents and is in need of refilling.
Here the father hands the cup of violence to the son, and
though the shape is there, the contents would drain out if
another living being did not keep the vessel filled. It is true
that the future generations of colonialists have inherited a
system that is a necessary *processus*, in which their own actions are alienated (hiring a Moslem at abominable wage
rates, treating him as an enemy because he has already been
made one by those before), but that *processus* was deliber-
ately created earlier by an oppressive *praxis*. It is furthermore true that past victories are renewed daily by the very
presence of the army in Algeria, as *la violence pétrifiée*.[55]
Responsibility may be tempered but never evaded, for "exploitation as a pratico-inert *processus* is identical with historic *praxis* realizing, determining, and controlling itself in
the milieu of passive activity."[56]

The *real* antagonism between oppressors and oppressed is
not easily determinable, since it is neither mere pratico-
inert *processus*, nor an open *praxis* of combat. Individual
relations of tension between colonialists and Moslems will
arise, conflicts which have a common signification but one
which is not directly realizable, since there is as yet no community among the Moslems and no common individuals, but
merely a seriality of Moslems and serial individuals.[57] The
Moslem, experiencing oppression in his daily life, carries a
resentment in his heart, even when he wishes "assimilation,"
and there is a certain negative unity, albeit a powerless one,

[53] *Ibid.*, p. 675.
[54] *Being and Nothingness*, p. 61; *The Tragic Finale*, pp. 25–26.
[55] *CRD*, I, p. 679.
[56] *Ibid.*, p. 684.
[57] *Ibid.*, p. 685.

in his being other than the "enemy," together with the other Moslems. The different groups among the *colons* have a more organized unity which is conditioned by the "climate of the colony," through their being other than the surrounding series and through their having in common a better living than their counterparts in the home country, an advantage that depends upon that series[58] (cheap servants, higher salaries for overseas personnel, etc.).

At times one can more easily ascertain the index of violence, as on the morning after a group of drunken soldiers has profaned a mosque. All the colonial employers will feel a disquiet and may punish or even strike a Moslem employee, not as a direct consequence of his conduct, but simply by virtue of his being in the other camp. If the employer, seeing a community in what is still series, considers his antagonist as a common individual of a group, he will hasten the day when he will become just that.[59] It is the colonial himself who is creating the opposing group as a negative unity. As the tension grows, the respective unification of the opposite camps grows until they are not mere negative unities but positive unities of action, and violence explodes on a grand scale. We have seen the results in Algeria—for the natives, it was the end of atomization and the beginning of liberation. Sartre excuses the violence of the rebels, for it was "nothing else but the violence of the colonial; there was never any other violence."[60]

Through this concrete example of colonial expansion and its culmination in bloodshed, Sartre has wanted to *show* that History is more than mere determinism, more than mere *processus*. It implies the *praxis* of men, men with projects, men who wish to overcome certain material conditions and who invent, plan and reshape their practical field toward certain ends. Similarly, class struggle cannot be simply identified with "a double contrary alienation of two serialities in

58 *Ibid.*, p. 684.
59 *Ibid.*, p. 685.
60 *Ibid.*, p. 687.

the pratico-inert"; the struggle between the classes is one of oppression and exploitation of the one by the other in its entire development.[61] Exploitation and capitalism cannot develop as a *processus* unless there is someone with the intention to exploit. If class struggle is nothing but molecular conflict and conditioning, History becomes positivism.[62] If, on the other hand, it is *praxis* alone, and the resistance of matter is not recognized, then "the human universe dissolves into an idealism of the Hegelian type."[63]

Sartre refuses to be either a positivist or an idealist in what he considers to be the Hegelian sense. Two remarks might, however, be made at this point. First, "idealist" is a term which Sartre and other contemporary philosophers apply to anyone who attempts a metaphysical interpretation above and beyond bare phenomenological observation and description. Hegel becomes a prime target because of his trend to let the human mind become the pervasive element in the composition of an intelligible world and to minimize the importance of material reality. In my opinion such an interpretation of Hegel is a somewhat one-sided one. As we have seen previously, the Hegelian mind does indeed pervade the cosmos, but it does not for that very reason exclude Nature. On the contrary, it is in the synthesis of Idea and Nature that a human world is born. Secondly, it is an oversimplification to state that the exclusion of positivism and Hegelian idealism leaves no alternative but Sartre's view. One cannot rest satis-

[61] *Ibid.* The word "oppression" refers to the individual direct action or *praxis*, "exploitation" to its objectification as *processus*. The colonialist or capitalist oppresses; his actions on the level of his class become exploitations.

[62] Sartre has of course attacked determinism in *L'Etre et le Néant*. Motives cannot be conditioned—ossified from all time, for all time— since "their whole value depends on my insight and on my continual evaluation" (*The Tragic Finale*, p. 97). The view has not changed in this later work but must be constantly restated, since this is the crucial point of divergence with "some Marxists." See *Being and Nothingness*, p. 440.

[63] *CRD*, I, p. 688.

fied that these three theories cover the field, for other interpretations could possibly be mentioned.

THE INTELLIGIBILITY OF THE CLASS STRUGGLE

Sartre considers his own interpretation of the class struggle to be a *via media,* since it gives a place to both mind and matter. Thus the basic material condition with which we are confronted, the fundamental given of our world as we know it is *scarcity.* Man is dominated by *need,* and it is to satisfy his needs that he acts. The actions of men satisfying their needs in a world which cannot satisfy the needs of all will necessarily conflict, one with another. This is so basic that Sartre now defines man as "a practical organism living with a multitude of fellow men in a field of scarcity."[64] The world in which he finds himself is a world of reciprocity, but that reciprocity, with scarcity ever posing a threat, can only be one of mutual menace.

Sartre's description of this "battle unto death" is striking and forceful, though harsh in its moral implications.[65] Thus scarcity, bringing a perpetual menace of death, makes each individual a risk of death for the other, and anyone who uses a product I need or want becomes superfluous. It is not only *my praxis* which counts, however, for the other, insofar as he is like me, can likewise consider me to be superfluous. He menaces my life even as I menace his, and we both become inhuman to the extent that we are human. It is therefore necessary that I (and my community) destroy the menacing *praxis*—and freedom—of the other (and his community). It is my freedom as an individual man which organizes the field of action and reaches the Other, not insofar as he is a simple object but insofar as he is a free being who is, in turn, capable of menacing my freedom if he is not held back. This of course implies violence, but the only violence which is conceivable is that of "freedom upon freedom through the

[64] *Ibid.*
[65] *Ibid.,* p. 705.

mediation of inorganic matter."[66] The freedom of the Other may be directly destroyed, as we have seen in the case of the colonists versus the colonized, who become the enemy or the *contre-homme*. Even the freedom of his own *brother* is curtailed, as in the case of *Fraternité-Terreur*, for fear of his becoming other and enemy. In both instances man is violent, whether it is oppression against the *contre-homme*, who threatens his way of life because there is not enough for all, or whether it is *terreur* against his brother, who must be kept a brother, by force if necessary. In both cases, it is freedom annihilating freedom, for fear it will itself be annihilated. When "certain groups of individuals band together with the idea of exacting labor that will be accumulated, in return for a regulated substandard consummation," we see the structure of capitalism.[67] This has arisen as a conscious *praxis*, with one group oppressing the other because of this perpetual battle of freedoms, fought on a battleground of scarcity.

This emphasis upon the free *praxis* of men in a battle for survival does not of course exclude the importance of the inert and of counterfinalities. Man works through matter, and Engels is right when he claims that the iron-coal structure has dictated class structure and created the proletariat. At the beginning the use of coal in the manufacture of steel created its scarcity, and the owners of mines were driven to discover new methods of extraction in order to meet the new demands, or they would be eliminated from the market. As we have seen before, the market was not a consensus of owners but a flight. It was as a member of a series that the newly born capitalist was obliged to cut his costs to increase his profits, and to stay on the market, and it was as a member of another series that the worker was reduced to a subhuman status. The exigencies came from the outside to the owners— the sudden demand for coal, and its subsequent scarcity— but it was necessary for him to *interiorize* that scarcity, and

[66] *Ibid.*, p. 689.
[67] *Ibid.*, p. 690.

to exercise as his free response the oppression of others in order to meet the new demands. Scarcity for the owner, after all, was not the menace of starvation but merely the possibility of not taking the fullest advantage of his heritage, the coal mine, by reorganizing the field and meeting the competition. Anyone who stood in his way became for him the *contre-homme;* whether his resistance was inert—not enough workers in a village—or active—sabotage, thefts, strikes—it was alike interpreted as antagonistic *praxis.*

It is true that the *être de classe* of the worker is produced by the mine (Engels), but it is also true that the *praxis* of the owner would not co-operate in the process unless the industrialist considered the worker as a *contre-homme* and an enemy.[68] There is a certain contradiction in the fact that the industrialist creates a whole mystique about the "free contract," as if he is negotiating with his equal, another member of the human race, and then proceeds to treat him as enemy, subhuman, member of another species.[69] The industrialist resolves the contradiction in considering the worker as one who freely sells himself; "man freely becomes merchandise."[70] Unlike in slavery, where there is no connection between production and payment, the "free worker" supposedly can increase his payment through increasing his production; he can sell himself at a higher price, or if one wishes, become more expensive merchandise. Since this incentive is necessary to keep up production, the worker must be allowed a measure of his freedom and his humanity, yet at the same time be hated and restrained as one whose freedom must not be allowed to resist the employer. The worker must always be watched as a *free* enemy, not merely as an object.

We might observe, in passing, that underneath his harsh views, Sartre hides what I would like to call a mild form of Manichaeism. Man is free, yet he has evil built-in, or rather,

[68] *Ibid.,* p. 692.
[69] *Ibid.*
[70] *Ibid.,* p. 693.

he is evil and menacing because he is free. His freedom is my menace. All this betrays a deep distrust of man in any actual predicament, not unlike the pessimism found in earlier writings. Sartre has always found the relations between men to be conflicting ones. Even before scarcity became *the* given, the Other was the enemy, whose mere presence was a menace to me. Wherever two subjects confronted one another, a duel ensued, for Sartre was obsessed by the idea that the glance of the Other diminished me, in making me an object. In order to avoid being made object, I must overcome the freedom of the Other. The only restriction to freedom which Sartre allowed in *L'Etre et le Néant* was the freedom of the Other infringing upon my freedom.[71] One wonders whether the Sartrian man could not upon occasion choose a different attitude, forbearance, for example, instead of distrust, or charity instead of hate. Sartre's descriptive narration of people and events "as they are" does not discover that form of behavior, and perhaps, as we will discuss in the last chapter where I offer my comments upon Sartre's text, the extremely negative attitude of the viewer himself gives the picture its drab coloration. In truth, if man were ever to be defined as "a practical organism living with a multitude of fellow men in a field of *abundance*" (a possibility which Sartre continually puts into parenthetical asides as being not inconceivable) one feels he would find other points of conflict in the new philosophy of freedom which would succeed an outdated Marxism.

FREEDOM AND THE CAPITALIST

In Sartre's opinion, the whole capitalistic regime constitutes a serial collective, with the complex structure of the market, profits and loss, capitalization, circulation of merchandise, etc., based upon the laws of alterity, as they have

[71] See my discussion of the Other as a diminishment of "me" in *L'Etre et le Néant*, in *The Tragic Finale*, pp. 67–93, 116, 117, 122. *Being and Nothingness*, p. 509.

already been explained elsewhere in this study. "Capital is not a totality but a flight."[72] This is to say that the capitalistic system depends upon the atomization, or the separation, of those involved, and is characterized by a methodical *non*-organization. This does not mean, however, that it is merely the sum total of unrelated capitalists. On the contrary, they are related serially, gathered together by the collective entity that is capital, in the accumulation of which all must share. There is a general movement that proceeds through a certain unity, even though that unity is one of alterity. Indeed, their unity is *by virtue of* their alterity, and its center, the accumulation of capital, is as man-made as the bus which we used in our first example of the series as a collective. Bus and capital serve the same function of making each member a mere Other among Others, with their relationship one of a common being-outside-themselves. The individual action of the manufacturer is objectified in a *processus;* "it comes back to him as *other,* and everything is defined through the *Other,* as for example, when one imports a new machine because the *Other* does it . . ."[73] (Or has not yet done it.) Notwithstanding its escape into alterity, every action nevertheless remains his own direct, free decision. The industrialist has to intervene, to decide, to consult, to plan, even though together with the decisions freely taken, the *processus* gets started and continues to unroll (upheld by other decisions, also freely taken). It is always *this* industrialist, in *this* factory who decides to replace a certain number of workers with a machine, and no gainsaying will make the decision other than "a direct action with a marginal alienation."[74] It will recover its serial sense later, for each operation of the capitalist has a redundancy upon other activities or events, and this continues into the infinite or transfinite where all series terminate. Although the sum of this chain reaction reaches into what Sartre has been calling the "trans-

[72] *CRD,* I, p. 696.
[73] *Ibid.*
[74] *Ibid.*

finite" and its actual structure is one of seriality, the individual intervention is accomplished in freedom. The capitalist chooses his machines freely and consciously as a means to tie down the freedom of others and to keep them—be they his workers or his competitors—under a perpetual menace. His actions are dictated by violence, and although he may rejoin that when he makes a decision, it is actually the Other who decides—"*Ce n'est plus moi qui opprime, c'est l'Autre*"[75] —or although he may defend himself as only a player of a ruthless game of economic laws, Sartre answers him with good reason, "It is not the things which are unmerciful, but man."[76] This Engels seems to have forgotten in his *Anti-Dühring*. It is after all man who chooses to play the game, man who is ruthless, talk as he may about the *necessity* of oppression. He knows that oppression has to be ruthless if he himself wants to survive, and since he wants to survive, he freely consents to it. The father did it, and the son quietly takes over the same unscrupulous methods. His taking over can only be interpreted as free approval.

The "liberal" theoreticians are aware that this seriality of producers, workers, and consumers must be maintained at all costs, and that it is maintained only in a system which is unorganized and structured (or actually non-structured) by separation. The system encourages a *false totalization* on all its levels, whereby everyone at each level acts like the Other, but that Other is ironically no one but himself *acting as Other*. "In the milieu of the Other, that is, in the pseudo-totality of concurrential flight, oppression changes into powerlessness not to oppress, or if one prefers, it becomes a necessity."[77] We have already seen in detail how the false or pseudototality, induced by the sovereign, operates, as in the case where the producers were united, whatever their respective rivalries, in persuading the consumer to buy more than he really wanted to buy. This same extero-conditioning

[75] *Ibid.*, p. 698.
[76] *Ibid.*, p. 699.
[77] *Ibid.*, p. 698.

applies to the producers themselves, who, as Other, buy machines, reduce salaries, etc. The capitalist, as sovereign, chooses this state of affairs which delivers to the *matière ouvrée* its power of stealing the freedom of others, and eventually of himself. His theoreticians ensure that it will be ever so; their "optimism" is based upon two contradictory principles. One, analytical in nature, asserts that "economic laws," not they themselves, are responsible for particular disasters. The other, falsely synthetic, argues that the "natural laws of economy" must regulate the accumulation of capital for the good of society as a whole.[78] The "good of society" seems to be equivalent to the good of themselves alone, however, for they are the human beings, who must be supported by the "other species," those who are not human beings. One recalls the Greeks of ancient times, who considered themselves to be the only civilized beings and all others to be mere barbarians. So also the bourgeois, in replacing an absent unity with the unity of a concept, shelters himself behind a bourgeois humanism, according to which only the bourgeois are human and all others are excluded.[79] Anyone threatening his way of life, based upon the accumulation of capital, is the *contre-homme* and must be treated with violence. The dimension of being of the bourgeoisie is based upon the non-human dimension of the worker, for the bourgeois needs him to be what he is. As a salve to his conscience and his theory, he allows the worker enough freedom to sign away his freedom in the "free contract," in other words, "freely to exclude himself from the bourgeois humanism."[80] The worker must always remain worker, for the system must have its barbarians, and Saint-Marc Girardin is quoted to that very end: "*Les prolétaires sont nos barbares.*"[81]

The roots of this "bourgeois humanism" are to be found in a strangely ambiguous attitude of each member of the bour-

[78] *Ibid.*, p. 699.
[79] *Ibid.*, p. 702.
[80] *Ibid.*, p. 703.
[81] *Ibid.*

geoisie. On the one hand, he upholds the seriality of his class when it is exigent; on the other hand, he considers his class as a possible totality, as when the workers resist the system. At this level, exploitation (on the level of *processus*) is taken to be a mediation of individual acts of oppression that makes them a *duty* of each common individual of the class.[82] In actuality there is no totality, and consequently no common individual, but the bourgeois acts as if there is always the possibility of a totality, though this is never actualized, and consequently, of a common individuality, though this is but an illusion. The failure to achieve an actual totality is always the fault of the others, according to each would-be "common individual," and his own individual acts of oppression thus become a duty carried out to uphold the class as a sovereign totality. Unlike in the aristocratic or theocratic regimes, where the nobles or priests oppressed others from their places in the totality, the bourgeois oppress from their places in a series and find their only unity in concepts, as the concept of bourgeois humanism, which justifies their actions as a defense of civilization (and incidentally, of their own continued existence). For the bourgeois class is not a group, not a hyperorganism, but merely a series of individuals kept together through their common oppression and exclusion of the worker. As Sartre will put it later, "Divided in the *processus* of exploitation, it is one and indivisible in oppression."[83] The only limit to their oppression is the need they themselves have of the worker. For without the worker, they themselves would not be.

CLASS STRUGGLE AS A RECENT HISTORICAL EVENT

Sartre next proceeds to give a detailed account of the struggle between the classes in France in the nineteenth century. Since much of this is of purely local interest, a summary for the English-speaking reader is unnecessary, but some

[82] *Ibid.*, p. 702.
[83] *Ibid.*, p. 706.

extremely interesting general observations emerge from the detail. Thus the worker is seen to have become increasingly aware of his exclusion from the "general good," both through particular instances of oppression and through the realization that the government was on the side of the bourgeoisie. It was not the impersonal laws of economics but the governmental troops which caused him finally to interiorize his situation and to unite. The bourgeoisie, in turn, found itself a class-object, and each member felt himself to be an object of hate, not as a particular but as a *common* individual. In the eyes of the worker, the bourgeois was a criminal by inheritance of all the past wrongs perpetrated upon the worker. The bourgeoisie thus acquired a *common being* from the outside, a status it never could achieve from the inside, divided as it was by a seriality that was the very foundation of its system and the preclusion of any regrouping. If the bourgeoisie failed to interiorize itself into a group, the working class nevertheless saw it as one. Were not the government troops, after all, put into its service? To the son of a worker killed in a massacre, the antagonisms of the *classe sanglante* are but a fine point; he can only see its members as unified in an organized, methodical campaign fed by hatred and fear, and it little matters that their consent was given only *as Other*.

"Each *other* bourgeois is led, through his being-object for the other class to see himself as a co-responsible member of a concrete group that is none other than his own class. It is necessary, of course, to turn the sign reading 'criminal-member' to read 'upholder of social values!'"[84] He is actually, in Sartre's presentation, a rather pitiable figure, confused both as to the nature of the enemy he faces (Are the workers united or not, are these workers in my factory "good" or "bad"?) and as to the nature of his own class-being, insofar as it has been induced by the Other, from the outside, and is not determined by himself as one himself totalizing a total-

[84] *Ibid.*

ity. In other words, his common being arises as object-hatred of the other class, the extent of which he is not always certain, and his only possible unity is in a common oppression of the worker, an uncertain unity since he is never sure of the totality he faces and since his oppression is always perpetrated as Other, as member of a seriality. This does not relieve the bourgeois from his responsibility, for his participation is in a threefold way. First, as a member of the bourgeoisie, he is with those who control the government and its troops, which are called out against the worker. Second, he supports the various pressure groups within his class. It was a majority of the Assembly which approved the use of troops in a particular massacre. Third, even if he was ignorant of the governmental action, even if he was far removed from politics, he belongs to the class of the massacrers as Other, and although it is "only tomorrow that he will learn that he has killed,"[85] he is guilty of participation through his passive attitude, from which he can only be absolved if he attempted to group together some of his confreres to protest the massacres and oppose the repressive measures. This third form of participation brings us to the delicate problem of "collective responsibility"; though "one has vainly attempted so to define it,"[86] it remains true that the definition of the class by the groups rising within it can only be carried through if the class-series is *dépassé* and manipulated by those groups. If each member is not directly involved, he gives at the very least his passive assent and becomes by default their instrument.

This assent has usually been to things as they are, to the *status quo*. Some have tried to effect a systematic, organized, responsible evolution within the capitalistic society itself, to enlarge the conception of the "general good," and incidentally, stave off revolution; such a visionary, in France, was Louis Blanc. The pressure groups within the bourgeoisie sabotaged all his efforts, however, for they preferred battle

[85] *Ibid.*, p. 709.
[86] *Ibid.*

to negotiation with the proletariat. (Negotiation would recognize its rights and its humanity!) These groups fought
under the banner of "liberalism," which for them meant non-
intervention so far as the economic laws of the bourgeoisie
were concerned (what if a few thousand workers were to
die during a "period of readjustment") and repressive intervention against the proletariat, when needed.[87] The patron
of the province, who lived far away from the capital where
things were decided, was as much a killer as those in the
group who made him an instrument of their *praxis*. Actually
neither may have picked up a gun—it is enough to close a
national workshop and send the workers away jobless to
have exercised "the fundamental right (of the bourgeoisie)
to kill."[88]

Sadly enough, the son, more than the father, constitutes the
class in a conscious and reflective way, for the son realizes,
more than the father ever could, what he is, and in this very
act, unifies past and present. It is he who interiorizes an inherited historical being, whereby he is the beneficiary of past
oppressions, and a social being, based on that "bloody" history that makes him the enemy in the eyes of the other class.
This he does from *within* the class; his interiorization and
acceptance of the total activity, diachronic and synchronic,
solidifies the past and constitutes the present and future. His
act of reflection supposes the same partial identification of
himself with the object which we have already seen is true
of the group member and the group. Thus since he is part of
the class, he cannot confront it as a separate and distinct
object, but only as a quasi object. This means that he can
never entirely divorce himself from the Other in the class,
just as the individual can never tear himself away from himself, or the group member from the group. He is the same as
the Other, and interiorizes what the Other wishes. The internal change brought through reflective totalization is of the
greatest importance, for it gives to the past a sacredness (as

[87] *Ibid.*, p. 712.
[88] *Ibid.*, p. 713.

the regulative norm) and to the present a duty to continue the oppression and never to yield to the worker. He expects the Other to be unyielding, since every concession brings with it the risk of a fatal evolution, and he himself stubbornly refuses to concede, since the Other conversely expects it of him. This refusal to yield on the part of each one takes the place of an oath, which would be given were it a group. Though it is not a group, and the oath is not explicitly given, there is a kind of integration, for the bourgeoisie is conscious of itself as a class which could be betrayed or denied. He not only knows the class but *comprehends* it, that is, reproduces the project of all the others, in other words, lives the existence of the Other. Thus whatever the Other does, he understands immediately because he is the same in refusing to concede and in oppressing.[89]

THE CLASS SUBSTANCE

The oppressive *praxis* takes many forms, one of which Sartre explores in detail, that of "distinction." Through this example, he leads up to the idea of a *class-substance,* a particular way of looking at things which the class members have in common, based upon the inertia of a totalizing oppression of the other class.[90] (The term "substance" here does not have all the metaphysical implications it sometimes has.) Thus in the second half of the nineteenth century a bourgeois style of life began to appear that has been called "humanistic puritanism," or "distinction." The life of a man of distinction was one of restraint and sobriety; his clothes were simple, his tastes modest, his wife frigid. In every phase of his living he suppressed his needs and claimed the priority of culture over nature. To the anonymous originators of what was later to become the public attitude of the bourgeoisie, "distinction" was a justification of their inheritance. The capitalist was distinguished from his workers in that he

[89] *Ibid.,* p. 717.
[90] *Ibid.,* p. 722.

was free from their needs; he was of another order of being, of a cultural order that need not submit to the ordinary demands of nature. The signification of puritan sobriety among the rich is obvious; through oppression freely exercised upon themselves, the oppression of the worker could be viewed as the oppression of nature by culture. Furthermore, if the patron does not overeat, he has a greater right to underfeed his workers. (Sartre comments cynically in a footnote, "The ascetic is a man rich enough to choose his poverty freely.")[91] This particular *praxis* was invented by certain inheritors in certain conditions as a justification of their inheritance, but it became alienated until "distinction as a serial *raison* becomes the dictatorship of the Other."[92] What was originally "*my* oppression on my own body has become the oppression of *all the Others* on my body."[93] Thus the various rites of distinction—puritanism, cultural salons, soirées—become the *praxis* of the entire class, as class; each member performs them, not as a particular justification of a particular heritage, but for the others. Each bourgeois comprehends sobriety or puritanism as Other and as a tactic of an organized oppression; "his class is totalizing itself under the form of culture and rejection of the body in the same movement which holds off the worker . . . who after all is nothing but a body."[94] The oppression of the worker thus continues on the social level, as each bourgeois destroys the worker in himself.

Through this example, we can understand the *objective spirit* of the class. The various actions comprised under the general term "distinction" are not only singular *praxes*, singular inventions of detail but also parts of an inert totality, a *totalité autre* that in its impassibility becomes a power, the power of the Other,[95] or as Heidegger would call it, the power of the "one," *das Man*. One acts in the way the Other

[91] *Ibid.*, p. 717, footnote.
[92] *Ibid.*, p. 719.
[93] *Ibid.*
[94] *Ibid.*, p. 720.
[95] *Ibid.*, p. 721.

acts in order to please the Other. Each judges and talks *en bourgeois* concerning art, literature, etc., and his opinion is no longer his own but that of the others, elsewhere. A particular novel or a particular painting is chosen, by no one and everyone, and later it is abandoned, by everyone and no one. It is not only appreciated as Other (each examines it insofar as it pleases the Other and in order to make himself Other) but it is even *produced* as Other, insofar as the painter attempts to anticipate the tastes of others. To comprehend and to produce are thus the same thing.[96] The comprehended object is the concrete mediation between the members of the class, though "the result can never be communication, since the comprehension in each one is identical and there is nothing to communicate.[97] The comprehension itself is a *compréhension-autre*. (Sartre here makes a distinction between *compréhension-autre* and *compréhension de l'Autre*. Thus the latter is direct, I reproduce the act of the Other and make him into myself, with the limits of my comprehension coming from the object, while the former is indirect, I make myself Other in order to understand the object through all the others, or to comprehend their comprehension, with the limitations coming from the Other, not from the object.)[98] The result is of course a false totalization; in a real totalization, every local event is a determining here, whereas in the *totalisation-autre*, which determines a milieu of circularity, the here is always an elsewhere.

This picture of the bourgeoisie which Sartre paints is hardly a flattering one. The bourgeois still emerge, as in his famous first novel *La Nausée*, as *les salauds*, with their very "class substance" consisting of an explicit or tacit oppression of the worker. Even their support of religion has as its motive his oppression through superstition and ignorance—if the worker believes in a paradise after his death, he will be less likely to seek one on earth. The bourgeoisie must sup-

96 *Ibid.*, p. 723.
97 *Ibid.*, p. 722.
98 *Ibid.*, footnote.

port the church financially, stand behind the power of the priest (who as Other oppresses elsewhere) perhaps even himself become a Christian. This comprehension of the usefulness of the church may be either cynical—when it is supported merely as the opium of the people—or sincere—when the individual bourgeois actually believes that the religion of the people is also the religion of man.[99] In either case, it serves as an instrument. Alfred de Musset was one of the first to equate the two significations of unbelief (offense to God, cause of social unrest) in his *Confession d'un enfant du siècle* (1836) in which he reproaches the bourgeoisie for having dechristianized France.[100] It is unclear in this volume whether his reproach is based upon their disavowal of a truth or upon their shattering of an illusion; in either case, it would have been better to have kept the faith, as a buttress against his own dissipation and addiction to ethyl and against the uprisings of the workers as well. True or false, faith has a practical usefulness, and even though it indeed be opium, a metaphorical opium is less harmful than real ethyl and real revolts.

THE CONTROL OF THE WORKING CLASS

By the turn of the century exploitation had become so ruthless that the inevitable happened—it came into conflict with itself. For since the exploitation of the worker for the profit of the employer cannot continue without the worker himself, and since the worker was on the way toward being exterminated by the free development of the *processus* of exploitation, the question arose as to how one could control that *processus* without limiting the profit.[101] In order to save their class, the bourgeoisie took refuge in Malthusianism. Through a doctrine which maintained that since population naturally multiplies faster than the means of subsistence,

[99] *Ibid.*, p. 724.
[100] *Ibid.*
[101] *Ibid.*, p. 726.

the lower class must inevitably suffer from poverty and hunger, the bourgeoisie could justify both their prevention of population growth and the low standard of living for those who were allowed to survive on the lower levels. Their *praxis* of oppression, in accordance with their doctrine, was threefold: (1) the prevention of births—the worker, in deciding that he could not support another child, was only serving "the sentence" imposed upon him by the other class;[102] (2) the refusal to enlarge the market, with its concurrent of a "provoked scarcity"; and (3) the encouragement of competition between the various milieus of workers, under the banner "Divide to Rule."[103] The employer increased his own income, though at the same time reducing production, through selling at a higher price, the larger firms setting their prices in accordance with those of smaller, less efficient businesses, but realizing a far greater margin of profit. This margin became even greater as worker was set against worker to produce more and thus himself to become more valuable merchandise to offer on the hiring market. No overt conspiracy on the part of the bourgeoisie was necessary, for everything went silently but smoothly through the power of the seriality. Sartre sums it all up succinctly: "Abortionist, famisher, divider, the bourgeois class continues the massacre."[104]

Sartre has chosen Malthusianism as practiced by the French bourgeoisie for his example, but there are of course still other means of control which might be and have been used, such as paternalism and "human engineering." (Sartre uses the English term.) The assertion that these practices

---

[102] *Ibid.*

[103] *Ibid.*, p. 727.

[104] *Ibid.* One cannot help feeling that Sartre plays the moralizer in these emotional passages, though he claims that he does not, or at least he has not yet clearly shown where his norm of morality lies. He is obviously on the side of the worker, with him against the *bourgeoisie sanglante,* but he does not clearly indicate why his attitude is the right one. We shall have a chance in our next chapter to explore this point in greater detail.

constitute the "motors" of History makes more sense than
does the flat generalization that "economics" are the motor of
History, but this is so only because it comes closer to the realization that the evolution of mankind is built upon the relations between the various collectivities (groups, classes,
etc.), relations which are practical: they result from free
praxis, whether this be in the form of help and support, or of
conflict and oppression. Reification and other elements of the
anti-dialectic play a part—they are the inorganic and the inert which have so often been discussed in these pages—but
one cannot limit history to these elements alone and reduce
man to a pure "moment of the inert."[105] Our analysis of the
dialectic should by now have abundantly shown that this is
not the case, but Sartre once more hammers in the point (as
he has throughout the book) that however great is the inertia and powerlessness of alterity, there remains nevertheless the power of man organizing and changing his field of
action, choosing the means to the end, adapting these means
and ends to a different environment. Alienation itself would
fall away if man were not a free being who chooses and prefers, resents his frustration, and attempts to overcome it. Even
the admission that there is a certain amount of reification in
man makes sense only if one presumes that he once was *not* a
thing, for one cannot reify that which is already a thing.[106]
Sartre is clearly remembering his old distinction between the
Pour-soi and the *En-soi;* his position here has not changed.

One must keep in mind that there is a difference between
individual *praxis*, common *praxis*, and *praxis-processus*, with
individual *praxis* being the free action coming from the individual, common *praxis* that coming as free deed from the
group, and *praxis-processus* being any free action *together
with* its sequel of necessary events. It is important to keep all
three strictly apart from a mere pratico-inert *processus*, which
is nothing but a mechanistic succession of events, with no

[105] *CRD*, I, p. 731.
[106] *Ibid.*, p. 732.

human intervention admitted at the start.[107] No attempt is made to deny the existence of this pratico-inert *processus,* but Sartre summons all the power of his dialectic to show that behind the concatenation of events stands the practical organism called man. Reciprocity implies man reciprocating, whether he helps or oppresses. *Oppression is definitely an act of man, as is the reaction in the form of a strike.* Each of these acts of man is different in a different situation, thus showing both adaptability and inventiveness. The future can only be realized by men themselves, and no one can safely predict what human insight and free choice will bring.[108] The worker is not a robot, however hard the other class tries to make him one; he nevertheless lives his time and takes upon himself the gradual fulfillment of history, and no one can prevent him from totalizing his class as a free entity which will construct the future. One concrete way of doing so is the strike, his refusal against all odds to keep the machines in the factories going. From all this an antagonism results, an antagonism which is reciprocal and "assumed," whether one likes it or not, and the bourgeois class undergoes and assumes a totalization by negation.

One can understand, finally, that the unity of each class results from its antagonism with the other class, and this antagonism results from deliberate *praxis.* It should be added that this *praxis* originates in a world where the fundamental but sad characteristic is scarcity. One can of course imagine other worlds, but we are charged with explaining ours, and in order to do so, we must confront the fact that there are classes. ". . . if *there are classes,* one must choose: *either* one will define them by way of inertia, that is, as the strata of society and with no more unity than the compact inertia of geological slices; *or* their moving, changing, fleeing, unseizable and real unity must be seen as coming from other classes, in this sense that the classes are all linked together through a

107 *Ibid.*
108 On Sartre's notion of future, see *Being and Nothingness,* pp. 126 ff. and 145; *The Tragic Finale,* pp. 39, 42.

practical reciprocity . . . This implies that the unity of each is dependent upon the unity of the other and, above all, that this dependency does not come from some dialectical magical entity but from a real project [human and free] of violence which integrates the other unity as a practical factor of its own unity."[109]

Sartre has presumed in the course of his argument the existence of two classes, although it will be remembered that he further divides the working class into three parts: the union, the *groupe combat,* and the seriality. (The bourgeoisie is also in three parts: the group-institution or sovereign, pressure groups, seriality.) All of these collectivities are what they are through their mediation with the others. This mediation implies a circularity, since the movement goes through the other and returns. When one class triumphs over another, this results in an intrusion of the freedom of the victor into the freedom of the vanquished, which on the rebound makes the victor more than ever aware of his own undamaged freedom, on condition of course that the freedom of the defeated is still alive. For to reign supreme over the dead is no thrill for the victor.[110]

The Awareness of the Dialectical Movement

The preceding analysis has to be placed in the flow of History, from the broader vantage point of which it will appear that since the past is neither forgiven nor forgotten, the heritage of mutual antagonism creates in the present and in the future a coherent class and gives it this stubborn and hard character which we know. Action and reaction solidify the mutual opposition until that day is reached when the working class can no longer tolerate "the impossibility of its

[109] *CRD,* I, pp. 735–36. The comment between brackets is mine. This is indeed the way in which the term "project" must be understood in Sartre's view.

[110] *CRD,* I, p. 736. For a similar dialectic among individuals in the domain of love, see *Being and Nothingness,* p. 364; *The Tragic Finale,* p. 85.

situation" and wants to create a new world through the destruction of the present.[111] While it is true that at times the worker was prepared for a more conciliatory attitude, as in England, where events did not lead to such violent clashes (extraneous factors were in operation such as profits from her colonial empire and a foreign policy which kept her out of European wars), or where other methods, such as paternalism, neopaternalism, and human engineering have masked the radical attitude of the employer, it appeared that in our example, that of France during the nineteenth century, an agreement became more and more impossible. The position of the worker was an intolerable one, for in the eyes of the employer he was not even considered to be a human being.[112] The worker carries upon himself the contempt of the employer and knows himself as he is known by the employer —in a typical Sartrian rebounding—"as a slave-worker enchained to do evil and as Other than man."[113] The worker naturally cannot assume and interiorize this Manichaeistic identity inflicted upon him by the employer, and in his refusal to define himself as evil and inhuman, which is a refusal of "bourgeois Manichaeism," he is contesting the claim of bourgeois humanism to be the universal, where his own role can only be that of playing the non-human. His task, then, is to enlarge the stage and make room for another humanism, a true and positive humanism, where culture is not a bourgeois monopoly and where he, too, is one of the players, with his rightful share of the intellectual and artistic life.

This is where the dialectical reason asserts its value, for it is the dialectic which overspans the vast, inexorable current of History and which gathers up as a mere segment within its moving ensemble the analytical reason. This the *petit bourgeois intellectuel* has understood. As an intellectual, he is in search of the universal, and this universal he discovers

---

[111] *CRD*, I, p. 737.

[112] *Ibid.*, p. 739.

[113] *Ibid.*, p. 740. See also *The Tragic Finale*, pp. 69 ff.; *Being and Nothingness*, p. 275.

in the working class. It is the worker who is the potential universal, for "*praxis* is the measure of man and the foundation of truth," not intellectual analyses.[114] The bourgeois, leaning solely upon the analytical, positivistic interpretation of world reality, rejects the dialectical movement as a menace to his own reasoned superiority and practical supremacy, but his protest is but a part of the dialectic, and whether he wants it or not, he and his class, with all its "immobile" analytical procedures, is caught up in the flow of dialectical History.[115] The intellectual, as interpreter of this dialectical movement, states what is and will be, and this he sees to be the dialectical *praxis* of the working class and its uprising against oppression and exclusion.

The *practical* understanding of the dialectical movement (the "*Raison dialectique*") in the working class Sartre has called its "objective spirit," an invention discovered to offset and negate its "dehumanization."[116] We will recall that the bourgeoisie also had an "objective spirit," which lay in its explicit or tacit oppression of the worker, but whereas the bourgeois oppresses as Other, the worker resists this oppression as himself agent. The class totalized by the Other must dissolve this unity induced from the outside by a real movement of totalization.[117] Alterity has been overcome and refused in the formation of the *groupe de combat*, and the worker who flatly says, "I will not do more than the Others in order not to oblige the Others to do more than they can, so that the Other will not oblige me to do more than I can," is "already master of a dialectical humanism not as theory but as *practice*."[118] Even though the *Raison dialectique* belongs to the working class and the *Raison analytique* to the bourgeoisie, some members of the bourgeoisie, namely its intellectuals, discover the *Raison dialectique* and by means of it and

114 *CRD*, I, p. 741.
115 *Ibid.*
116 *Ibid.*, p. 743.
117 *Ibid.*, p. 741.
118 *Ibid.*, p. 743.

of the class which denies them, discover themselves and their own class as well. These "traitors" to their class give the *Raison dialectique* its theoretical expression, as we see, for example, in the work of Marc Bloch and Georges Lefebvre. Not mentioned but tacitly accepted as the *petit bourgeois intellectuel* par excellence is of course the most talented of them all, Jean-Paul Sartre himself.[119]

The contradiction between the two types of rationality, dialectic and analytical, in the bourgeois class is not properly our subject. Sartre wishes, rather, to insist that we grasp the rhythm of History itself, and that the intelligibility of this rhythm be dialectic. In a world fashioned by scarcity (again, as he so often has, Sartre posits as an aside the possibility of worlds where there would be no scarcity)[120] it is inevitable that one class exploits the other, and the result is a reciprocal antagonism, a conflict of classes. One might wonder at this moment whether the individual caught in the dialectic of History can really "comprehend" it, whether he can decipher its complex mixture of freedom and inertia. Sartre believes

---

[119] This idea appears more and more frequently, that the dominating class can discover itself and achieve freedom only if the dominated class is liberated and a truly universal humanism prevails. It is undoubtedly true that the Negro revolution in America has caused all Americans to question their own lives and motives. See, for example, the following reflections of Thomas Merton in a review on William Kelley's *A Different Drummer* (Garden City, New York, 1962), a novel by a young Negro writer: "The real tragedy is that of the white man who does not realize that, though he seems to himself to be free, he is actually the victim of the same servitudes which he has imposed on the Negro: passive subjection to the lotus-eating commercial society that he has tried to create for himself, and which is shot through with falsity and unfreedom from top to bottom. . . . Is there really a genuine freedom for the person or only the irresponsibility of the atomized individual members of mass society? . . . The white man is so far gone that he cannot free the Negro because he cannot even free himself. Hence these books are not in any sense demanding that the whites now finally free the Negroes. On the contrary, the magnificent paradox they utter is that the Negro has a mission to free the white man: and he can begin to do this if he learns to free himself." *Jubilee*, September 1963.

[120] *CRD*, I, p. 744.

that the best answer is that of Diogenes, who solved a theoretical question with a practical answer: he stood up and walked.[121] The analogy is a pointed one: we do indeed struggle with or against our class, and when in the last paragraph the word "invention" was used to describe the practical understanding of the dialectical movement, the choice was not accidental. It is man who discovers and invents, understands and acts. In the conflict of classes, everyone knows that he faces free men, not things, and that in the planning of a strategy, one has to be aware of what the opponent knows and of what he knows of my knowing him. The dimensions of freedom are multiple. One has to view oneself not only as acting subject but as the acted-upon object of the Other as well.[122] No one would deny that there is an inorganic or material element—Sartre calls it somewhat facetiously *matérialiste*—which includes the material conditions of time, space, environment, means of action, etc. Dialectic for Sartre is freedom built around matter, while a positivistic interpretation takes into account matter alone.

Sartre finds as a natural parallel to the human condition of class warfare upon a battleground of scarcity the actual situation of men in a war. There the thingification or gradual objectification of freedom is something which happens to the loser under the pressure of the winner. Before the battle lines are drawn, each unit already has a certain amount of materiality which makes it object, or inorganic, in the strict sense of the word.[123] Any weakness in that line, any ignorance of what it can or cannot do, or of what the Other can or cannot do, is fatal. Freedom is the skill to foresee, to go beyond *what is*, to calculate what can be done and what can "be taken in" from the opponent. This is no question of extero-conditioning but rather of planned calculation. Prevision thus concerns the material impedimenta insofar as they are haunted by freedom. The *praxis* of the other must be known, and it is

[121] *Ibid.*, p. 745.
[122] *Ibid.*, p. 747.
[123] *Ibid.*

only to the extent of this awareness that one can attempt to go to the end of one's own capacities. Freedom incessantly measures itself against freedom.[124]

Even in a group of soldiers that is surrounded and will be exterminated, this freedom, though by now a desperate freedom, is still there. Although their annihilation appears inevitable and their totally "becoming object" practically certain, they still continue the battle because deep in their hearts remains the will to go beyond the "alienation" which the opposing group has inflicted upon them. Their mutual combat is in a way an agreement upon "freedom," which although transcended in the one camp is still for both an object of antagonism. The continuation of the battle is an admission of "fault" on one side—aware of our mistake, we continue the battle—but on the opposite side, it is a free decision to exploit that "fault" and bring about the passive objectification of the enemy.[125]

All struggle is a combat of freedom against freedom. Therein lies, against a background of *rareté*, the profound menace of man for his fellow man: man is the being through the *praxis* of whom man is reduced to the state of haunted object.[126] The error of the loser is always a defeat in freedom. We see this in the example of a woman who, even as she jumped from a moving train, fell beneath the wheels, and was carried to her death in agony, kept repeating, "I should not have jumped! I should not have jumped!" Powerless to reverse her fate, she had nonetheless fully chosen it herself; such is indeed the power of man over things.[127] One will recall that one of the main theses of *L'Etre et le Néant* was that remorse is an assertion and proof of freedom, since it clearly implies that one could have acted differently.

Where the struggle lies between man and man, the struggle is one of freedom against freedom, subject against sub-

[124] *Ibid.*, p. 746.
[125] *Ibid.*, p. 749.
[126] *Ibid.*
[127] *Ibid.*

ject, project against project, with the definite hope on each side of transforming the Other into a subhuman object, into a thing. Together with the (free) *praxis* and the combat born in the dialectic of opposition, there is always and there always must be the attempt to comprehend. This comprehension is not unlike that which happens in a chess game, where the highest skill consists in foreseeing as far as possible and with the greatest possible precision the move, or *praxis*, of the opponent. This could eventually become an object of mathematical calculation, at which level one wonders whether there are still two players or only one, the winner. The game nevertheless started with two players, two projects, two freedoms, and the loser is only the loser to the extent that he becomes a passive object. *To the extent that he is unforeseeable, he is not an object.* The chess game serves as a simplified symbol of actual life. The "scandal" is not that the Other exists, as Hegel would imply, but the fact that the Other must exist as a menace so long as *rareté* is a factor in this sad world of ours. In the Sartrian understanding, the resulting violence is not blind, but presupposes, rather, a reinteriorization of the situation, the situation of all of us in *rareté*.[128] If one of the "*combattants*" is no longer able to comprehend, that is, if he is no longer able to size up the *praxis* of the other with all the possible combinations, he becomes the loser and an object for the other. It is impossible to underestimate the importance of a clear insight, or what we have been calling "comprehension," for the loss of comprehension is the loss of freedom itself.

[128] *Ibid.*, p. 752.

Chapter IX

A PROBLEMATIC UNRESOLVED

Such, then, is the content of the *Critique de la Raison Dialectique*. The reader who courageously plunges into it will discover the conquest to be a laborious one, for the book is cumbersome, repetitious, and in a superfluous way, extremely difficult. It is unfortunate that the construction of the *Critique* pays so little heed to the eventual reader, for it will undoubtedly discourage many. Simone de Beauvoir, ever ready to come to the defense of her friend, has attributed the chaotic nature of the work to be due in part to the influence of the tense period during which it was written. Although its content had been in his mind for years, Sartre did most of the writing between 1957 and 1960, when France was deeply shaken by the war in Algeria and by the transition from the Fourth Republic to the regime of Charles de Gaulle. All this deeply affected Sartre and he sought "to protect himself in working furiously at the *Critique de la Raison Dialectique*. He did not work with the usual interruptions, erasures, tearing up and rewriting of pages; instead, working for hours at one stretch, he dashed from page to page without rereading what he had written, as if he were caught by ideas which his pen could not overtake even at a gallop . . ."[1] The writing and composition of the *Critique* was such a gigantic effort that it actually made Sartre ill for a while. Of this his opus bears the marks, and although Mlle. de Beauvoir did a great deal of proofreading, it would be unfair to make her responsible for the editing of such difficult

[1] *La Force des Choses*, p. 407.

and obscure pages. This most devoted of Sartre's readers loyally did her utmost, and felt herself amply rewarded: "I spent hours in reading and rereading the manuscript of the *Critique de la Raison Dialectique;* I groped my way through obscure tunnels, but once in full daylight, I was often carried away by a pleasure which made me feel twenty years younger."[2]

One can readily agree that the tunnel is indeed one which is well-worth traversing, for the *Critique* is an impressive work and carries a forceful message, one which might be briefly formulated as follows. Man is not matter; he is more than matter. Creator of himself, creator of the group, conditioned in his liberty, controlled by oath and *terreur,* subjugated by authority and institution, man *qua* man does not die. His freedom is indestructible. If he is the worker, he freely signs the contract which will exploit him; if he is the employer, he shrewdly plans and decides how to subjugate worker and competitor alike. Man is both free and not free, creative and inert, master and slave, rebel and prisoner, builder of the Bastille and its destroyer as well.

From a methodological point of view, the book reveals once again Sartre's unusual phenomenological skill. He is a master in describing what he sees, albeit he sometimes sees only what he wants to see. The most subtle nuances emerge from amid an incorrigible verbosity, for the writer thinks aloud until he reaches the perfect expression for his thought, then does not bother to turn back to erase the preliminary gropings. Faithful to a method described in *La Nausée*—"*Il faut écrire au courant de la plume; sans chercher les mots*"—Sartre writes on and on, unhampered by the lack either of words or of ideas.[3]

We have seen that the influence of Husserl went hand in hand with that of Hegel, and the discussion of Hegelianism in the second chapter was an attempt to prepare the reader

[2] *Ibid.*, p. 499.
[3] *La Nausée,* p. 77.

for a recognition of Sartre's skillful use of Hegelian reciprocity in his phenomenology. It would be hard to cite any publication since *The Phenomenology of Mind* itself in which the rebounding concatenation from man to man or from man to matter is more heavily exploited. If the universe of the past was one in which men were merely juxtaposed, that of the present is one in which men are tied together by an invisible link. Sartre claims that although this link is not matter and is therefore not empirically perceptible, it is nevertheless phenomenologically observable and the mind of man is able to discover the dialectic. In this description of the relational link between men, Sartre no longer uses the *look* and the reactions of shame and pride called forth by the look, as he did in *L'Etre et le Néant*,[4] but in closer imitation of Hegel, he shows the Self to be born through the awareness of the Other, the relations between X and Z being construed by the third man. Hegel's famous synthesis no longer has any external fulfillment, but lies, rather, inside man himself. To be man, or freedom, or totalization, or synthesis is all one and the same thing. The whole enterprise is an onward movement, of which the living individual is the present inheritor. In his function of recipient, it is he who adds up the dialectic.

ETHICS: THE ANSWER OR ANOTHER QUESTION?

A question which naturally comes to the mind of the reader of the *Critique de la Raison Dialectique* is whether or not it can be considered to be the long-awaited expression of Sartre's ethical position. In an attempt to answer this question, we would do well to take a brief look at Marx's ethics, for it is only in the light of Marxist morals that Sartre's position becomes intelligible.

Marx himself had no direct interest in the search for an ethical norm. His clearly avowed purpose was to liberate the proletarian and thus enable him to reach personal satis-

---

[4] *Being and Nothingness*, pp. 252 ff.

faction. Unfortunately for Marx—and this is no less true for any social reformer—the ethical question in one way or another keeps coming up. Then the answer came: ethics was part of the superstructure, hence as with all manifestations of the superstructure, it would result from the material state of affairs of a nation. Ethics, in other words, is grounded in economics.[5] Just as feudalism was the prelude to a capitalistic world and a capitalistic ethic, so also capitalism will give way to socialism and to a socialistic ethic. Whatever class is in power dictates the moral code which will support it and keep it in existence. Since the proletariat is the growing class, it is only natural that we can expect its ethics to be the ruling ethics. What these ethics are or will be is not made precise, but we may surmise that in a general way the Marxist moral is and will be to free man from his alienations. It is considered unfitting for the time being to explore beyond the day when this happy situation will have been reached.

Turning to Sartre, we are struck by the fact that wherever we can discover any ethical statement, it has a strong Marxist flavor. Sartre also strongly objects to any universal and abstract norm of ethics. Thus he said upon one occasion: "The moralist is like a driver: in driving his car, he watches the curves of the road." He agrees with Marx that the proletariat is the class of the future and that "truth lies in the look of the poor." The attempt of the proletarian to realize this truth in the conquering of the world is consistent and unavoidable. *Value* itself is presented as that toward which my *praxis* tends, as it does toward its future.[6] The *ought* is of a temporary nature, for with the gradual elimination of man's alienations, these values themselves will no longer be necessary. They result from our living in an inferno of exploitation and oppression, and thus are needed for the present, but after the revolutionizing of our social structure, they will return into

---

[5] Karl Marx, *Critique of the Gotha Program,* p. 10. See also *The German Ideology,* p. 14.

[6] *CRD,* I, p. 302.

nought.[7] The perennial protection of values which belong to a tradition is often a mask for systems of oppression and exploitation. It is the rich man who is "virtuous" and wants everyone else to be. His "values" are a defense of the *status quo*.[8] Once in power, however, the proletarian will dictate the ethics of a classless society, one in which scarcity will have been overcome. What these ethics will be in the concrete is no clearer than what the new philosophy of freedom will be. The two are equally inconceivable at the present time, for we cannot see beyond the bend of the road.

Although these and similar assumptions seem to bring Sartre close to Marx in the realm of ethics, it should be kept in mind that while he agrees with his master that "matter" shapes History and therefore all cultural and ethical expression as well, it is in Sartre's view "matter" as shaped by *free* man. He bitterly complains that present-day Russian Marxists have kept alive a semantics of moralism without showing that value makes sense only when connected with (free) *praxis*. As a consequence, they are unable to make intelligible the concepts they use.[9]

Be this as it may, Sartre himself would be the first to agree that the ethical implications contained in the *Critique* leave many questions unanswered. He might add that the *Critique* is a sociological study and has no ethical pretensions. This, however, would merely postpone the problem, for in that case one might wonder whether or not a sociological stand as defended by Sartre could ever give birth to a normative ethics.

Although one might applaud Sartre's efforts to spiritualize a materialistic world interpretation, it is not easy to demonstrate that the "deviation" of Marxism as preached in the

[7] *Ibid.* Sartre himself wrote in his unpublished notes: "A moral attitude appears when technical and social conditions make a positive behavior impossible. Morality is an ensemble of idealistic tricks which help you to live in the way the lack of resources and techniques compels you to live." (Quoted in *La Force des Choses*, p. 218.)

[8] *CRD*, I, pp. 302, 303 in footnote.

[9] *Ibid.*

communist milieu is necessarily wrong, once one has made it clear that every epoch deserves the thinking of its doing. If thought reflects the manipulation of matter by man, and philosophical doctrine is merely an echo of that interference in a world of matter, why should a Marxist "deviation" be wrong? What allows me in a succession of human intellectual performances to distinguish the true from the false, the right from the wrong, if no fundamental norm stands as immobile and no value survives perennially? Sartre may retort that all that counts is *man*. The debate begins, however, as soon as precisions are asked for: what man deserves our attention and what is it in man that calls forth our utmost defenses.

Another ambiguity has struck me in reading the *Critique*. I can not shake off the impression, still in the realm of ethics, that at times a strange form of Manichaeism emerges from its pages. Obviously Freedom is defended as something precious, but no less obvious appears the menace that threatens this value and slowly but irrevocably chokes the divine in the heart of man, the menace of the inert or the anti-dialectic. The inert is something omnipotent; as the enemy of liberty, it can only be an omnipotent Evil, changing Freedom into Coercion, and into Destiny. Destiny in Sartre's view does not present us with a determinism built upon the mechanistic conception of a succession of cause and effect, yet it is so pressing and weighs so heavily upon man's decisions that by a strange contradiction with Sartre's fundamental view on absolute freedom, it tends to threaten freedom altogether, or at least that which is its most cherished concomitant, responsibility. *Praxis* is always in danger of becoming *processus*.

This Manichaeistic trend, quite pronounced in the *Critique*, is also present in Sartre's little book on Cuba, which serves to betray his thought to us, even though it was written without scholarly pretensions. Sartre, in describing what he sees, makes it clear that what he sees has to be. The Cuban revolution may be childish and immature in some of its manifestations, but it must be taken for granted. Here is a Sartrian Plato finding the program of *The Republic* being happily fulfilled. *Que sera, sera.* Is Revolution responsible for its crimes or are they merely facts? Could things have gone differently and better or are they the unavoidable results of a society in turmoil, hence without moral connotation? Is Evil, like Destiny, written in the hearts of men as an indestructible mark? One fact appears more and more distinctly, that the Revolution seems to be devoid of all moral obligations save one, and that is to succeed. No wonder that any individual who stands in the way of History—and History is the gradual growth of a classless society, we must remember—can only be a monstrous being. The employer above all appears as violent, cruel, and inhuman. His living *praxis* is oppression, and oppression is "permanent violence, that is, insofar as it exercises itself against the anti-human species . . ."[10]

Since all of us have known employers who show a deep sense of charity, this may appear to be a one-sided judgment. Must we philosophers ignore them? Is charity a shame in this world where Nietzschean harshness is the rule? The reader of Sartre catches himself with mixed feelings: while admiring the brilliant defense of freedom as a value, the deep compassion for the underdog and the persistent attempt to lift man above matter, he cannot help questioning the exclusive emphasis upon violence and the attendant implication that charity hampers the flow of History. In the pages of Sartre the Sermon on the Mount finds no followers anywhere, and worse still, it should not, for such a spirit holds back progress. This is a world where "man is violent . . . against the anti-man (that is, against any man) and against *his Brother*, as being such that he can at any time become an anti-man [*un contre-homme*]."[11]

[10] *CRD*, I, p. 698.

[11] *Ibid.*, p. 689. In *Les Aventures de la Dialectique*, written many years before the *Critique*, Merleau-Ponty discovered a link between the Cogito and the Sartrian type of violence. Wrote Merleau-Ponty: "*Dès que la conscience intervient, elle intervient en législateur souverain, parce que c'est elle qui donne le sens, que le sens n'est pas plus*

At this point the objection might be made that the present situation is provisional. Since the remote cause of evil, or what might be called Sartre's original sin, is scarcity, once scarcity has been taken away from this universe, violence will equally disappear. This is indeed the hope of all of us. Yet the question unavoidably arises: Will man be better when there is no more scarcity? When there is enough of everything, will evil disappear from the surface of this earth? An affirmative answer is doubtful for anyone who remembers the conclusion of *L'Etre et le Néant,* where man is dramatically described as an incessant failure. How can man, who perpetually transcends his achievements, ever be satisfied? I can always dream of better even when I am no longer hungry; in this respect the lives of our American millionaires are not exactly comforting to contemplate.

To this writer, the Sartrian man still appears in this work to be incurable. He is subject but as subject compelled to fight and striving to win, he must "submit" to the Other and become the "common man." He subsequently lives under oath and in *terreur.* He becomes member of a group, which eventually turns him into an "institutionalized" man. He moves ever in a circle in which freedom becomes slavery and slavery turns back to freedom recaptured. Man is a profoundly frustrated being and always will be. Why does Sartre, who knows man so well, look for another man? Are the conclusions of *L'Etre et le Néant* notably altered? Our attempts to discover any definitive ethical answer in Sartre seem to result only in a further questioning.

---

ou moins, qu'il ne se divise pas, qu'il est total ou nul. On reconnait le cogito. C'est lui qui donne à la violence sa nuance sartrienne" (p. 214). *Violence* became a more important part of his theory than one would expect on the part of a man who is at heart a generous person. "Sartre avait réalisé à Cuba la vérité de ce que disait Fanon; dans la violence, l'opprimé puise son humanité." De Beauvoir, *La Force des Choses,* p. 619. Compare with Sartre, *Les Mots,* p. 210. See on the same topic the article written by J.-M. Le Blond: "Histoire et Liberté chez Sartre," in *Etudes,* July–August 1960, p. 74.

TOTALITY OR TOTALIZATION

One thing is certain. *Praxis* is better than idle speculation, for only action overcomes the contradiction inherent in man. We are told that the main character of Sartre's play *The Devil and the Lord* is an attempt to incarnate his ethical man, not because Goetz commits a murder but because in committing a murder, he *acts*. It is at this point that I must disagree with a thinker for whom I have a great respect. For me the writer of the Gospel is still right when he specifies the origin of the act in the opening words of his narration: "In the beginning was the Word"; for Sartre, who has lost his belief in truth for its own sake, only Goethe can be right: "In the beginning was the Deed." This divergence has its consequences.

To Sartre's definition of man as freedom must be added the qualification that this freedom, since it is perpetually productive and creative, exists only in the *act*. Man is act. And since action prevails, cognition and culture in general can only stand in its service and manifest themselves through it, through action. Free action is not action for its own sake, however, as the study of *L'Etre et le Néant* may have led us to conclude. Sartre now asserts more firmly that action and creation should be placed in the service of a political ideal. Writer and philosopher alike are committed men, men who belong to a Cause. This involvement has, moreover, a noetic implication. It is in its very being an act of understanding, since to be a reformer is to illuminate History for oneself and for others. The writer, then, is a reformer—his is an ethical commitment—but this activity is also a cognition: *commitment is an act of learning*.

The implications of all this are clear: History is a process which every living individual totalizes and encompasses, but in order to encompass it *in truth*, one must consider and consult the poor. Their look is an accusation, for in it we see both what the social order is and also what it should be.

Any philosopher worthy of the name must accept the challenge of their plea and express the wishes and hopes of a new world; the historical situation of the present draws him irrevocably into the combat for one ideal: the defense and propagation of liberty. Those who are ignorant of or indifferent to that ideal are summarily dismissed by Sartre, and only those who have understood the need for a socialistic Europe can number among his elect. It is to the fulfillment of these hopes that he himself devotes, as he has for years, all of his literary craftsmanship and immense intellectual energy.

It should be noted emphatically that although Sartre's commitment is incessant, it has never overlooked the Self, which has always been well protected. The Sartrian Self has always been free from all dogmatism, even the Marxist, and has ever been fluid in its manifestations, save for the uniformity of a vague sentiment against the bourgeoisie. Sartre himself did not marry, nor did he join the Party; his relations with Communism are fraught with hesitations, half commitments, and denials. Freedom has never been forgotten . . . nor have the caprices of the Self. Sartre's totalization was above all one of a splendid isolation.

This attitude is ambiguous, to say the least, and calls for some questioning. One may even wonder whether it is still philosophical, or merely a subtle play of the mind caught in its own game. No doubt Sartre has chosen Marxism as *his* philosophy, but within Marxism he has cut himself a costume of his own size. No *engagement* could appear more candid and yet at the same time less dogmatic. The ambiguity lies in the term *totalization*, implying as it does perpetual action and creation. As we know, History is totalization, as is also man himself. The Sartrian Self demands an incessant departure; Sartre himself tells the story that once when he had to choose a symbol of maximum speed from several drawings, which included a galloping horse, a soaring eagle, and a motorboat gunning its motor for a rapid take-off in a race, he chose the boat because of its phenomenal force in the launching.[12] Man is *that* power of creation which starts ever anew and with a vigor that overcomes all obstacles. Sartre has made it very clear that he is against any form of totality that is beyond concrete human achievement. If we now observe more closely the reason behind this denial, it appears that for Sartre totality is out of place because it implies *immobility*. Sartre's philosophy can only accept a swift-moving Self in pursuit of a world which it itself creates. For the same reason knowledge is carried on in motion and action and is denied that static character which the Greeks cherished in their νόησις της νοήσεως, the quiet storm of the Pure Act, undoubtedly active, yet immobile, caught in self-contemplation and by essence self-contained. There is no place for the contemplative in Sartre's restless, onward-moving world. In short, he is *against any form which as totality or as immobility encloses the totalizing reality called man.*

This is, I believe, a fair account of Sartre's position. To me, the serious question arises as to whether such a totality can be left out. Does the motion of the motorboat make sense without the immobility of the lake? Does totalization exist outside a norm, which as an immense dome overspans the *praxis* of man? Is totalization *really* a creation or is it not rather an accomplishment—within a pre-existing totality? These are some of the questions which legitimately can be asked, it seems. This writer does not claim that he can answer them himself, but he at least hopes to show through a clarification of terms that Sartre has left in this field a problematic unresolved.

Sartre himself, as previously mentioned, considers *totality* to be merely the material result of human achievement, as, for example, the tool that the *praxis* of men has manufactured or the work of art that he has executed. There is no objection to this conception of the term—one is free to define one's own terms—but Sartre's refusal to extend its domain beyond

[12] Sartre, *Les Mots*, p. 193.

that of human achievement reveals nevertheless his refusal to accept any other totality. I should like to suggest that Sartre has left out, by definition and by intention, any totality which is immobile and might be considered to be an entity englobing the individual man, to which he belongs as part or fragment. The encompassing entity which I have in mind is double: it is cosmos, and it is human *totum*.

If we consider Totality as cosmos, we do not limit its meaning to that which has been achieved by the hands of man or to what lies in front of him as his tool or his opus, but we also include that which is prior to man's deed, as that out of which he has drawn his object. The Totality or whole would then be the immense container of matter in which he lives. How far this cosmic Totality reaches, where it starts and where it ends, we do not know. Whatever its limits are, the creativity so highly praised by Sartre can only start from *there*, that is, from this spatiotemporal totality, and it cannot reach beyond these terrestrial frontiers. Totalization, then, is not *mere* creation, uninhibited creation. This is a deceptive term. Totalization is movement, a movement which goes away from the subject and calls upon all his forces, but it is confined within a path and poised toward a future which is partly determined, since it is only within an immobile *totality* that the moving and "creating" takes place. That expansion of a cosmos which is *already there* englobes my creation. Though my act may appear to be performed in the instant, the cosmos has a way of being ahead of my totalization through its inexorable laws, which, although not yet applying to what is not yet, nonetheless are there awaiting my free act. This act of mine is carried in the continuity of the dimensions of the universe as Totality. However free and spontaneous, it is caught by a certain number of rules which come to its encounter: they are the presence of a future which when added to an accomplished past constitutes the totality within which every totalization finds its place and its moment and from which it can in no possible way sever itself. One is always here and now, no doubt, but the values of the here and now are safeguarded with the instruments of past and future. Past, present, and future are aspects only of a surviving *totum*. It is laudable for man to prefer the present and the existential, but it is imperative for the philosopher to see the present "angularity" hanging in the span of an enduring cosmos.

But—and this is another point which Sartre has overlooked —the acceptance of an *enduring cosmos is only possible because of a tacit faith in a human totality*. I have attempted to show elsewhere how the individual man himself is the undivided fragment or *atomos* of this human *totum* and how he is entrapped within its nets.[13] This *totum humanum* implies a past, a present, and a future which does not exist as yet but commands through its lawmaking procedure the internal growth and cohesion of the *totum*. The act of procreation is itself testimony to the oneness of a gigantic totality. The hypothesis of a being who is alive and rational but neither results from nor tends toward procreation would indeed be a totality unto itself. This is not the case with man. For the existent called man as we know him is both *from* and *toward,* and through this very dimension attests to the existence of an englobing human totality. Although one can speak with Sartre of totalization as performed by the living individual, this "summing up of the past" must in my opinion be understood not as a *conclusion* but as a *provisional* synthesis, for man is a transmitter. He does not really conclude anything; as in the Olympic Games, he is merely one of the runners and must pass on the torch. In short, he is but a relation between past and future and his synthesis can never be considered to be finished in depth.

It follows, then, that although the future of mankind as physical totality is still the *absent* wing, this future is nevertheless *present* in the structure of man as relation. Mankind in its physical expansion is not an entity existing all at once —this we concede gladly—but it should be added that mankind as a whole *is* through its internal law of procreation and

[13] *The Planetary Man,* I, p. 21.

transmission beyond the present and beyond its living repre-
sentatives. As *totum* it has an atemporal character, although
its constituents themselves come in succession. For all their
mobility, their activity is merely part of the game played out
under the dome of the *totum*, intelligent play, but partial play
nevertheless, since its finality is never wrapped with the
player solely and completely.

The whole question is whether the future, although not
yet visible or present in the act, still can motivate an actual
event.[14] On this point Sartre and this writer clearly disagree.
Sartre himself accepts a shaping of the present through the
future, but only in the realm of individual existence; he completely ignores the same influence in the actions of the collective upon its internal parts. The Collective is denied any
"project." Since Sartre claims that the moments of an individual life must be understood *"à partir de sa totalité,"*[15] we
might ask why he could not go further and admit that the
individual and his totalization must be understood against
the background of the Collective and the Totality as well,
even when this Totality has not completely unfolded through
time.

Immobility and *Praxis*

Sartre makes a remark in *Les Temps Modernes* to the effect
that there are certain people who write books with a vision
sub specie eternitatis, yet whose publications carry a date.
The wit of the paradox should not mislead us into believing
the underlying assumption, for there is nothing wrong with
the attempt to make a pronouncement *sub specie eternitatis*
and yet to write it, as one must, on a certain day, in a certain
month, of a certain year. Sartre's own statement is such that
he hopes it to be a truthful one and in its truth-content to
stand forever.

[14] I have used the term *remote completion* for a slightly different
application of a similar idea. See *The Planetary Man*, I, p. 28.

[15] Simone de Beauvoir, *La Force des Choses*, p. 57, in footnote.

What Sartre's pun overlooks is that man, though he be part and fragment of an enveloping world, probes that world and expresses the results of his probing in a *judgment*. This judicative act is made under the obsession of the absolute, even though that absolute be a myth. It is this character of our judgment to which we now turn.

Observing the behavior of men and the efforts of philosophers to prescribe some rule for moral behavior, we discover that there are a great many moral norms, such as the Hedonist, Utilitarian, Stoic, etc. This is not the place to express any ethical preference. Let us merely point out that man has always searched for some norm and that this norm, whatever it might be, has always constituted a limit, a self-made area within which he accomplishes his deeds. It erects by hypothesis an invisible wall, beyond which he believes he should not venture. The implication is that X, and only X, is good (and therefore ought to be done). That statement may be indeed general, but somehow it is there.

Sartre himself has made great efforts to keep this "absolute" out of sight: by intention his world is not a circumscribed, self-enclosed entity that is complete within itself. Its occupants wander in open spaces with no ultimate norm or general strategy to guide them through the void; they have only stratagems and what in a crude way must be called "expediency." This was the main objection of Albert Camus against his old friend and has no doubt left many a disciple at a loss, for he is given no map with familiar landmarks, but must follow his own road winding off into the unknown.

The motivation behind this moral labyrinth is philosophical. Sartre's position is both Marxist, in its pragmatic character, and existentialist in its insistence that there be merely incessant choice and never-ending creation. Sartre, when asked for an ethical norm, has kept silent. His silence is eloquent, however, for it clearly shows that any formulation like X *is good* implies a concession to the immobility of the absolute and of the abstract. This he has wanted to avoid at all costs.

Yet in my opinion, the attempt was in vain, for the strange thing is that Sartre is himself caught in the necessity of the dogmatic and the oracular, whether he wants it or not. He makes it repeatedly clear in the *Question de Méthode* that there can be no global view of History. Negating the possibility of any historical totality, Sartre once more sees History as a mere succession of man's changing manipulation of material things, together with its correlated expression in a philosophical doctrine. There is no transhistorical view. Each philosopher is the philosopher of his epoch, an absolute of his own times, but he becomes merely a relic of the past as the sequel of events goes on. New answers fit new times, and the expression of our age can only lie in Marxism. Yet we might ask here what right Sartre has to find in a purified Marxism the decisive expression of our age. His pronouncements concerning History seem to be as absolute as those of Spengler. It seems difficult, moreover, to make this assertion—granting that a man who believes only in totalization has a right to do so—without some sort of a transhistorical grasp of the totality, including past and future.

The fact is that dictates do not lie in the intention of the philosopher, his to make or not to make; they lie in the structure of the human mind, which tears down with great energy the walls of the absolute, only to build up new ones with no less alacrity. It seems that man cannot not judge. It is his obsession to make an ethical statement in an absolute form because in *any* statement he makes, he faces this temptation toward absolutizing. When he claims that X *is good* (and ought to be done), he formulates a proposition which has practical implications, how to behave in the world of things and of men. When he makes a speculative judgment, X *is* Y, he reflects this Reality itself without immediate practical connotations, but both judicative acts equally denote or attempt to denote Reality. In their vision of the Real, they are absolute. Who escapes the seduction of the attempted vision? No one. When man judges, he comes to the fore, takes a stand,

and implies *that things are such*. In his judgment, in a moment of absoluteness and immobility, he visualizes an identity of subject and predicate. The absolute lies in the grasp of
the object, which his vision internalizes. This is not to claim
that the "mystery" of the real is solved, or that the "knowledge" contained in the act of judging is exhaustive, or even
less that it can be totally reached by *one* man. All this would
be presumption. It is merely stated, as it was earlier in the
paragraph, that man cannot not judge and that his mind is
caught by necessity in an "immobility."

The judicative act of the philosopher is of course more
complex than the same operation performed by the man on
the street, but he is no better off than his fellow men. His
vision draws a circle around the world and around men: as
man himself, he is *in*cluded; to the extent that he *is* vision,
he falls *out*side. Although coming from a certain point of the
globe and formulated at a certain time, Truth gives his act,
as it gives any judgment, a value of universality and lifts it
to the dimensions of the immobile and the timeless. He
stands on the bank of the river, and his judging reveals that
which is static and enduring in the moving reality below him.
When Sartre states his belief in the *praxis* of the individual
existent, he is making a statement that in its very formulation and vision transcends *praxis*. When Bergson states his
belief in the eternal *mouvant*, his judgment is the immobile
echo of a *perpetuum mobile*.

It is true that Bergson's intuition of the *mouvant* or Sartre's comprehension of the project imply that at the very core
of cognition motion is built-in. To this I must respond that
to the extent of the overlapping of consciousness and the
mobile, the former is itself a process, but to the extent that
consciousness becomes an act of discernment, it is no longer
motion. It surfaces from the flux into immobility. At that moment takes place the *theoorein* (the seeing or visualization),
which is by itself not a negation of the motion, still less its
destruction, but is, rather, its consecration, or motion *as un-*

derstood. At this stage vision is rest, immobile and static. Only because his act of noesis itself is made from a point of rest can the philosopher absolutize the relative as relative, that is, for what it is.

From the preceding, I would like to make these concluding remarks:

(1) Learning is the process of transposing ontological density into vision. History is that learning as it progresses; though the last comer sums it up and encompasses it—an accomplishment for which the term *totalization* is not unsuitable—it still remains true that his vision *qua* vision is immobile. Totalization is a useful term when understood as the *praxis* of man achieving history, as long as one keeps in mind that *this very act stands between a double immobility, that of the human vision, and that of a cosmos that as timeless and interminable totality reaches beyond all* individual *acts of totalization.*

(2) It is only natural that any attempt toward immobility is also an attempt toward non-alliance. Philosophy is not a sword but an inquiry.[16] In order to discover Truth, the philosopher must be *non-engagé.*[17] Every philosopher is in proper fact a meta-philosopher. Since he must outdistance himself as individual, who is engaged in the world, he attempts to be the philosopher of his own philosophizing; there precisely lies his meta-philosophical attitude. His whole conatus is above all one of disengagement. The closer he comes

---

[16] In *Les Mots,* Sartre has lost some of his combativity: "*Longtemps j'ai pris ma plume pour une épée: à présent je connais notre impuissance*" (p. 211).

[17] I can only subscribe to the words attributed to Nathalie Sarraute in the course of a lecture in Moscow: "*Quand je m'assieds à mon bureau, je laisse à la porte la politique, les évènements, le monde; je deviens une autre personne.*" This remark was quoted, with disapproval, by Simone de Beauvoir in *La Force des Choses,* p. 211. In an interview with Mme. Sarraute, she informed me that this quotation, although true in spirit, was not exact in its formulation. Mme. Sarraute has elsewhere emphasized this need for a "realistic" and unprejudiced approach. See, for example, *The Age of Suspicion,* trans. Maria Jolas (New York, 1963), p. 134.

to this position, the closer he comes to a level of immobility. Since vision itself is not action, commitment as such does not solve the problem of cognition. On the contrary, it is more likely that incessant commitment hampers cognition and vision. Any "declaration of war" before the inquiry is finished is an undue act of alliance. At that moment the philosopher is no longer meta-philosopher and becomes pamphleteer instead; since he is no longer the critic of his own commitment, he belongs to a Cause and not to Truth.[18]

The philosopher's non-engagement, as this writer understands it, does not imply that an individual vision is ever exhaustive, nor does it posit the attitude of non-alliance as one of complete objectivity. Although the philosopher is not intentionally implicated, or willingly a participant, his view, although aiming at total noesis and "immobility" in truth, is caught in its very origin in what I call the *angular,* that is in the individual and the partial.[19] That sort of "engagement" catches him in the rear by the very fact that he is *Dasein,* with the residual content of suchness in him. It is neither chosen nor wanted, it is a result of his being thrown or "*geworfen*" into a certain materiality. In limitation he is born.

This limitation is imposed, not sought, unlike the Sartrian limitation, which is explicitly intended and wanted. The philosopher, in the hope of reducing the "partial" within himself and the unavoidable trial and judgment of the *Totum Genus Humanum* above himself, tries to elude any frontal engagement *when philosophizing*. At that moment he is the "will to the *Causa Prima*." With that aim in mind he divorces action and cognition and seeks totalization and progress through individual *praxis*, but only as performance *within* a Parmenidian Totality. This Sartre has ignored. He is pure

[18] On the problem of capricious choice, see the penetrating criticism by Alvin Plantinga in "An Existentialist Ethics," *Review of Metaphysics*, XII, pp. 249–50.

[19] I have defined in *The Planetary Man* the angular vision as that vision which belongs in exclusivity to an individual. *Angular* in my definition does not mean erroneous. See Chapter III, p. 35.

mobility and incessant commitment, and his *praxis* takes place outside an all-encompassing dome. We can only conclude with the statement that to be a victim of *time* leaves still another problematic unresolved.

Chapter X

THE LAST OF THE CARTESIANS

If, for Sartre, individual totalization is supreme, it is because the Self is supreme. Totalization *is* the Self. Undeniable as the influence of Hegel and Husserl upon his philosophical methodology may be, Sartre is in my opinion fundamentally French in his spirit and in his ultimate vision of the world and of man. I hope to show in the following pages that as the power of Descartes is the power of Sartre, so also is it his weakness.

THE SELF IN COMMAND

Freedom, for Descartes, is that unearthly quality of the *Cogito* by which "in affirming or denying, pursuing and avoiding the things suggested by the understanding, we behave in such a way that we do not feel that any external force has constrained us in our decision."[1] Free will thus expresses itself in a variety of ways: it can be a positive force of self-determination, but this capacity of proceeding toward and of preferring certain things includes the power of negation as well. The text from the fourth Meditation clearly implies that the capacity of denial is also part of the dimension of freedom. In actuality this idea was already present in the first Meditation, where the possibility of doubt presumed freedom "on the lowest degree." At that time doubt was pre-

---

[1] Meditation IV, in *Meditations*, trans. by L. J. Lafleur (New York, 1960), p. 51.

sented as the capacity of not-embracing, the *posse non am-plecti.*[2]

When we turn from the observations of Descartes to the work of Sartre, we see immediately that he has seized upon the negative aspects of freedom. If, for Sartre, what counts is the Self, it appears that for him, more than for many others, it takes the shape of negation. Someday perhaps in the psychoanalysis of a remote childhood, the seedbed of Sartre's fundamental project will be revealed. But it can be said already that this descent from the book into the author (as he himself maintains can and should be done) would consistently reveal a character of refusal. Whatever may have happened in his life, one can say that he is a vitality which has savored its reverse.[3]

The first negation in Sartre is the negation of the infinite. *Nous sommes pour une morale et un art du fini.*[4] The finite can deliver only the finite and has no opening into the absolute except to affirm its negation. It is only the infinite which gives birth to absolutes, but this infinite I have not been able to find in Sartre, except as a vague nostalgia and a feeling for the endless motion of this earth. Galileo of the noesis, he moves through the sociological strata and discovers their motion, but having abandoned the absolute, he gives us a universe that has neither sun nor any other center of stability. Man builds over the ages his tomb and his prison, resuscitates and liberates, only to destroy again and to rebuild anew in a never-ending cycle. Sartre's philosophy is a phi-

---

[2] See *Principia philosophiae* (1644), I, 37. On freedom as positive force, see Lettre à Mesland, 2 mai 1644, A.T., t. IV, p. 117. Compare also with the concept of the Will refusing to choose in Meditation IV, p. 53.

[3] This was written before the publication of *Les Mots,* Sartre's own account of his early life, which in a strange way seems to confirm my words. Writes Sartre: "I shall tell later what acids corroded the deforming transparency of my Self, when and how I became the apprentice of violence, discovered my ugliness, which for a long time was my negative principle and the quicklime in which the marvelous child was dissolved . . ." (p. 210).

[4] *Les Temps Modernes,* I, 1945, introductory article.

losophy of finite life looking at itself and discovering only the contingent and the continuation of the contingent. There is no paramount remedy, no dogma of salvation, only this universe and this man, the universe incessantly tempting man and man perpetually responding.

Another negation, which may seem surprising and yet is very Sartrian, is the negation of matter. On second thought, Sartre's revolt of mind against matter should not be too surprising, since mind, too, is an underdog. He has carried on a lifelong struggle to protect what the French so aptly call *la lucidité,* which is of course Descartes' old *Cogito,* the privilege that mind alone has of not being earth, or any kind of matter. In the depths of his doubt Descartes discovered one certainty, namely, that he thinks, and therefore is a spiritual being. *Lucidité* is that unique light that, containing a world of sense data, itself stands outside and above the world. This is Descartes' defense against a world that is myth—*mundus est fabula*—and Sartre, as a descendant of the Cartesian tradition, introduces it into his own life and doctrine as the negation of matter. Mind alone is supreme and free. In the Cartesian view, thought contains the complex activity of perceiving, knowing, willing, and desiring. Yet knowing is not exactly desiring, since the latter has no limits. Only because you know as a man can you desire as a god.

This Sartre has inherited, but he has eliminated God from his inheritance and replaced him by man, who now has absolute freedom. Sartre complains that in the days of Descartes an established order of truths, a dogmatic and even a dictatorial structure of society prevented man from being creative in his freedom. Man was "infinitely free" only insofar as he said no to evil, that is, insofar as he walked in the footsteps of God. His freedom was not a creative invention but merely a refusal. That sort of freedom of course displeases Sartre, to whom freedom which is not creative is not worthy of the name. It is, moreover, not even freedom. He writes, "If man does not invent his God, if he does not construct Knowledge, he is only nominally free. Cartesian freedom here joins hands with Christian freedom, which is a false freedom. Cartesian man and Christian are free for Evil, but not for Good, for Error, but not for Truth. God takes them by the hand and through the conjunction of natural and supernatural lights which he dispenses to them, leads them to the Knowledge and Virtue he has chosen for them."[5]

The conclusion for Sartre is obvious: man must take over the freedom of God. The freedom which man has a right to conquer and to possess is the freedom of Orestes in revolt against Zeus—we recognize the theme of *The Flies*. Descartes' description of God's illimited and creative freedom is for Sartre nothing but a sublimation and a transposition of human wishes into divine fulfillment. "The God of Descartes is the freest of the gods that have been forged by human thought."[6] For Descartes it was clear that Freedom and Creation were one, and that God alone fulfills this ideal of creativity that is unrestrained by the demands of time and space. In God, willing is creating, and we still have not left the grounds of St. Thomas Aquinas, who, although above all an intellectualist, would also claim that *Amor Dei est creans*. Sartre would have us leave these enclosed grounds and step forth on our own, with the result that there is no longer for him a human freedom limited by a divine freedom but a human freedom that is unlimited and unrestricted.

This was not the only modification which Sartre introduced into the famous *Cogito*. By a strange irony, at the very time that the Ptolemean system lost out and man's world was no longer the center of this universe, man's Mind asserted itself to be an omnipotent and powerful center of a world of Knowledge. Galileo and the discoverer of the *Cogito* were contemporaries. The earth might have been set in motion around the sun, but the mind was to discover a power of immobility, for the rationalist of those days trusted that his truth, like that of mathematics, was irrefutable and universal.

[5] Sartre, *Literary and Philosophical Essays*, p. 193.
[6] *Ibid.*, p. 194.

This form of absolutes in immobility Sartre could not accept, since between Descartes and himself, Hegel had appeared and placed motion in the mind itself. Under the impulse of the Spirit—divine or not—man's ethical and cultural expression, caught in a world of time and space, evolves with History. Marx inherited this Hegelian view but stripped it of its idealistic content. The origin of History now is material, based upon the need and economy of man, but historical succession remains. Under this Hegelian impact, the Cartesian Subject could no longer be equated to an eagle soaring above time and space, but was reduced to a bird caught between mountain tops. The pronouncements *sub specie eternitatis* were gone—so we are told—for although Hegel himself was still the *aquila metaphysicans*, his followers were not.

Existentialism as professed by Sartre is an abandonment of the immobile Reason but not of the Subject. It is Descartes corrected by Hegel. This does not necessarily imply a greater modesty, for upon reflection it will appear that the *human Subject brought into existence by the Cartesian Cogito has with Sartre reached its zenith.* The fundamental intuition in both *L'Etre et le Néant* and the *Critique de la Raison Dialectique* claims accomplishments of the Ego which are immense.

In *L'Etre et le Néant,* it is the core of a creative noesis which reveals and organizes a world, dominates its surroundings, escapes determinism, is immensely free, lives instant by instant, is lawgiver to nature, and in the reverse of William James's words, stands firm while nature accommodates itself to him. The omnipotent and absolutely free Cartesian God, whose *creatio continuata* kept a universe afloat, has found a replica in Sartre's *Pour-soi,* who from now on in this age of *Götterdämmerung* takes care of a world. One cannot help remarking how in this age of ours the philosopher's effort aims at replacing the old God by the new one, the new one being, of course, man himself. There is always need for an explanation, and although that term is for the time being taboo—one does not explain, one merely describes—the moving force of the philosopher's work is a strenuous attempt to replace the Cause by the cause. I should add that even the term *cause* is antiquated, and we must replace it by *clarification*. This is exactly the need which the *Pour-soi* fulfills. In inventing the *Pour-soi*, Sartre has dispelled the mystery once more, and the world is nothing but the *Pour-soi* in act.

In the *Critique de la Raison Dialectique* Sartre has taken a similar stand: What makes the group? The individual. What moves the inert? disturbs the sociological strata? starts the revolution? expels the king? The individual once more. Neither God nor devil, neither State nor society, only man is responsible for man, only the individual man makes and assembles the totality through his *praxis*. There is nothing but the individual self and its unexplained and unexplainable power of synthesis.

In the light of this enormous emphasis upon the Self, we might expect the Other to be overshadowed, as indeed he is. In a well-known article, "The Transcendence of the Ego,"[7] a remote preparation for his philosophical position in later books, Sartre cancels the Ego as the ontological core and substance of the individual. The Other at that time was ignored by virtue of the fact that there was no ontological entity to which he could be linked. In *L'Etre et le Néant,* the Other was no longer ignored, but he became the enemy. The literary corollary of this philosophical stand is famous: *L'enfer c'est l'autre!* In the *Critique de la Raison Dialectique* the Other remains a menace, but he is nevertheless needed for my salvation. The group is born through *me* as individual and for *my* protection. The constituents of the group are such through *my* act of totalization, and by this Sartre means that the group is a collection of *entia rationis*, which my *praxis* calls into being. Their "membership" is *my* creation. The group holds no ontological dimension other than that

[7] In French, "La Transcendance de l'Ego," *Recherches Philosophiques*, VI (1936–37).

which the individual Self wants it to have. Such is the power of the individual *praxis*.[8]

When the Other is no longer a help, he becomes, in a world of scarcity, a danger. On such a globe as ours, where there is not enough for all, he appears as menace, scandal, *contre-homme*, perpetual opponent. No wonder that the exclusive emphasis upon the subject as the supreme value and the *Ens Realissimum* excludes any philosophy of love. Philosophical subjectivity, which starts with the Self and measures everything from the viewpoint of the Self, is a form of speculative egotism, just as unselfishness is a prelude to charity. Sartre's *Pour-soi* in *L'Etre et le Néant* meets an opponent at every turn, as does the individual man in the *Critique de la Raison Dialectique*. Since there is no *we*, but only *me* in this age of decadent Cartesianism, we find neither charity nor benevolence.

What Sartre wants to make clear through all the obscurity of his prose is that the Individual is "sovereign" and that the Other is completely incidental. Neither group nor totality of any form stands above the individual. It is necessary for us to examine this claim, for, although Sartre has erected an impressive defense of the Subject, in order to clear the way he has had to tear down the scaffolding of the Intersubjective.[9]

THE SELF WHERE IT BELONGS

The problem of the Group and of the Intersubjective should not be misconstrued as being merely an ethical

---

[8] Merleau-Ponty wrote in *Les Aventures de la Dialectique*, p. 156: "*Pour Sartre la prise de conscience est un absolu.*" Sartre has not altered his stand in the book under study.

[9] Professor Herbert Spiegelberg was well inspired when he wrote in 1954: ". . . from the philosophical angle its ["it" referring to Sartre's social philosophy] prime weakness appears to be the lack of a theoretical foundation . . ." "French Existentialism: Its Social Philosophies," *The Kenyon Review*, Vol. XVI, No. 3 (Summer 1954), pp. 446–63. The *Critique* has opened new horizons, given us some revealing descriptions but it has not fundamentally belied Spiegelberg's statement.

question. Upon sober reflection one discovers it to be an ontological or, better still, a semantical problem. The term opponent—the opponent of the individual subject, that is—is
nothing but a product of *individual semantics,* that is, of a
semantics which is made *upon the size of the individual.*[10]
Such a semantics, the product of man working and thinking
and inventing as an individual, is and was the semantics of
Western thought, which reached its highest point in the philosophy of Descartes, whose *Cogito* was the subject par excellence. Only on the basis of the *subjective* and as a consequence, only on the basis of the defense of the subject, do
terms like opponent and menace-for-me make sense.

Discovery is dependent upon the chosen *point de vue.*
Sartre's problem—and it is actually the problem of Western
thought at this stage of its evolution—can only be solved
through a radical change, a change in point of departure
from the *Individual* to the *Totality,* whether this *Totality*
(or *Totum*) be the *Totum Genus Humanum,* that is, mankind as a physical whole or a *totum* of a smaller size, custom-
arily called a group. When a *totum* is considered as
Subject, it will be a kind different from the individual subject, since it will contain the individual men themselves as
its physical constituents. Individuals, then, are in fact fragments, unique and unequal, of the collective *totum.* The
totum itself presents a basis of oneness, which is made up of
the individuals as parts, but this oneness neither prevents
nor hampers their individual freedom. They keep their mobility against a background of belonging. I still do what I
want, I say what I wish, I move freely, etc., but this "freedom" does not cut the fundamental tie with the Totality.
Within the oneness of the total Subject, the *we*-awareness
makes sense for the first time. *We* are constituents of the
totum, since we—not I—constitute the totality and the Subject. This *we*-element must not be misunderstood. It is not a
vague sentimental unity expressed by the word "together-

[10] I would like to refer the reader here to *The Planetary Man,* I, the
Introduction and Chapter VI.

ness," a term which has recently gone through a brief period of success. We-awareness is the unemotional confrontation and acceptance of a reality, the reality namely, of a *totum*, of mankind as a physical totality that is fragmented, with each of us a fragment of that *totum*.

In this view, the Self can no longer be considered to be an independent and metaphysically solitary entity but rather as a relational dimension, or better still as a *persona* in the etymological sense of the Latin word, that is, as that "through which the sound comes."[11] The individual Self is thus *an* opening of the Totality upon the world. It is through each individual that the *totum* is given the possibility of approaching a world.

The reader who has followed us thus far has no doubt understood that the *totum* is no longer being considered here as a *logical totum* or *class*. Here again I underline a topic brought up elsewhere,[12] but the re-emphasis is necessary for the understanding of my opposition to Sartre. Sartre's mistake in the making of a philosophy of the *group* lies in his use of the *logical* class only, that class or category which we have inherited from Aristotle's Logic. Containing objects *A, B, C,* etc., on the basis of certain similarities, its categories offer the plurality of human minds a possibility for identical thinking and identical understanding. Within this approach, which is in my understanding followed by Sartre, no ontological provision is made for the unequal and the unique, both of which are simply overlooked.

The *totum physicum*, unlike the logical class, is a totality resulting from the addition of different individuals, each of whom brings his own unique and exclusive contribution. This *totum* is in the opinion of this writer the archetype upon which all grouping must be construed. By this I do not imply that the logical class must be dropped altogether. Its use will always remain the pedagogy for the understanding of the similar and the essential but one should keep in mind that

[11] See *The Planetary Man*, I, p. 71.
[12] *Ibid.*, p. 13.

however pervasive it has been in Western thought, it dis-
torts the texture of the real as much as it reflects it, for in its
search for the similar, it makes no room for the different and
the unique. It is here that the leveling technique of stand-
ardization finds its roots. If the *logical totum* has killed the
unequal, the addition of men in the *totum physicum* implies,
on the other hand, an acceptance of their uniqueness and a
recognition of individual character.

When we probe Sartre on this topic, we are first of all confronted with a firm stand on ontological equality: "A man
cannot be more of a man than other men because freedom is
similarly infinite in each individual."[13] What this absolute
freedom means we have examined in the study of *L'Etre et le
Néant* and it will not be necessary to return to it here except
to add that in the concrete this absolute freedom does not
exist. For all practical purposes infinite freedom in man has
inevitable limitations. Even Sartre would make such a concession. If we accept this less-than-absolute freedom in the
individual man, where then lies the uniqueness of a man? The
Sartrian answer seems to be that what characterizes the individual is *his project*. We have already observed that through
the project Sartre makes an eloquent defense of the individual, coming back to the topic again and again, as if to make
sure that we have gotten it.

If we accept Sartre's defense of the uniqueness of man as
lying in his project and his transcendence, we may nevertheless still ask from where this choice or original project
comes. If instead of merely observing the outward manifestation of this project, one goes back into the individual man in
an attempt to discover the motivating basis, one finds nothing
but the psychoanalytic and the sociological. Sartre has un-
covered these elements most skillfully in the case of Flaubert,
through delving into the relations of the author with his
father and with society through the medium of his family.
These observations are admittedly very sensitive, but it
should be noted that they only serve to bring out precisely

[13] Sartre, *Literary and Philosophical Essays*, p. 183.

that which Sartre wishes to avoid. For this emphasis upon the psychoanalytic and the social underlines the fact that Flaubert is caught in the whole, or conversely stated, stresses the impact of the collective upon that "portion" we call Flaubert. No doubt it is Sartre's intention to preserve the uniqueness of the individual, but his skill as an analyst convinces us instead of the enormous part played by the collective in shaping Flaubert, who was pressed by the *totum* into being the genius which he was.

We should of course make it clear here that if without the *totum* there would have been no Madame Bovary, it is equally true that these influences (of the *totum*) upon Flaubert are not themselves Flaubert. They merely constitute the past (and future) working upon Flaubert: only Flaubert himself can carry the present. However heavy is the weight of his milieu and his ancestry, it is still Flaubert who is that irreplaceable entity in whom the project is rooted and through whom it obtains its unique character. I would like to suggest at this point that this process which we have followed of the author incessantly transmuting what he has absorbed into what he is and "projecting" it into *"cet ouvrage monstrueux et splendide, Madame Bovary"* gets its maximum intelligibility only when and if we grant the *totum* an ontological status, thus providing our doctrine with a metaphysical basis for inequality and uniqueness. The acceptance of the *totum* as a physical whole would then result equally in the acceptance of its constituents as *parts* and *fragments*, the subsistence and ontological depth of which must be unequal and unique in order to ensure the survival of the *totum*. The surviving *totum* provides an answer to the fundamental inequality of men and the singularity of the particular fragment which constitutes *that* man. This does not imply that the transcendence which is proper to man ought to be cancelled or that *project* has to be ignored, but it adds to this the all-important point that the project is such and such only because it has its roots in the particularity of the individual himself. It is because individual X is *such* that he has *such* a project. But the suchness of individual *X* is meaningless in isolation. Only because there are others within an englobing Totality can *X* be *X*. What Sartre does not see is that the unique implies the unequal and that inequality fulfills itself within "organic" oneness.

Finally one might add that here, as is so often the case, the semantic confirms the ontological. If *X* appears to be unique, it can only mean that he is different from others *in* that *totum*. The term "different" in its etymology denotes the meaning of "*dis-ferre*," but only if one is somehow *related to* can one be *carried away from*. The words themselves imply that only in the circular plurality of a "physical" *totum*, where the many are parts, can the many be unequal parts, and in being unequal, be unique as well.

The uniqueness of the individual therefore has no meaning without the presence of other individuals. In *X* lies the slumbering core which against the others but within the global configuration of the totality gives him his distinctiveness. Each individual is an inimitable segment indeed, but he is such only against a background of belonging to a *totum* . . . and I must add, at the price of that belonging. For if uniqueness is his glory, it serves also as an instrument toward the total achievement of mankind. Ontological diversification or individual uniqueness (which goes with it) is intelligible only when segment *X* is part of a totality which *qua* totality resists disappearance. The grandeur of individual *X* never means independence. This has been the tragic metaphysical mistake of recent centuries, and Sartre is only one more victim of the illusion.

Sartre sees dependency as a menace for the *Pour-soi*. In his fear of anything which resembles the *Gestalt* or of any oneness which even remotely might be considered *organic*, he shuns this solution and chooses instead a position where the many are juxtaposed but in no way co-ordinated. Lacking a philosophy of the collective, his doctrine presents us with a series of units which are fundamentally equal, although on the surface diversified. They act and "project" in a diversified way, but no explanation is offered for this diversification *in* them. Ontological equality has not been abandoned, and the Logic of Aristotle has merely been strengthened through the influence of Descartes. Thus individuals are all alike, but since they are *subjects*, each of them, they wander freely, the lonely proprietors of an empty globe. Sartre himself pokes fun at those who discover similarities in crabs, start studying them, and triumphantly present us with the "eternal crab."[14] Sartre has no intention whatsoever of discovering the eternal man. This must be stated emphatically. Yet *having killed the organic, he has, in my opinion, unwittingly killed the unequal.*

In Sartre's defense, it should be mentioned that together with an incessant defense of the subject, there is a continual attempt to protect a dialectic of reciprocity. This may appear at first glance to be a protection of the *intersubjective* as if Sartre did believe in an interpersonal status over and above the condensed activity of the *Pour-soi* or subject in action. This is actually not the case. What happens is—and the reader may remember the scene of the *petit bourgeois* gazing from his hotel window—that *A* views *B* as he works and in his visualization gives him a status both of *object* and of *subject*. *Object*-ification always happens through matter, for every individual, although not matter himself, is sunk in materiality. All this is part of the game of the *Pour-soi*, which is in itself nothing but the revelation and manipulation of what it is not. *A* considers *B* as a subject as well and knows that under the materiality lurks the danger of Freedom, which will later appear to be both a menace and a help. The subject will be shown to be *praxis* and an active support in the creation of the group. Although Sartre would for all this vehemently reject all accusations of idealism, it should nevertheless be stressed that *no* interpersonal status is present nor accepted *beyond that which proceeds from the subject,*

[14] *Les Temps Modernes* (octobre 1952), in the article "Les Communistes et la Paix," p. 727.

whether from A or in the reverse from B. Some may see the "intersubjective" in this, but I would be inclined to think that there is much "subjective" but little "inter." The Other is merely an *alter ego*. Sartre juggles with *alter ego's*, but *alter ego's have nothing unique*, they are merely the same.[15]

It should be remarked further that this structure of unity-in-diversity that is characteristic of the *totum* is so natural, and I should say so elemental, that it is present *before* any organized grouping. The fragmented *Totum Genus Humanum* is the group par excellence, the model and matrix of all subsidiary group formation. Sartre did not observe that already among those waiting for the bus on the place St.-Germain-des-Prés we had this inequality in depth, since it is, notwithstanding the seriality, a crowd of unequals struggling to survive and doing so through a diversity of occupations, through a division of labor. The group is *there* in a latent and potential way.

To construct outside of this elemental group which is the *Totum Genus Humanum* another grouping, whether it be one which aims at the conquest of the Bastille or one which wants to protect the rights of the worker, is only natural—and no one would contradict Sartre on the point—on condition that the prototype of all grouping is kept in mind. Any one of Sartre's groups is nothing but an imitation of that most essential structure, the structure namely, of the segmented *Totum Genus Humanum*, surviving the menace through internal inequality and diversification of jobs. The individual man is ontologically and in depth *group-fragment*. Survival is possible only where the dissimilar *fragments* complete one another. It is this ontological inequality—not to be confused with juridical inequality—which results in a division of labor and thereby in a salvation of the *totum*, whatever may be its

---

[15] Cf. *CRD*, I, p. 426, where in the text, *"Dans l'Autre, qui agit avec moi, ma liberté ne peut se reconnaître que comme la même, . . ."* Sartre confirms his fundamental position, and where liberties are presented as equal and juxtaposed, not as unequally grounded and converging or completing one another.

size. The *group*, then, *appears as a physical sum of the diverse resulting in a defense of the constituents.*

THE MANDATE OF THE GROUP

Although Sartre refuses to give the group a status all by itself and makes it exclusively dependent upon the creation of the individual self, he does not deny that the growth from seriality to group and later on to institution results in a serious loss of freedom for the individual self. These passages are in my opinion among the most impressive of the whole book. Actually he has done so well that, for me at least, he has reversed his own thesis: he has convinced me that the *group* is more and other than the *individual*. I am thinking, for example, of that force of fatalism which comes so strongly into the foreground as the book progresses. The term fatalism is obscure and I would like to return to its eventual meaning later, but at this point one thing emerges with force and clarity, namely the fact that within the growing trend of organization, it appears that the *subject is no longer sovereign*. The least which can be said is that the acceptance of a fatalistic trend means a limitation of the subject *qua* Sovereign, since it posits a power above and beyond that of the individual.

We observe also Sartre's detailed description of the seriality as it appears, for example, in the world of business, where he clearly implies that the plurality comes first and the individual only later. A striking example in that field is the notion of *interest*. Something interests me not because it is useful to me but because it is wanted by the plurality. With these words Mill's form of Utilitarianism is rejected and the collectivity, that anonymous and strange power, is placed in charge of value judgment.[16] The plurality dictates my *Credo*. At a certain moment Sartre mentions the forceful obligation which reaches the individual, but it reaches him from

[16] *CRD*, I, p. 279.

nowhere: *"C'est une fuite infinie."*[17] Its origin is lost in the darkness of the infinite. He also elaborates at length upon *"la grande peur"* and convincingly shows that all through history, groups or nations are at times caught by a great panic. No single individual is responsible because everyone is.[18] We are one step removed from Sartre's analysis of *processus*, according to which *praxis* and its unavoidable evolution chooses a certain direction which no one individual can alter. Things once more appear to be irreversible. They are above any individual power, and Sartre would agree, but if they escape the control of the omnipotent[!] individual, where do they belong but in the hands of the plurality?

Furthermore, we recall that Sartre was relentless in pinning upon the group a collective responsibility for its sins of commission and omission. As the son of a bourgeois, I am not better than my father and I inherit his sins along with his money. In these pages, Sartre joins hands with Dostoevsky "Believe me, everyone is really responsible for all men and for everything"[19]—only he is more violent, sparing no insults for the *bourgeois massacreur*. Sartre seems unaware that in proclaiming a collective responsibility of the group or of the class, he is endowing that group or class with a dimension of being that is totally alien to the individual endeavor. *Only when the group has an ontological status can one bestow it with moral guilt.*

What does all this mean? It means: above the individual hangs a strange power, a power which he cannot shake off, but which guides him irresistibly, instills the collective guilt into his heart, and is in every way stronger than himself. Sartre may call it *marche irréversible, destin, processus,* or *fuite infinie;* all these are words, and their meaning is not always the same, but they all converge on this one point: the individual man is not really a Sovereign. Forces pursue him and hold the Prometheus in chains. Sartre's semantics

---

[17] *Ibid.,* p. 349.
[18] *Ibid.,* p. 343.
[19] *The Brothers Karamazov* (New York: Modern Library), p. 344.

are in fact a subterfuge which attempts to hide the fact that the group has a power and that it has a power because it has an ontological status. In my opinion, there is no destiny, but there is a *freedom of the group*, which formulates its decisions above and beyond the choice of the individual, decisions which are at times bitterly resented by the latter. The group *is*, and *decides* as such.

Philosophers of the past have always made exclusive use of what I call *individual semantics*, since they claim that every term can carry its full meaning as understood by the singular individual. Sartre provides in this respect no exception. I have attempted to show elsewhere that there are terms which for their complete understanding require the intervention of the *group*.[20] They belong to what I have called *group-semantics*. What appears unintelligible to the individual may very well be intelligible to the group. What looks like destiny to the individual man is merely the disposition of certain means toward an end that is visualized by the group. The group, whether existing in its elemental and natural way or in a man-made form (for a particular purpose), confronts a problematic situation and adopts a solution. It has a "freedom" and makes a choice. *This "choice" quite often appears as a mystery to the individual existent but it compels him, nonetheless, as destiny.*

The increase of the birth rate during and immediately after a war is a characteristic example. Individuals do not consciously reflect upon that need, yet this drive toward procreation imposes itself upon them in the form of a quasi obligation. The group manifests itself *in toto* and chooses a certain solution. We might also observe the renewal which at times takes place within a group. If the group is a religious one, the believer may consider the rejuvenation to be of supernatural origin. Should this be true, it still remains a fact that in its actual and present fulfillment it is a group decision. The individual member feels totally inadequate or ·

[20] *The Planetary Man*, I, pp. 80 ff.

even impotent until the group *as such* begins to move. I can also very well visualize the *prise de la Bastille* as the result of a group decision. Here once again we see the group at work, the group *being born before my articulate awareness of it* and before my reaching the Boulevard, yet in its decision englobing all of us and provoking the response of each one of us. The entity "group" sweeps in some remote and invisible way (invisible to the individual perception) all individuals, men and women, onto the *boulevard St.-Antoine*. It is a "free" decision, motivated by the circumstances no doubt, although one which does not necessarily coincide with my individual choice. The group decision may force me into action, at times to the detriment of my own interests or while appearing "unreasonable." To the extent that the group takes a clear-cut shape, it may even seem to be a prison and then of course the term *destiny* comes to mind, yet it is in fact nothing but the *group acting* in self-defense, as a group must, even at the price of some of its unwilling "fragments." We have already mentioned the relentless, irreversible pursuit of *The Informer* in John Ford's film of that title. Whatever might have been the sympathy of the group members for Victor McLaglen in his role of the half-idiotic culprit, his condemnation to death had to stand, for the sake of the group. The decision could not be changed by or for an individual, or even by a few individuals, who understood all the nuances of this muddled, bewildered life. The organization, a supra-individual entity, had decided, and nothing could reverse that decision, for it belonged to a different dimension.

From our preceding analysis, it follows that *when individuals revolt against Authority*, be it Stalin or Louis XVI or the Grand Inquisitor, *that revolt has silently been in the hearts of many long before it could receive its explicit formulation through* praxis. In other words, the group has been born but its members are unaware of the birth. The group is *there* before the individual has a clear consciousness of its existence. *He belongs to the unborn group and he does not know it.* His conscious co-operation will be free, that is, it will be based partly upon his own choice, but at the same time his actions are made possible by the global freedom which surrounds him. When Sartre describes skillfully and in great detail the rush of the rioters on the Boulevard toward the Bastille, he nevertheless overlooks the fact that the individual's conscious response is a response to the group as an ontological and massive entity that already exists. More precisely, Sartre accepts such a response in the form of individual interiorization, but he does not see that interiorization *is merely a symptom of synchronization, not a creation.* It responds to what is. Grouping comes to the individual man from the rear: it seizes him because of an urge emerging from the *totum* itself, an urge which is in depth a drive for survival. Grouping in its ultimate intelligibility is a necessity imposed upon the individual; as such it is in him before manifesting itself through *praxis.* In my opinion the group is born from the group. The individual no doubt contributes, that is, he consciously co-responds to its conscious genesis, but as fragment of that particular *totum,* he was already involved in its pre-logical birth. Once the group is well on its way to its stages of organization and institution, this co-response will be asked less and less frequently as a free and voluntary *praxis,* for then—and here Sartre will of course agree—we observe the birth of the inert and of the anti-dialectic, of the overpowering hold of the group as group. I confess that we have as yet no clear semantics to express the status of the group. The hesitancy about giving it a name nonetheless does not imply that it should be denied an existence. Sartre may be right in rejecting the term *organism.* If this term is incorrect, however, it is not because in one way or another it reflects a certain hampering of individual wishes but because the group cannot without danger of gross oversimplification be placed on the same footing as the individual.

There is obviously no objection against calling man himself a *totum* or even a sovereign but it must be with the clear understanding that man is sovereign only toward his own internal constituents. His freedom or power of decision is pure and complete only within himself: he chooses and wishes, he desires and wants, he denies and affirms. Nevertheless, he will collide with external resistance when he starts executing, since execution involves the transition from his being a *totum* in relation to his own inner dimensions to his being a *fragment* in relation to the enveloping dimensions of a superior *totum*. Man is a god in the depth of his dreams only. *There* he is truly sovereign, but once the self steps outside its kingdom, it realizes that it is but a part of a universe, not master of it, that it is a fragment of a *totum*, not a factor of it.

Sartre's subject attempts in vain to dominate the group, just as in *L'Etre et le Néant*, his *Pour-soi* was a vain effort to conquer the Other. The appropriation of other men and of the world was doomed to failure, just as is the domination of the group through the subject, for the obvious reason that neither individual man nor *Pour-soi* are made for domination of what is above and beyond. The world is ours, not mine, and what I cannot accomplish, no doubt the group will, but it should be well understood that the group does not consist of *me* alone, but is an internally diversified and higher *totum* made up of many *me's*.[21]

[21] Sartre has not made clear the distinction between that which provokes the group into existence and the group itself. Versailles may very well have provoked the turmoil in the *quartier St.-Antoine* and my demands may have started the grouping and organizing of the postal services; still, the outsider *is* not the group. Cause and effect should not be intermingled, for the one is definitely not the other. Kurt Lewin, whom Sartre mentions without reference, considers the boundary erected by the outsider to be a condition of group structure, but he does not consider it to be the essential feature. The group is in his terms a "dynamical whole" which is definitely more than the sum of its parts. "It has its own structure, its own goals, and its own relations to other groups." (See Kurt Lewin, *Resolving Social Conflicts*, pp. 84 and 164.)

THE CARTESIAN *En-soi*

There is within the Sartrian frame of thought more than the Cartesian lucidity, which Sartre has transformed into his *Pour-soi*. In addition there is what might be called *mutatis mutandis*, a Cartesian *En-soi*. Sartre far from ignores "matter" in the *Critique*. On the contrary a considerable amount of attention is devoted to it, much more than in *L'Etre et le Néant*, and the extreme entanglement of matter and mind at times comes to the fore very forcefully. I am now thinking of certain passages where "men appear as autos" and "autos as men," or where man, in imitation of Zola's *Bête Humaine*, is viewed as losing himself in becoming a *thing*. "Thingification" is not new to the French Existentialist; it is mentioned frequently in his previous writings.

Nor is the problem itself new; it is one which has confronted philosophers of every age. Although one might thoroughly disagree with Descartes' solution, one cannot deny that he had seen the intricacy of man's constitution. For if man is basically not matter, how can and does he respond to matter within himself and to the quantum which surrounds and penetrates him? The answers of Descartes are well known and this is not the place to repeat what others have already analyzed. Let me merely point to the fact that one can discover in his work a double path leading to the acceptance of matter in and around man.

The famous dualism of body and soul appears as the conclusion of a Cartesian deduction in the fourth part of the *Discourse on Method*. But there is another aspect of his method which receives less attention, that where the presence of the continuum is somehow directly felt by Descartes as a phenomenon. So, for example, he describes the muscular movements which appear to us from within and the strange weight of the body bearing down upon the soul.[22] In this occurrence he mentions the fatigue felt by the soul in carry-

---

[22] *Réponse à la sixième objection.*

ing a body, a fatigue which at times is so heavy that one envies the angels. Descartes states in the fifth part of the *Discourse on Method* that "it would not suffice to place the soul in the body like a pilot in a ship, . . . but that it must be more intimately joined and united with the body in order to have feelings and appetites like ours, and so constitute a real man."[23] This general awareness is not unlike the sensation of "internal space" which Maine de Biran has revealed with great finesse. He sees man as the discoverer of space through the use of his organs. That discovery is at first merely a vague awareness of the voluminosity of the body, felt by children and no doubt even by animals. Gradually, in attempting to overcome the resistance and the volume of the bodily organs in oneself, the Self itself is born, for opposition increases the awareness of the Self. The Self arises, enveloped in a material embrace from which it can no longer release itself.[24]

It is interesting to note, then, that already before Sartre, philosophers like Descartes and Maine de Biran had drawn attention to the ponderosity of the inert *within* man. Moreover, Descartes did more than merely mention the felt presence of matter "within" the soul; he also presented it as a mutual negation long before Hegel and Marx. In his *Entretiens avec Burman,* he pointed to that attitude of the mind where it says *no* to matter and where matter says *no* to the mind, although both are condemned to live together in their mutual denial as one.

When Sartre himself came on the scene with *L'Etre et le Néant,* he brought a new semantics and a new ordering through the use of the *Pour-soi* and the *En-soi*. I have sufficiently explored the meaning of these terms in a previous publication so that it is not necessary to do so now. It can

---

[23] *Discourse on Method,* trans. L. J. Lafleur (New York, 1960), p. 38.

[24] Maine de Biran, *Fondements de Psychologie,* Première Partie, sect. II, chs. 3 & 4. See also Raymond Vancour, *La Théorie de la Connaissance chez Maine de Biran* (Paris, 1944), p. 183.

briefly be stated that *En-soi* is that which does not choose but is chosen, that which does not know but is known. As such it is opposed to human consciousness or *Pour-soi*, whose function of discovery and conscious desire, of knowing and choosing, places the human individual in the dimension of *nought*, that is, in the dimension of not being matter.

This would seem to settle the problem, if it were not for the fact that the *Pour-soi* is contaminated by matter through the presence of the Body. Avoiding a Cartesian dualism within man, Sartre wrote a penetrating chapter in *L'Etre et le Néant* on *The Body*, the implication of which was that there is no dual structure within man, but that man's consciousness in a world of material things *"exists"* a body. Through this psychic body man himself is a center of references and is definitely *une présence au monde*.[25]

This solution may have appeared to be satisfactory in the days of *L'Etre et le Néant*, but in the *Critique* it has lost its effectiveness. The propinquity, even the actual interpenetration of mind and "matter"—terms which are not Sartrian, I confess—have become such that it is no longer possible to keep the concept of matter (or its corresponding term) out of the definition of man. A new semantics is not always a cure for old problems. There is a danger of eliminating the ghost and saving the machine, but there is no less peril in choosing the ghost alone, in the hope that the machine will be forgotten. It is my clear impression that Sartre's definition of man as propounded in *L'Etre et le Néant* does not warrant the formidable impact of matter upon man which is shown and defended in the *Critique de la Raison Dialectique*. Or to put it differently, if "men become autos," perhaps the reason must be sought in the fact that there is something of an auto *within* man. The question may be asked whether the *En-soi*, which Sartre in *L'Etre et le Néant* has carefully kept outside the inner dimension of the *Pour-soi*, has not, or

[25] On this topic see *Being and Nothingness*, p. 326; *The Tragic Finale*, p. 78.

rather should not, become in the *Critique* an integral part of man. We begin to wonder whether it really suffices to consider the body as a "contingent presence" rather than as an essential part of man in order for us to live philosophically at ease in a world of earth and stones, that is, whether one meets matter *without* if there is not matter *within*.

If gold means so much to man—as the *Critique* so emphatically states that it does—something *within* man must be essentially dependent upon gold. If machines affect him so deeply, something "cybernetic" must be hidden *within* his structure. The excitement produced by the discovery of the steel and coal complex in the Europe of the nineteenth century surely proves that the definition of the *Pour-soi* purely as creative freedom and transparent lucidity is patently deficient. Within the texture of man we must discover as an *essential* part that which can carry gold as an inner complementum and saturation, and we must incorporate this into our *definition* of man. *L'Etre et le Néant,* in not doing so, has not prepared us for coping with the heavy invasion of matter in the *Critique*. In the previous study, human consciousness was defended as absolute freedom. Sartre's *Pour-soi* had nothing to lean upon and did not really confront matter: it could afford to be volatile, translucid, and absolutely free. But now the Sartrian man, threatened with the elements, can no longer appear as mere freedom. Sartre, aware that a concept like the *Pour-soi* is too frail to combat a world of resistant materiality, has quietly dropped the old terminology. Sometimes he employs the term *organism,* which is more neutral than mere consciousness, but he has actually made no real attempt to redefine man. Forgetting that one confronts matter *without* only when reinforced with matter *within,* he has sent this angel of light unarmed unto the earth, there "to negate" and "to conquer."

The spirit and content, once more, are French and Cartesian, betraying a dictate of mind above matter, however Hegelian and dialectical might be the semantics and the method. I would even be inclined to say that this combination comes naturally, not only because of the powerful influence of Hegel and of his philosophy of mobility upon all Continental writing but also because of the fact that dialectic carries the obscure more easily. One may even go so far as to wonder whether perhaps dialectic does not result from an introspection that attempts to clarify the twilight zone of matter and mind within man, but failing in its effort, brings it to the fore by way of externalization: what man has not been able to clarify within himself, he has transposed outside himself. Dialectic then would be the obscure reciprocity of two entities and their no less obscure synthesis. What we can no longer consider to be distinct and "discernible" we bring together as one and call "synthesis." It is neither one, nor two: it is synthesis. Thus is dialectic born, and the rare zones of light within its mysterious depths are considered to be analytical and proper to the world of mechanics.

Dialectic is, in my opinion, Sartre's answer to the problem of the relation between matter and mind. It is clever, for it enables him to avoid the quantifiable, hence to preserve freedom within the inscrutable movement of the dialectic. It is clever for still another reason. Philosophy can survive only in a world of the non-mathematically measurable. In an age where Metaphysics is in a decline, Hegel's dialectic appears as a last attempt to salvage from the analytical and the quantifiable a margin of being, that being which sages of the ancient world and of the Middle Ages had safely placed in the realm of the invisible and the immobile. There, static and real, it was called "metaphysics."

Sartre's approach showed great versatility indeed. Unfortunately his outwardly turned dialectic—man *versus* external "matter"—still did not solve the problem under discussion, the need to increase the inner density of man and to enable "matter" to become an integral part of a definition. By his omission Sartre showed once more what he included. Man is the dictator of the earth and the manipulator of the organic. Stripped down to the naked *Pour-soi*, he faces a world.[26]

This is, however, only the beginning of his seclusion. Man is not only separated from matter within, but when he is confronted with matter or with any human operation outside himself, he does so *in loneliness*. Sartre misses that collective noesis which, in my opinion, the approach to this universe requires. Only the a priori acceptance that *we* occupy this extramental real can warrant *my* own fragmentary exit, or in other words, *I* can reach outside myself into a real world only if *we* are there. A lonely *Cogito* on a bare planet would forever hang between dream and reality. Only the acceptance of the Other can make *that which is between us* something real. The current emphasis upon *my* world, which the penetrating analyses of Heidegger and of Merleau-Ponty have brought to the foreground, implies the existence of *your* world, since the distribution of worlds among individuals presumes the existence of a World, immense and gigantic, wherein *my* portion fits, juxtaposed to *yours*. This aspect contemporary thought has neglected. And yet it is from a World collectively owned by the *Totum Genus Humanum* that derivatively, the appropriation, noetic and otherwise, must be inferred. The *Totum Genus Humanum* knows the world it occupies and strictly speaking, no other. This is tantamount to saying that the subject is not the *I* but the *We*.[27] The human totality in its physical envergure is subject and *within* itself there can be no doubt concerning the existence of its inner constituents. It can be said, therefore, that it occupies a world which it divides among its inner constituents and gradually humanizes. *We* embrace a world, *we* negate

[26] I had already written all this when I read in *Les Mots:* "Every man has his natural place; neither pride nor value decide about its height: his childhood decides it. Mine is the sixth floor of a Parisian building with a view over the roof tops . . . I breathed there (again) the rarified air of *Belles Lettres*, the Universe stretched out at my feet and every object humbly begged for a name, which to give was at the same time both to create the object and to seize it" (p. 46).

[27] *The Planetary Man*, I, pp. 7, 81 ff.

the inert, *we* humanize matter, etc. What *we* embrace is inclusive of a world, since the world is nothing but what is between *us,* whether this "known" be a physical "between" or merely a noetic "between," as in the case when the mind of the astronomer wanders in the galaxy and in this way brings remote distances within *human* range.[28] Hence when Sartre wants *"un regard situé,"*[29] the look upon the world *from* a person engulfed in his own materiality, it should be kept in mind that epistemologically speaking, this look is open to correction and reaches a truth of a *generic* level only when supported through multiplication. The objective is nothing but the subjective multiplied in a world where a fragmented *Totum Genus Humanum* occupies a *totum universum.*[30]

We can now observe how the Cartesian psyche gets its origin. Within space the fragment, or human individual, has mobility. It is this mobility, however, which brings confusion and presumption, since it induces the *fragment* to believe that it is what in fact it is not, namely, independent. The individual is not independent, he is merely free. Forgetting that he is dependent upon the surrounding matter and upon others, he takes for granted a power and an independence

[28] *Ibid.,* pp. 6, 97.

[29] *CRD,* I, p. 31, footnote.

[30] I am not ignorant of the fact that through his judicious use of intentionality, Sartre ties his *Pour-soi* in with the *En-soi,* with the clear hope of avoiding all accusations of subjectivism. I would like to make two remarks in connection with that approach. First, the link between the *Pour-soi* and the *En-soi* is revealed in the pre-logical depth and results from a reflective attitude, which is itself prior to the recognition of a universe. Hence the Subject dominates. Second—and this merely confirms point one—within the life-world the movement toward a world (my world) starts from the subject. Sartre introduces intentionality as an attempt to reconquer the real. But this approach overlooks the fact that the real is already an occupation of the *we* and only afterward, within this closed circle, tacitly accepted, conceded to the expansion of the individual Self. Sartre's weakness (and to a lesser extent Merleau-Ponty's) is anthropocentrism. A similar accusation was made recently by John Wild against existentialism in general. See *The Journal of Philosophy* (October 24, 1963) in the article, "The Philosophy of Martin Heidegger," p. 677.

which he does not have. *The Psyche of the Cartesian subjectivity is built upon that presumption* since it confuses mobility and distances on the one hand with independence on the other. Reality teaches us differently. It teaches us that power and skill belong to the *totum*, whatever may be its size, that within the *totum* the individual subject is merely a response to the solicitations of the *we*, and that the same individual subject accepts the group as an established fact, not something he himself "wishes" into existence. Consequently, to visualize the individual as a sovereign upon this spatially constructed universe is merely to play with words. Whatever lives upon this globe is plurality, though it be under a variety of forms—serial, grouped, or institutional. It occupies this earth, subject to the unavoidable rebuff and mishaps of all occupation—Sartre's analysis of counterfinality contains much truth—but it occupies and conquers as a collective. For a world in which the solitary adventure gathers meaning only within a collective enterprise, Sartre's philosophy is not prepared.

MARX REVISITED?

In the opening lines of the *Critique* Sartre made it emphatically clear that he was a Marxist. Whether or not he deserves this name depends of course on the meaning of the term. Unfortunately the meaning has become so elastic by now that its application means little. Official interpreters range from Engels to Mao Tse-tung, and the scholarly commentators are legion. If, summarizing what I have said in the second chapter of this book, I attempt to give a definition, I believe that one can consider a Marxist to be one who sees History as progressing under the moving force of economics and man himself as a being of action, no longer held back by myth and speculation, but attempting within the progress of History to free himself of all alienations, whether they be political, economic, or religious. The ultimate fulfillment of these dreams will be the classless society, where all will live in freedom and total equality.

This definition may fit many, it may even fit Sartre. Unfortunately one element was left out, which, ironically, constituted the main topic of our study. We may at present call it the "humanistic" dimension, since it asks what is the importance of man himself in the fulfillment of History and what is the nature of man and the power of his intervention. We know well Sartre's view on that topic by now, and to summarize once more what has been said in the preceding pages would be useless repetition. On this point, there is no similar certainty concerning the attitude of Marx himself. Here the controversy rages. Is there only one Marx, who consistently defended the same view? Did Marx evolve gradually and, without any radical break, merely express toward the end of his life what was already in him as a young man? Did an older Marx, under the influence of Engels, break off with his past and launch into a more scientific view of the evolution of History? Did Marx agree with Engels on the defense of the dialectic of nature? All of these positions have been defended and it appears that no clear-cut answer is available.[31]

Sartre himself wants a consciousness which is situated in the world and which through its negation posits things and englobes them in a dialectical appropriation. Consciousness is then "une négativité située," that is, a negating act which is itself caught within the contours of time and space. No doubt this negativity needs "matter" in order to be—it knows "matter," negates it and gets hold of it—but it is itself more than "matter." It is creative freedom, it is discovery of a world, it is totalizer of the group. It is the Force Constituante, which interiorizes and synthesizes. It is all this. But if it is all

[31] For detailed information on this controversial topic, see Calvez, La Pensée de Karl Marx, pp. 413 and 425. See also L. Dupré, "The Challenge of Marxism," in Cross Currents, Summer 1962. On the diversity of interpretation within the Communistic camp, see G. A. Wetter, Sowjetideologie Heute, I: Dialektischer und Historischer Materialismus (Frankfurt, 1962), pp. 51 ff.

this, is it still Marxist? In my opinion the answer is no. There is no place in the writings of Karl Marx for a Self with such an amplitude. Sartre's free Self is an *ens amplissimum*. As far as the impact of the infrastructure upon man is concerned, the term itself is usually loosely defined by Sartre, but upon occasion he makes it very clear where he stands: *"Ce ne sont pas les choses qui sont impitoyables, ce sont les hommes."*[32] Man is the responsible being. If Sartre does not fit smoothly into the framework of Marxist semantics, it is because of his persistent intention to place subjectivity at the start of the revolution. No influence whatsoever has made Sartre deviate from his fundamental assertion: *The Self* is Sovereign.[33] Sadly enough this is not the way in which Marxism has been lived in the countries that have practiced its tenets, for there at least, few subjects have been "sovereign" and only the dictators have been free.

The irony of Sartre's situation is that while dreaming of a free and powerful Self that is variously creative and to whom is given the charge of a world, its organization and departmentalization, its grouping and institutionalization, Sartre has in fact created an entity *too isolated in a hostile world* to be ever successfully committed to a group or to anything. Descartes did not beget Marx. The Cartesian *cogito* was not a prelude to a Marxist collective, nor could "the king of creation" ever become submissive to the performance of the group. In my opinion Sartre's combination is an explosive one, especially so in that it is not held by way of the paradox of two contrasting views which are kept separate in their organic totalities and viewed merely as supplementing one another; the views are held, rather, as a unified synthesis, where both theories have lost their own individual character and are now supposedly united in a homogeneous whole. In fact Sartre has not abandoned Descartes. Although his de-

[32] *CRD*, I, p. 31.

[33] A similar point is made, although based upon a different approach, by Professor R. Kwant in a very thorough article: "Het Marxism van Sartre." *Tydschrift voor Philosophie*, December 1960, p. 674.

fense of the individual man as a free being deserves praise, it has gathered the defect of its virtue as well, for in blowing up the subject beyond measure, it has killed the status of the group and of the intersubjective. This is, I believe, the flaw of his brilliant argument. One is not what one wants to be, but merely what one has never given up being.

BIBLIOGRAPHY

Since this study was concerned with a well-defined topic, the bibliography will be limited as well. I have not deemed it necessary to enumerate all the works of Jean-Paul Sartre. This list is by now easily available. I myself have given one in my book, *The Tragic Finale*. A more detailed list is offered by Philip Thody in his penetrating book, *Jean-Paul Sartre, a Literary and Political Study*. To my knowledge, books other than mine commenting on the *Critique de la Raison Dialectique* are not available. Georges Gurvitch in his book *Dialectique et Sociologie* devotes one chapter (twenty pages) to the *Critique*.

In addition to the articles in *Les Temps Modernes*, those works of Sartre used in the making of my book are as follows:

Sartre, Jean-Paul: "La Transcendance de l'Ego" in *Recherches Philosophiques*, VI, 1936–37. English translation by Forrest Williams and Robert Kirkpatrick, *The Transcendence of the Ego*. New York, 1957.

————*L'Etre et le Néant, Essai d' Ontologie Phénoménologique*. Paris, 1943. English translation by Hazel E. Barnes, *Being and Nothingness*. New York, 1956.

————*Critique de la Raison Dialectique, précédé de Question de Méthode*, Tome I, *Théorie des Ensembles Pratiques*. Paris, 1960. *Question de Méthode* has been translated into English by Hazel E. Barnes under the title *Search for a Method*. New York, 1963.

————*Les Mots*. Paris, 1963.

————*Literary and Philosophical Essays*, English translation by Annette Michelson. New York, 1962.

WORKS OF OTHER AUTHORS

Calvez, Jean-Yves: *La Pensée de Karl Marx*. Paris, 1956.

Camus, Albert: *L'Homme Révolté*. Paris, 1954. English translation by Anthony Bower, *The Rebel*. New York, 1954.

Carlyle, Thomas: *The French Revolution*.

De Beauvoir, Simone: *Privilèges*. Paris, 1955.

——*La Force de l'Age*. Paris, 1960. English translation by Peter Green, *The Prime of Life*. New York, 1962.

——*La Force des Choses*. Paris, 1963.

De Waelhens, Alphonse: *Phénoménologie et Vérité*. Paris, 1953.

Desan, Wilfrid: *The Tragic Finale*. Harvard University Press, 1954; rev. ed., New York, 1960.

——*The Planetary Man*, Vol. I. Georgetown University Press, 1961.

Engels, Friedrich: *Anti-Dühring. The Peasant War in Germany*. French trans. Brache, ed. Costes. 3 vols. Paris, 1931–33. New York, 1926.

Feuerbach, Ludwig: *The Essence of Christianity*.

Forster, E. M.: *Howards End*.

Fromm, Erich: *Marx's Concept of Man*. New York, 1961.

Goldstein, Kurt: *The Organism:* A Holistic Approach to Biology Derived from Pathological Data in Man. New York, 1934.

Green, Norman N.: *Jean-Paul Sartre, the Existentialist Ethic*. University of Michigan Press, 1960.

Grégoire, Franz: *Etudes Hegeliennes*. Louvain, 1958.

Gurvitch, Georges: *Dialectique et Sociologie*. Paris, 1962.

Hall, Edward T.: *The Silent Language*. Garden City, New York, 1959.

Hegel, G. W. F.: *The Phenomenology of Mind*. English translation by J. B. Baillie. London, 1931.

——*The Philosophy of History*. English translation by J. Sibree. New York, 1956.

Jeanson, Francis: *Sartre par Lui-même*. Paris, 1958.

King, Martin Luther, Jr.: *Strength to Love*. New York, 1963.

Kojève, Alexandre: *Introduction à la Lecture de Hegel. Leçons sur la Phénoménologie de l'Esprit*. Paris, 1947.

Lefebvre, Henri: *Le Matérialisme Dialectique*. Paris, 1949.

Lewin, Kurt: *Resolving Social Conflicts*. New York, 1948.

Maréchal, Joseph: *Le Point de Départ de la Métaphysique*, cahier V. Paris, Louvain, 1926.

Marx, Karl: *Capital*. English translation by Samuel Moore and Edward Aveling. New York, 1936.

———*Critique of the Gotha Program*. New York, 1938.

———*Economic and Philosophical Manuscripts of 1844*. London, 1959.

———and Engels, Friedrich: *The Communist Manifesto*. New York, 1948.

———*The German Ideology*. New York, 1939.

Merleau-Ponty, Maurice: *Les Aventures de la Dialectique*. Paris, 1955.

Nietzsche, Friedrich: *The Philosophy of Nietzsche*.

Ong, Walter J.: *Ramus: Method, and the Decay of Dialogue*. Harvard University Press, 1958.

Proudhon, Pierre-Joseph: *La Création de l'ordre*. Paris, 1927.

Sarraute, Nathalie: *The Age of Suspicion*. English translation by Maria Jolas. New York, 1963.

Thody, Philip: *Jean-Paul Sartre, a Literary and Political Study*. New York, 1961.

Thomas Aquinas: *Summa theologica*, Pars Tertia.

Tucker, Robert C.: *Philosophy and Myth in Karl Marx*. Cambridge University Press, 1961.

Weber, Eugen J., ed.: *Paths to the Present: Aspects of European Thought from Romanticism to Existentialism*. New York, 1962.

Weil, G.: *L'Eveil des Nationalités et le Mouvement Liberal, 1815–1848*. Paris, 1930.

Wetter, Gustav A.: *Sowjetideologie Heute*. I: *Dialektischer und historischer Materialismus*. Frankfurt, 1962.

INDEX